ASK UNTIL IT IS GIVEN!

Give Me 15 Minutes – I'll Give You

God-Like Power To Have It All !

By

Matthew David Hurtado

ISBN: 978-1-717-05198-1

LEGAL DISCLAIMER

Remember: I'm not a doctor. This information is for entertainment purposes only. You must do your due-diligence and act like a responsible adult. The statements in this book have not been evaluated by the FDA. This material is not intended to treat, heal, prevent or cure disease.

Be a Part of My Media Empire!
http://www.FigLeaf.Tv

Table of Contents

FREE GIFT FOR MY READERS:

As a way of saying "Thank-You" to my readers, I have a special gift for you. Click the link below, and you'll have instant access to a SUPER technique to ***Attain Your Desires*** Without Struggle.

DISCOVER AN "UNDERGROUND" METHOD TO GET ANYTHING YOU WANT, FAST!

A controversial RITUAL selfishly protected by Nobility and the Knights Templar—*who used this ritual to control and amass vast resources and wealth*—is now in **your** hands.

Watch the **WEBINAR BELOW** and follow the step-by-step instructions. Do the ritual only once per each desire.

Webinar: http://www.MatthewDavidHurtado.com

INTRODUCTION

Imagine you're frustrated. Not hard to imagine, is it? You've been trying to build that internet empire, start that new business, or get that promotion that's long overdue?

Maybe you want to pick those hot cryptocurrencies or stocks. Or perhaps you want to manifest the lover of your dreams and live happily ever after? Maybe there's a block you want to do away with?

Do you have a nagging health challenge or some burden standing in the way of your happiness? Somehow, is something still amiss even though you've tried everything you can think of doing?

I have good news for you: your worries are coming to an end as you dive-deep into the pages of this book. Here's why:

You can be, you can do, and you can have it all. All you have to do is clear away the confusion. You need real answers, and those always come from within yourself.

You've been told to create your reality, right? But how do you do that? I mean, how do you triumph in the face of adversity everywhere you look? How do you ascend past your fears, doubts, and disbelief—especially in yourself?

What if your worries about the world or future of humanity seem to stand in the way of your ability to LIVE the dreams inside of YOU? Whatever it is, the solution is inside of you. Not in some far away distant reality. It's here, now.

The world will deceive you. This book leads you within, where you'll discover the light at the end of the tunnel. The God-within (your real identity) awaits your recognition, and this immutable force is 100% ready to serve you, right now.

GIVE ME 15 MINUTES, AND I'LL GIVE YOU "GOD-LIKE" POWER TO HAVE IT ALL!

The truth is; if you haven't yet discovered health, happiness, romance, and a luxurious lifestyle, you've missed something about life.

It's not supposed to be a series of tasks as a means to pay bills and scrape by. You're supposed to live in the mystery, following your joy or highest excitement—moment by moment.

Within these pages, you will find your ***childlike*** **essence** that has been deteriorated by "happiness-draining-parasites" camouflaged as "professionals" in society. These misguided souls mistakingly led you astray into the land of conformity and approval seeking.

When you realize how SNOWED the masses are into believing they are serfs—subjects, chattel, sheeple—you'll cringe at the thought of doing anything "their way" ever again.

From the first chapter, you'll experience an immediate WIN by understanding the cause of virtually all "poverty" (a mindset manifesting as poor health, lack of finances, and unhappy relationships).

Almost everyone you know is hard-wired this way. When you escape you can show them the way.

You will feel compelled to complete your journey here on Earth in the best way possible after you return to your innocence.

Victimhood will be intolerable to your new identity, as you shed false reality concepts—for good.

ASK UNTIL IT IS GIVEN! will deliver outlandish ideas in a way you've never considered before, urging you to explore them and redeem your "pro card" in Law of Attraction.

Are you ready to seize your AUTHENTIC POWER—guiltlessly and unabashedly walk in fields of gold, or Bitcoin?

Can you handle having it all, living life on your terms?

If so, let's get you on the throne. Your coronation is TODAY. There is no one greater than you in your universe.

Read this entire book. It will serve you well.

Selah!

You might ask how I know all of this to be true. It's because I've experienced it first-hand, many times.

However, I need to add a caveat: life will never be perfect. According to Clotaire Rapaille, *death* is the (USA) culture code for perfection, so don't expect it.

Yes, you CAN be, do, and have it all, but to "attract" something new is also to attract the lessons required. That's why I'll also show you how to deal with any perceived "negativity" that shows up when you begin working with proven techniques provided inside.

Who am I and why should you listen to me?

I am the #1 Bestselling Author of **ALLOW—Mastering the Law of Least Effort to Receive Your Desires!** I am an ordained minister, dubbed the Minister of ALLOWING.

I've done what this book aims at helping you achieve; my health, relationships, and finances rapidly improved—using the techniques I'll show you.

In 2009, I began this journey. I was bankrupt and bedridden. Lyme disease almost took my life.

At my lowest point, a series of these miracles led me to the amazing discoveries you'll learn about in **ASK UNTIL IT IS GIVEN!**

It felt like being *born under a lucky star*, and you'll feel this way, too. The same power is inside of you!

After rediscovering how to claim my God-given power, I recovered my well-being and built a multi-million dollar wellness empire in a few short years.

My mission is to share the discoveries that catapulted me from my sick-bed and penniless estate to a vast empire of wealth in all its forms—health, relationships, money, and happiness.

A revelation you will want to see immediately is that I didn't get here without assistance. Incredibly talented **mentors** poured their wisdom into my life in my darkest hours.

The difference between winners and losers is that winners finish what losers only started. Decide to be a "finisher," and I promise you this book won't let you down.

It is with great love that I pour my legacy out—right here in black and white—so you can obtain the same MIRACLE CONSCIOUSNESS I dialed-in during my greatest triumphs.

If you want more out of life, this book will deliver the missing piece to the puzzle. At some point, you will set this book down and think to yourself, "This is the answer, I feel it, and I know it!"

These pages are alive with transformative energy, beckoning you to take the plunge and immerse yourself in the strategies. You are called to this material because it is YOUR TIME for miracles.

Before we begin our journey, I want to share something Dr. Pillai—a mentor of mine—wrote on Facebook:

"Right now, it might be easy for you to get caught up in life's problems because we've been conditioned to believe that the external world is everything.

The Yogis, Siddhas, and even modern Quantum Physicists have understood that it's the internal reality that matters and that everything on the outside is dependent on what happens on the inside."

You don't have to work hard and struggle in the outside world; you can make the change within, and allow reality to transform around you.

Let the path that led you here be the end of "problem-consciousness" and the beginning of BEING the solution to the obstacles standing in your way.

Together, we'll prove how **powerful you are**. Stay committed to the natural tasks I'll present to you, and you'll taste victory! Success is supposed to be fun, and it will be.

Let us begin...

CHAPTER 1.

Anger is the Cause of Poverty and Proof of Defeat

The odds are favorable; if you're reading this book, it is because you are experiencing some poverty, and you are sick of it.

You don't want to live in a state of poverty, but you aren't sure what to do to change it. I'm not just talking about financial challenges when I use the word poverty.

For the scope of this material presented in the book, I'll use this definition of poverty: *the state of being inferior in quality or insufficient in amount.*

Since our natural instinct is to compare ourselves with others, this habit is typical for virtually everyone to some degree. Someone else is always stronger, more prosperous, happier, healthier, and better looking.

So what do we do to eradicate the hidden poison pockets of poverty lurking in our consciousness?

Well, you can't change it until you know what is causing it. Just like you can't live on aspirin to cover up physical pain without understanding and treating the cause of the pain.

You also can't work to cure poverty without understanding where your (spiritual) debts originated.

Poverty is more than just the lack of material wealth.

There are people on this planet who have vast amounts of money but who are still poor. Likewise, many people have very little to enjoy when it comes to assets, but they are very wealthy.

Poverty is a poverty of spirit—an inability to live the life you want to live in the manner in which you want to live it.

Anger Is The Secret Cause Of Poverty

According to my evaluation, anger is the cause of poverty. But don't worry – you can do something about it, and I'm about to tell you what it is.

Anger is one of the major things that will block you from being able to ALLOW what you want in your life. Anger = poverty. You have to understand what these words mean before you can address them in your lives.

Poverty is *the state of being extremely poor.* Again, my definition entails the 'perception' of how we inaccurately see our world. As you progress through this book, your consciousness will shift.

If you do the exercises, including the SUPER BONUS webinar at http://www.MatthewDavidHurtado.com, your life will change. I promise.

Let's talk about the traditional idea of poverty.

It occurs when you lack sufficient money to live at a standard considered comfortable or "normal" in the society in which you live. When that is the case, there is inevitably a lot of anger.

So which came first? The poverty or the anger in the genetic expression or the genetic code?

Anger and (spiritual debt) poverty can both be passed down from generation to generation in your DNA and your consciousness. It is also *programmed* into your consciousness.

Here's another definition of poverty that might be helpful: *a condition that is worse than is usual, expected, or desired. Something that is of a low or inferior standard or quality. Someone who is poor is a person considered to be deserving of pity or sympathy.*

How do people become poor in consciousness?

Anger itself is a reaction. Clotaire Rapaille, the brilliant French psychiatrist and marketer, author of *The Culture Code* says that culture gets imprinted on the brain stem—the reptilian, impulsive part of the brain—during childhood.

The prefix "re-" symbolizes a return to the inceptive cultural imprint. It refers to "home." In other words, it brings it home in a karmic sense. When you are *re*acting, you are acting as you did in your original home.

Please pause and reflect on what you just read, let it sink in. Every time you capture a nugget that makes you think, "I never saw it that way before"—pause and reflect.

Karma arises from taking action. Action creates a cellular memory, an imprint in your subconscious brain. It establishes your go-to reaction in any given situation. Including anger.

Here's the etymology of the word, anger:

*Middle English: from Old Norse, angr "**grief**," angra "vex." The original use was in the Old Norse senses; current senses date from late Middle English.*

Now, look at the meaning of the word, grief:

Noun

1. *Keen mental suffering or distress over affliction or loss; sharp sorrow; painful regret.*
2. *A cause or occasion of keen distress or sorrow.*

When you see me use the word ANGER, I'm using it in the context of the uneasy feeling birthing a sense of defeatism, due to our perception of being powerless.

Our evaluations (opinions forming beliefs) become our reality, according to how The Law of Attraction works.

Anger is the second step (after fear) you took towards a perceived danger, to assert your boundaries. *Flee*, or be forced to fight! So anger is just a *re*action, an effect.

When someone asks us why we are angry, often the answer is nothing more than "because...just because." We make up excuses.

We don't want to be paralyzed by fear, and at the same time, we don't want to feel threatened continuously, forcing us to fight. If the world is "out there"—we are always under attack.

Do you feel like you're always in danger of a health threat, money problem, or relationship issue?

Does it seem like the media and other news outlets remind you that the world is "unsafe" and you need a savior?

Is there always someone offering you safety in exchange for freedom, inviting you to conform to someone else's way of thinking for you to live in peace and harmony?

Yeah, we'll touch on how the *harm* in harmony is selling you down the river in a few moments. First, let me make one thing clear and precise:

"Your world is nothing more than a reflection of your ATTITUDE towards life, reflecting itself back to you."

What we are doing is looking at our reflection of the world, mirrored back at us. This mirror-projection is an indicator of our attitude towards life. If our external "echo" comes back to us, we know this is the effect.

When we respond to our echo with internal irritation, we are reinvesting in another karmic tantrum. These repeat episodes engrave yet another cellular memory, another imprint upon our brains.

This pattern establishes another excuse for us to use another circumstance to blow up and huff about again.

The poverty that we see in the world is just a reflection of the cycle of anger we have created. It gets played out over and over again and it is difficult to break. It is anti-human, and it is anti-prosperity.

WHERE DOES ANGER COME INTO EXISTENCE?

At the outset, anger comes from trauma. In Freudian psychology, the "id" is the disorganized, instinctive part of our personality. It is the reactive part of who we are.

Trauma creates a psychological id. When we experience trauma—or unexpected shock, a new persona, a new set of instinctive reactions gets created. And these reactions are all perturbed.

Look at anger, and see it for what it is. You can see it as a schism—a break between strongly opposed parts of your personality.

I'll go as far as to say that the unexpected upsets we experience and derive our unhealthy counteraction from **opens a parallel reality.**

We know that our "persona" injects itself into consciousness, yet most people miss the obvious elephant in the room:

If a person with multiple personalities can change physical features (like scars disappearing and illnesses going away) as they change "personas"—we're witnessing a different doppelgänger, from a different universe, appearing before our eyes.

Why do I say this? According to German New Medicine, the unexpected emotional upset (shock) triggers what we perceive as illness in our (so-called) physical bodies.

Based on my observation, when I busted loose from Lyme disease—resolving the conflicts in my psyche—the reality of a healthy and vigorous version of myself emerged, which is thought to be "impossible" to present-day medicine, to say it lightly.

We are always shifting in and out of multiple reality constructs.

You can see distemper as a manifestation of your id—the instinctive, irrational part of your personality. Or you can see it as a *holodyne*—a holodyne being the physical manifestation of an idea or thought as it imprints on a cellular level.

Think of a holodyne this way: it is the way memories get stored on a cellular level. It is the way certain things get passed down or ingrained in our cells on a fundamental level.

This "default-storage" can be a good thing—in the types of foods that give us comfort, or a bad thing—in the kinds of things that trigger adverse reactions.

You don't get apples off of pear trees—you get apples off of apple trees. If your home was one in which the response to negativity was anger, then you will do the same thing.

So consider the word "reacting" once again. You have "re" which represents "home." And you have "acting." So who was acting at your home when you grew up in this way that you are now mirroring? What happened that became a karmic episode which created an imprint on your very DNA?

Poverty is Inherited

Poverty gets passed down from generation to generation. This "spiritual debt" becomes a part of your id, your holodyne.

Poverty is the harboring of too many judgments; we feel out of control.

Like judgments on a credit-report, "spiritual debt" is inflicted on us by our **judgmental-attitude** about life and what we are experiencing.

We want to step into control. The irony is; *surrender is being in control.* When we try and use force, we are acting out of control with behavior that the ego surmises will change the situation. It reinforces the karmic episode and repeats the lesson.

We create a lack because when we "want" something it means we lack it. Anger becomes our (immature) solution to powerlessness. We learn to become provoked as a means of masking the feeling of learned helplessness.

In fact, this is just an immature holodyne making itself known. It is not healthy, and it will keep you in a cycle of poverty consciousness.

Where did I get this word "holodyne" that I'm using, you may ask?

Dr. V. Vernon Woolf, the creator of holodynamics, taught me about holodynes, and Toby Alexander (a mentor) taught me about how we create "ids" in our persona.

When you discover common denominators amongst various teachings, you find the essence—or power.

I'm going to remind you of your GOD-LIKE POWER throughout this book.

In fact, the symbol on the front cover of this book can be used to stare into and alter your brain waves.

In 1984, researchers at Moscow University used an EEG machine of a few individuals asked to use the Sri Yantra.

Researchers found that within moments, user's brainwaves came down to an Alpha brainwave. Alpha is known for enhanced creativity, relaxation, meditation and intuition.

The Sri Yantra symbol has been proven to do this, and it represents one of the most potent ways to change your life. I'm talking about the use of symbols to affect the crystalline structure of the light-body. Symbols program consciousness.

USE THE COVER OF THIS BOOK TO YOUR ADVANTAGE

If you want to gain the most advantages from this book, stare at the cover of it for 3-minutes before you pick up your reading where you left off. The insights will sink in deep for you to shift awareness with every further reading.

Do not rush to finish this book. When you glean over something that gives you an 'aha' moment, put the book down. Or, go ahead and read it straight through anyway (I'm not here to tell you how to do what's best for you.)

Back to our discussion about anger, for a deeper understanding of how we got here in this mess.

To escape poverty consciousness, we must overcome; we must ascend these holodynes, imprints, ids, whatever we choose to call them. We must be able to react in a *prospering* way. To undo this, we need to understand these three keys to evolve our actions beyond anger:

1. ***Vulnerability equals strength.*** I learned this when I was on my couch, dying of Lyme disease, at the will and mercy of the world around me. I had no strength left. I had no human might, so I was forced to surrender to my spiritual nature. Why do you think most of the elite-class who reign supreme over their counterparts usually appear so tenuously built? They know that all influence over others begins and ends with their non-physical power.

2. ***Surrendering is you being in control.*** When you try to control your life, you are acting out of control. The modus operandi behind trying to be in control and asserting strength and dominance stems from a feeling of being out of or lacking power. If you knew that you were a being that could have anything you could ever want, you'd have nothing to prove. With no need for approval, you would have nothing to fight with or push against to validate self-importance.

3. ***Relaxing is allowing.*** Relaxing to "receive your desires" is a significant insight. Anger restricts the FLOW. It prevents your cash flow, your fluidity, and your currency. These are symbolic words. Anger constricts the flow of your life energy—and this includes your money. Money is just an acronym for My Own Natural Energy Yield. So when forcefulness (derived from anger) calls the shots, you will not receive what you want. I'll show you two techniques in this book to empower you—The Safe Touch Method™, which I created in a

three-day meditation (downloading the insight from the Divine), and Ho'oponopono.

So we know now that poverty is a state of being that arises from reacting in anger over and over. It's like you're in a hypnotic spell. It's time to *break the spell.*

If you are poor in your consciousness, your reaction is to be infuriated. This emotion is so close to anger. It's an inferior reaction.

So how would you like to upgrade your reaction? In the past, when you were triggered, your response may have been hot-headed or you *inverted anger with guilt*, calling for self-punishment. If so, you learned it at home.

To push against something is also to reinforce it. When you resist something, you lock it in. You are *re-e*nforcing.

Reinforce. Someone showed force in the home, and you are activating your cellular memory, your karmic episode repeated.

Force vs. Power[1]

Remember—(force-backed) coercion is not power.

---

[1] If you want to learn more about this concept, read "Power vs. Force" by Sir David R. Hawkins, M.D., Ph.D.

Governments exist today via the use of force-backed coercion. These institutions of authority do not possess the creative capacity to initiate advancement on any level.

Instead, the improper use of power (under the color of law or authority) is beguiling only to war-mongers and thieves.

Clotaire Rapaille describes bureaucracy in this way: *extreme power given to extreme idiots.*

It reminds me of the story of little Sam who was caught by his parents with a broom in his hand, stirring up so much dust they could barely breathe.

Upon entering the kitchen, they found Sam sweeping piles of dirt back and forth -- appearing to be busy and productive -- while accomplishing nothing but an exacerbated debris; creating a smokescreen of progress.

Sam's parents said, "Sam, what in the heck are you doing?"

"Helping!" Sam replied.

Sam has grown up now. Here are seven words you never want to hear from Uncle Sam: "I'm with the government. I'm here to help."

Power is what you want: you don't want to have to force things to happen, you want the ability to **ALLOW the game to come to you!**

When you manipulate through coercion, you disconnect the natural flow. It is an inferior method, and it can make you infuriated.

Instead of "kinking the garden hose" of the stream of life, *ALLOW* the flow of life that is trying to come through you: it will support you and take care of your needs.

For now, let's keep it simple. Let's talk about engaging with an alternative solution that will work for you instead of against you the way force will.

Your DNA has been pre-programmed to react in an upstream, resistant way. But we can change this program as it derives from the mind as we engage the six-degrees of separation.

My book **ALLOW - Mastering The Law of Least Effort!** will explain the six-degrees of separation through three kingdoms, as the "fall of man." If you want a copy, I suggest grabbing one whenever it feels appropriate.

(Free Digital Copy) http://www.ALLOW.ws

If we struggle to get ahead and remain bound and entrapped in our circumstances—we are repeating our karma. We keep recreating the same things by re-engaging our mind and reacting the same way. It's mostly unconscious.

The worst thing we do is to engage our thinking mind and try and solve the issues (using the same level of being that is creating the problems, unconsciously).

We can **align** with real power, if we want to shift our circumstances. We don't have to force anything.

Power comes from vulnerability. We live in an upside down anti-civilization; irrationality often trumps common sense.

Have you heard it said that *doctors destroy health*, and *lawyers destroy justice*? All these memes show up in our world, and we go through years of education without questioning the hogwash we devoured.

Where did our history originate? Who wrote our history? *Conquerors did.* #CriticalThinking

No matter which side of the coin you choose, you lose in an upside-down anti-civilization, as long as you sustain its might by conditioned-response behavior.

Whatever you push against, you reinforce the opposing viewpoint and subject yourself to its lesson. We want to eradicate the ignorance behind our anger.

We can create the path of least resistance and change our world, by changing our inner world.

We know that things aren't always as they appear. Deep down we know that if we act in newly-empowered ways, we can break the spell.

It begins with a change in our attitude and perceptions about life. Once you know the world is inside of you, you awaken to your full potential.

REVERSE SPEECH: the door to the unconscious

A great technique to prove this is the use of David Oates' method of **Reverse Speech**.

I've been using Reverse Speech for several years. Our consciousness is a two-way mirror; we reflect our reality outward and internalize our perceptions inward.

Reverse Speech is our soul's method of communicating the inward perceptual motivation behind our unconscious intentions.

As Mr. Oates says, "The voice of the unconscious never lies!" Want to know what someone is going to do? Reverse their speech and listen, carefully.

About every fifteen-seconds, the unconscious mind will give you a reversal or some clear indicator of the unconscious intent.

I've solved complex challenges and experienced impenetrable *lie-detector-like* shrewdness in business dealings by listening to messages with Reverse Speech technology.

In addition to these benefits, I've discovered that using POSITIVE AFFIRMATIONS works far more efficiently (in my experience) by speaking them out, **reversing them**, and chanting them in their reversed-speech language.

Example: "I am a millionaire now!"

Saying, "I am a millionaire now!" is a normal affirmation. Most people chant this way and let's be blunt: it usually ends up wasting their time.

Their conscious mental filter kicks it in the storage bin as "junk." It's not believable for most people.

However, if you reverse it (using a free reverse speech app on your smart-phone), "I am a millionaire now!" sounds like, "one ran ding ling mama!" *When I speak it, it sounds this way.*

MY DISCOVERY AND THEORY: REVERSE AFFIRMATIONS:

By chanting "one ran ding ling mama!" (your reverse speech sound may differ a bit), the conscious filter doesn't see it as a threat to the ego's "baseline reality," and the unconscious mind takes it in, immediately!

Try it on for size and see how your results differ if you are currently using positive affirmations.

It's all about non-resistance (removing the anger and force-backed coercion).

Think about this; government means "mind control."

The ideal reality is one where we have intelligence enough to self-govern through the use of non-violent communication.

Let me give you an example of how non-resistance creates transformation by eradicating the type of anger-programming I'm talking about—*ignorance masquerading as experience.*

Consider this example: when I used to have panic attacks, my mentor told me that as long as I feared a panic attack and suppressed them, it would only get worse. **My instinct was to fight against these attacks.**

As a result, I started to have them all the time. What my mentor told me to do was to stare my panic attacks in the face and demand more of them. He taught me to reverse engineer the cause of why I kept reacting and recreating the panic syndrome.

After a few attempts, I was able to break the spell of the fear behind a panic attack. Each time the panic episode would reach a pinnacle of terror, as I asked for more and more—the waves of fear would calm, and peace would flood my body.

Eventually, the panic attacks left for good. My attitude towards the phenomenon I once feared shifted. **I stopped fighting and used my vulnerability as my power.**

Vulnerability As A Weapon Against Ignorance

Let me back up for a moment and tell you some more about vulnerability. It is the difference between real power, and force and anger. Force (threat) and anger (violence) are nothing but ignorance surfacing to be "cleared."

The first step is to recognize when you reactivate a feeling of powerlessness, and you feel overwhelmed.

If you habitually engage in battle with your hologram (your creation), just observe what you're doing and surrender your need to fight against yourself.

Be in control!

Surrender doesn't mean give up and give in—it means relax into the control that you already have as The God-like human being with all of the answers to the problems already buried within your consciousness.

Again, just read these words and reflect (for now). The exercises in the book will be SIMPLE and more efficient than you can imagine.

I'll show you how to **relax and allow**, to shift consciousness, move to a parallel universe, and walk in miracles, every day.

How do I know this will work for you?

You are already born as an entirely whole human being, endowed with the power of your creator.

At Last, Moving Beyond Mind-Control

When the problem shows up, the solution shows up as well. Duality perpetuates with a "Problem-Reaction-Solution" framework perception, while wholeness means the solution exists within the perceived problem. #YouAreWhole

David Icke talks about how humanity is mind-controlled by a program of "Problem-Reaction-Solution." Our reactions are due to the **false belief we hold in two-powers; good and evil.**

RETURN TO INNOCENCE!

You were born as an expression of the God-force. You surrender to the situation by relaxing and allowing the solution to appear. Allowing is the opposite of forcing and fighting against it. Fighting against your hologram creates more to fight against, more struggle.

Let's now reason for a moment: if anger and force are poverty states of being, relaxing and allowing (through surrender) is the wealthy person's antidote to the **mass hallucination that implies the world is outside of us**, subjecting its will upon us at all times.

This idea of "wholeness" is a different awareness from what you learned in your household, school, or cultural programming. Don't initiate force—force is just powerlessness in disguise.

Yes, I played hockey for years and was a defensive enforcer on the ice. Eventually, all that force came back and after four head concussions—there's a reason I never groomed my children to pursue contact sports. They are free to engage if they desire, but I'm not an advocate for violence of any nature.

So what happens when you choose the non-violent and non-aggressive path to allow things to happen for you?

Once you have made this decision, you align yourself with your God-like power. Being in this flow is the expression of heart-centered love and being vulnerable.

It is your natural state of being—innocence. After all, it is your attitude towards life reflected back in your circumstances.

#ChildlikeInnocence

war is powerlessness declaring itself mighty

Look at it this way: the war on drugs creates more drug problems. The war on cash creates a public demand for cash.

The war on another country creates radicals who become violently aggressive as their family and friends lose their lives by the use of bombs, drones, bullets, and foreign invasions.

What is behind all this? You may not like my opinions, but I'm going to speak my truth. Here's the setup:

Anger. (Spiritual ignorance).

A program. (War cult-ure).

A hypnotic spell. (Patriotic duty to support a War Flag).

Look, if you served your country under the pretense of preserving freedom, you were doing what was right in your heart.

You deserve to receive the respect you earned for your sacrifice. At the same time, many people find out (a little too late) that war is a profitable business and the "Expendables" isn't just a movie title.

Bodies get buried while loved ones depart forever, and who wins? The families that lost their loved ones? Or the ones who sell the ammunition, guns, bombs, tanks, and missiles?

Casualties of war are usually never the ones who initiate the battle. Instead, war is a racket (profitable) by funding both sides and spinning a narrative that is *culturally mesmeric.*

By the time the soldier returns from battle, the horrifying reality of war leaves a permanent wound on their psyche.

Want to change the world? I promise you already have GOD-LIKE POWER to do so, and you won't be the first person to have this power and utilize it. Fighting won't change the world, ever.

All great men and women, who have tapped into LOVE'S power (not violence) and used it to fuel their life's work, eventually discover this realization.

By now, you're probably figuring it out: I'm not going to give you any power that you don't already have. I'm reminding you how to turn on its full potential and open the throttle for maximum thrust!

YOU WILL change the world if you do exploit this potential inside yourself.

In chapter 12, you'll see how Dr. Len has done it and how fast the results can occur. Please don't skip through unless you desperately have to get to work "clearing" immediately.

There are many insights I've planted in this book to cause a *Sutra-like* alteration of perception; perception is our reality. A new world will emerge if you're ready for it.

YOU ARE THE CENTER OF YOUR UNIVERSE

You are standing in the middle of your creation. You are looking out to your circumstances. There is no such thing as absolute reality. What we see has no meaning until you give the events meaning.

If something happens to you, it is neither good nor bad: it has just materialized.

Ten years from now, you may say that what felt like the worst thing that happened to you at the time was the best thing that ever happened to you.

Perspective can change how you view the events with hindsight being 20/20. You assign meaning to your life, but without perfect vision—you risk prematurely throwing out the baby with the bathwater.

"Only the good is true" if you want only the good to be real, as it is your attitude towards life as the mirror of consciousness revealing itself to you. #RepetitionLearning

You CAN set up the game to win.

Instead of the old reaction of anger, which just creates more poverty, more lack, more frustration, and more infuriating circumstances, come from non-resistance.

You can, and you are going to stand in your power this way because *relaxing and allowing* will attract wealth and prosperity.

You were born spiritually-endowed. You are a deity. You were born with sufficient means to succeed already in your genetic code.

You DO create your world from the inside out. Self-mastery is an inner game: **you can** act in a vulnerable capacity by expressing love. **Love obsoletes** all forms of violence and **ignorance**.

Non-resistance (vulnerability) is an affirmation of absolute command over the forces operating in your environment.

The "Jedi-Force" in you becomes awakened in a surrendered, relaxed state of being. **Surrender begins with non-judgment.**

Cracking the whip on your circumstances affirms you're ensnared in the ties-that-bind. Again, I'm referring to the labyrinth of the mind and the six-degrees of separation.

EDEN: BEFORE THE KNOWLEDGE OF "GOOD AND EVIL"

When you master allowing, you are surrendering your firm and fixed hard attitudes towards life.

You are "being" in control, by letting go and becoming vulnerable. Hard circumstances occur because of hard attitudes towards life.

We are going to soften that process to step into peace and prosperity. A new response will create a new cellular memory—a new consciousness—which will produce a further reaction and a new outcome.

We must revoke our propensity towards "less-than" thinking. As in, "I'm less-than others because (fill in the blank)." #NoJudgment

All self-esteem issues are a manifestation of poverty consciousness. You get to the root of it. The source of it is the tendency to react with anger, resistance, and force-backed coercion.

From now on, think of your reactions and what drives them. Be aware of the perceptions that you have and the meanings that you assign to things as they happen.

I'm not asking you to go to counseling and sit for hours on a couch. I'm not Dr. Phil. Just be cognizant that patterns repeat themselves because of our reaction.

Karma Is: Action, Cellular Memory, Reaction

No matter what happens to you, recognize that at some point you created an action which created a cellular memory which generated an automatic response within you.

We'll "clear" all this junk out, later. The action of clearing is when miracles happen—sometimes instantly.

Our Behavior And Thinking Is Pre-Programmed

You find yourself wanting to re-enforce the use of force that you learned in your home, tribe, school, or cultural program.

Heck, every time we salute our troops, are we doing so because we are grateful for their service, or are we excited about the next action movie with an act of violence every five minutes?

I'm not judging. We have a legitimate purpose for a military presence (within our borders) to protect us from all enemies, both foreign and domestic.

Many of my friends have served their country and are great men and women of honor. And, at the same time—have we taken things a bit all over the world as if we are the world's police? #TeamAmerica

We've gotten so accustomed to violence in our American culture that Clotaire Rapaille tells us the cultural code for "sex" is "violence." We are (literally) getting off on it, while the vast majority of the world's public wishes for abstinence.

I'm merely observing how amplified our penchant for violence in America has become. And, how does this tie into our economic situation? $20 trillion in debt and counting, with no end in sight.

If a government can print money out of thin air without any consequences or audit for their reckless spending, someone is going to get screwed.

I'm not sure about you, but I didn't see my friends and family get any vaseline in 2008 when the markets bent them over.

I tell you this because we are perpetually at war. ***Commerce is war!*** Let me say what I mean, and why it is essential to think outside the mainstream "idiocracy farm" they call the educational system or *public fool* system.

Here's Where Your Slavery Began And Ends

Our core structures that lead to our social structures (law and money) permeate everything.

Law permeates everything; it is what holds us all together. We built our foundation of money on our system of law, over thousands of years. M.O.N.E.Y. is the acronym for your energy field. My Own Natural Energy Yield.

Law has been used to bind and control our energy and assets—with trustees, wardens, rules, regulations, and mental constructs we adhere to as "law-abiding" citizens.

A citizen is the property of a government; a franchise — an artificial construct—operating as an individual (corporation).

Property and franchise relationships were designed to expand into a monetary system (with insurmountable debt) and then, collapse. All the way back to ancient Egypt, Sumer, all the way back for thousands of years, this cycle has repeated.

We are all under military occupation today, and it is the responsibility (under The Lieber Code of April 24, 1863) of the military to maintain all the public systems, and establish rules if the population becomes belligerent.

The United States is the military occupier of the planet. *Team America wasn't just a cartoon movie.* #PlainSight

We're under perpetual war and perpetual emergency—giving all power to maintain military occupation.

We call this "public policy"—**public policing**. (Who needs policing? Criminals; guilty people).

The Trading With The Enemy Act of 1917 excluded persons in the United States; in 1933 F.D.R. (after the *purposeful* collapse in 1929) proclaimed a national emergency.

#ProblemReactionSolution #MindControl

March 9, 1933—The Emergency Banking Relief Act, amended the Trading With The Enemy Act to **include U.S. Persons, declaring them as an "enemy of the State."**

This amendment gave the president singular authority, pre-approved to make executive orders.

The Pen is Mightier Than the Sword, Remember?

The Trading With The Enemy Act was amended to *include every citizen and every transaction* and any form of national emergency.

Trading With the Enemy Act Sec. 5(b)

"During time of war or **any** other period of national **emergency** declared by the President, the President may, through any agency that he may designate, or otherwise, investigate, regulate, or prohibit, under such rules and regulations as he may prescribe, by means of licenses or otherwise, **any transactions** in foreign exchange, transfers of credit between or payments by banking institutions as defined by the President, and export, hoarding, melting, or earmarkings of gold or silver coin or bullion or currency by **any person within the United States** or any place subject to the jurisdiction thereof; and the President may require any person engaged in any transaction referred to in this subdivision to furnish under oath, complete information relative thereto, including the production of any books of account, contracts, letters or other papers in connection therewith in the custody or control of such person, either before or after such transaction is completed."

On March 9, 1933, Roosevelt issued Proclamation 2040. It referred to the national emergency and again asserted Sec. 5(b) as authority for it.

Roosevelt then proclaimed that the Proclamation would remain in full force and effect until proclamation by the President. *It is in force to this day.*

***My observation**: in short, you're in a constant state of danger and ready to react in fear or fight mode for an unconscious reason; your DNA is influenced by your environment—epigenetics. (Symbols, language, cult-ure).*

The mind doesn't consciously recognize what you did not know, until now, but your crystalline structure—DNA Light Body—certainly knows. The

TRUTH was placed in plain sight to hide it from you, while the Father-of-Lies sold you a False-Reality Matrix.

*You've been living in an environment that is in **a state of emergency and perpetual war**. #DeathCulture*

THE BIRTH CERTIFICATE –"DEAD, LOST AT SEA!"

Since the Cestui Que Vie Act of 1666, we've been living under contract with the Crown (The Crown Corporation), born into an estate (trust), abandoned as collateral into a trust—a vessel in commerce—**a secured, bonded surety for all debts.**

Once debt-based collateral systems create fiat currency, the mathematics ensure a collapse is inevitable. #HistoryRepeats

If we remain entrained into "believing we're going to be saved by some external means," we are **energetically lifted into a containment field to build our prison**. Our life energy becomes the "booty" (claims of a war on the land and sea) ensuring the survival of those parasitizing off us.

Our consumer society ensures its very demise. So, in essence, we have an insatiable appetite for destruction. As we exchange our M.O.N.E.Y. in commerce, we reprise our currency back to the sovereign to maintain the war.

#ModernSlavery #SovereignCROWN

The collective (world system: the Beast in Revelation) hologram has captured our consent in a matrix that has been pre-programmed by *Lucifer*, the master architect of FALSE REALITY.

Public Fool System: All you learned in school was to be spellbound by lies and false reality "programming" to keep you subordinate.

Now that your history lesson is complete, here's what you can do about **choosing** the world your offspring will inherit.

Taking Back Free-Will With Sovereign Currency

Remember: a government is a collective out-picturing of mass-consciousness, reflecting itself back at us.

We created the mess we perceive to be in, on the brink of another world war and economic collapse.

What fuels it? Reminisce about what you just read. It begins and ends with you. And me. #WeGotThis

Cryptocurrencies are the first proof of the matrix disintegrating in our consciousness, due to the awakening out of the collective (Beast) trance we lived subordinate to for thousands of years.

A sovereign currency represents the end of the dismembering and our willingness to be separated from ourselves. We are becoming one and equal within our being.

We'll discuss cryptocurrency as a sovereign currency in Chapter 11.

The Art Of War Is Not The Science Of Happiness

Let's assume we decide to wage war on something in our "backdrop" external reality.

Since we are pre-programmed to do this as the culture code in the United States for "perfection" is "death"—we unconsciously seek resolution through death.

The religions of the world have taught us that Heaven (outside of ourselves) is the place of perfection.

So why not talk about how we want to "kill it!" or, "crush it!" We speak our cultural language.

Maybe we could "blast through" our problems, or "nail" that exam, *or that woman*? We spell-cast this stuff all day long.

Do you see it now? It's a death culture with "sex" and "violence" being equals; death is perfection and the means we use to establish our use of force and *willpower, our intent to "destroy"* what we perceive is in our way.

Since the United States exports its culture all over the world—*our most significant exports are debt and entertainment*—this "programming" affects more of the world's population, year after year.

Taking The Harm Out Of Seeking Harmony

We have to wake up from the dream-consciousness (false reality) that puts harm into everyone's path by *perpetuating force and violence to find harmony*. #SeemsLegit

It's the assumption that we are separate from the good we seek that divides us when it's all an illusion.

Nobody is there to attack, but yourself. We argue for our position to be "right" instead of "happy." More judgments.

When we argue to be right, we are only reinforcing the circumstances we are attempting to resolve. This only locks in what we are trying to undo. It keeps us stuck in the problem.

But it isn't unsolvable, not anymore. The way you solve it will be repeated multiple times in many ways throughout this book. **You must stop seeking authority outside of yourself.**

Only then can you break the spell, and dispel the illusion that the world is in control of you. You were *born* in control.

Prosperity has been your birthright since birth, so step into it and express the absolute perfection that you already have.

You will never cease to exist. As an eternal being, you can remove the false belief in "two powers"—the knowledge of good and evil.

Your surrendered state of being that allows you to relax into *allowing*, administers your command over the storms and raging winds.

You may feel vulnerable at first, like floating in a sea of turbulent waters. As you learn to "clear" the source of the sorcery, as we proceed further on this journey together, wisdom will be your reward.

"*Wisdom is the Greatest Magnet for Riches.*"

-Dr. Mike Murdock

CHAPTER 2.

Give me 15 Minutes and I'll Give You God-Like Power to Have It All

This book isn't just full of positive self-help information. Instead, it is a description of the quantum mechanics of the universe.

ASK UNTIL IT IS GIVEN! is a guide to take control of your hologram—the "whole"ogram. There's a lot of information to cover here, so let's get started.

All issues you will encounter in life can be broken down into three basic categories: financial issues, relationship issues, or health issues. All of these categories comprise parts of the "situations" we all face.

All of the internalized ATTITUDES we hold about ourselves and life, show up in our hologram. Your hologram is your extended world. This mirroring is what you are projecting outward towards your universe.

You make the rules in life and the only one judging you is you. If I can get your FOCUS to change, accepting the idea that the *world is inside of you* (including parallel universes), you'll have reclaimed GOD-LIKE-POWER away from the false-reality matrix.

Let's talk more about the architecture of this false-reality matrix and how it's influencing your behavior...

So what are the factors that influence your attitude? Where do these attitudes come from? How do we change them?

As crazy as it first appears, Freemasons and occultists have known for centuries that SYMBOLS run the world. **Symbols program consciousness.**

Symbols affect the emotional brain, tied to the reptilian brain. Here's an example: when I wanted to get in the best shape of my life, I began wearing the Navy SEAL "trident" symbol—every day.

HIJACKING SATAN'S TRIDENT TO "SEIZE" HIS POWER?

The trident is symbolic of Satan's power, so I hijacked the COURAGE it provides. Let's face it; it takes brass-balls to take God head-on, I mean, you gotta be bat-shit crazy or just plain fueled by stupidity?

I guess Frank Zappa was right when he said, "I know how stupid you are" to Satan in his song *Titties and Beer.*

Forgive me, I was being cheeky...

The trident symbol creates courage. *Lo-and-behold*, guess what happened? Courage became my constant companion as the trident influenced my subtle-bodies (astral, etheric, celestial, logoic).

You have a logoic body, hence the word "logo" being used to describe the symbols on products you buy all the time.

The Nike logo (swoosh) represents the greatness of Michael Jordan, Wayne Gretzky, Bo Jackson, and many other iconic athletes.

The slogan, "just do it!" is a neocortex alibi; the motto is an excellent sounding adjunct to the symbol itself.

In other words, the logo influences us at the level of our crystalline matrix, while the idea "just do it!" represents the logical alibi we need to back up the decision to BECOME GREAT.

It's important to notice what you're buying when you wear the logo you're compelled to associate with; using these symbols has adequate proficiency when it comes to unconscious compliance.

Wearing the trident symbol every day, I got in the best shape of my life. My behavior shaped and molded by wearing the logo itself. It gave me a false sense of dominion over my world (in a physical way).

Why do you think a pyramid, the all-seeing eye, and other Masonic symbols appear on the fiat currency we use?

The dollar we are accustomed to using as paper money is a "dead president" **occult ritual** we agree to perform. The bill has a magnetic strip, a signature, and a face on it.

As we engage with the bill, our currency (bioelectric, magnetic) interacts with the DOLL-ar (like a voodoo doll) to siphon our current into the power structures—via symbols on the dollar—and it brings that "dead president" to life!

I recognize this may have stretched your disbelief a bit. I'm only dropping breadcrumbs to get you to open up to the possibility of such a thing, even if you suspect it's science fiction.

What I'm talking about so far could be another book all unto itself, for now just observe the symbols around you. Become aware that they are everywhere and, unconsciously, these symbols influence you to some degree.

Symbols run the world by programming consciousness.

Reflect.

You can consciously choose symbols to INFLUENCE YOUR CRYSTALLINE STRUCTURE, through the chakra system and the Nadi's.

When you willfully take charge and program yourself with the symbols representing your values, you gain cooperation in the subtle energy fields within your bioelectric grid.

Here's an observation I want to share: the flag that we call the American flag (with horizontal stripes), is a war flag.

The "other" American flag with vertical stripes, U.S. Civil or Peacetime flag, shockingly isn't saluted at sporting events. Peace sells, but nobody is buying. #MegaDeath

How do symbols run the world? They PROGRAM CONSCIOUSNESS through the chakra system.

Understanding the chakra system can help us understand our reactions to life as it appears to us.

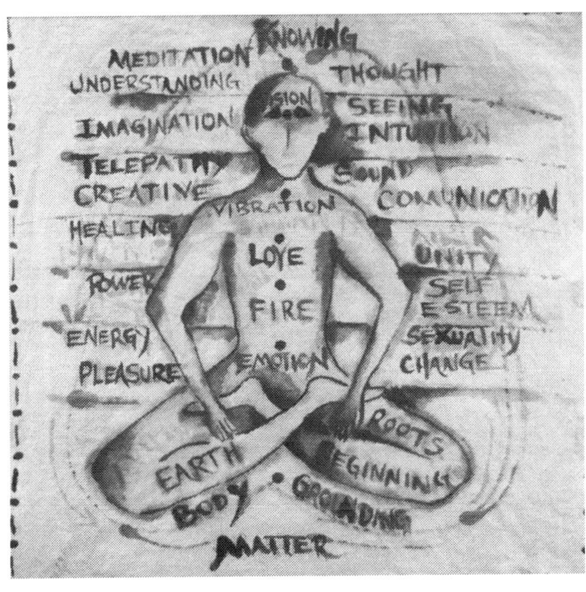

In the chakra system, prevalent in Eastern medicine, there is a meridian system which runs through your body. On these meridians, or lines, that run through your body, there are nodes or energy hubs.

It's like a grid that overlays your body that has some central focus points, called chakras.

Chakras are what we utilize in acupuncture. Eastern cultures have been aware of this for centuries—western civilization is only now catching up.

It's not profitable for medical doctors to teach EFT (Emotional Freedom Technique) or acupuncture, popular in Eastern medicine; profits are all that drive the "sickness" industry. Big Pharma has a stronghold in Western medicine.

Your chakra system isn't just "inside" your body. Now, this is where you must rethink things: your world is inside of you.

Therefore, your chakra system is representing your energy in your perceived "outer world" also...

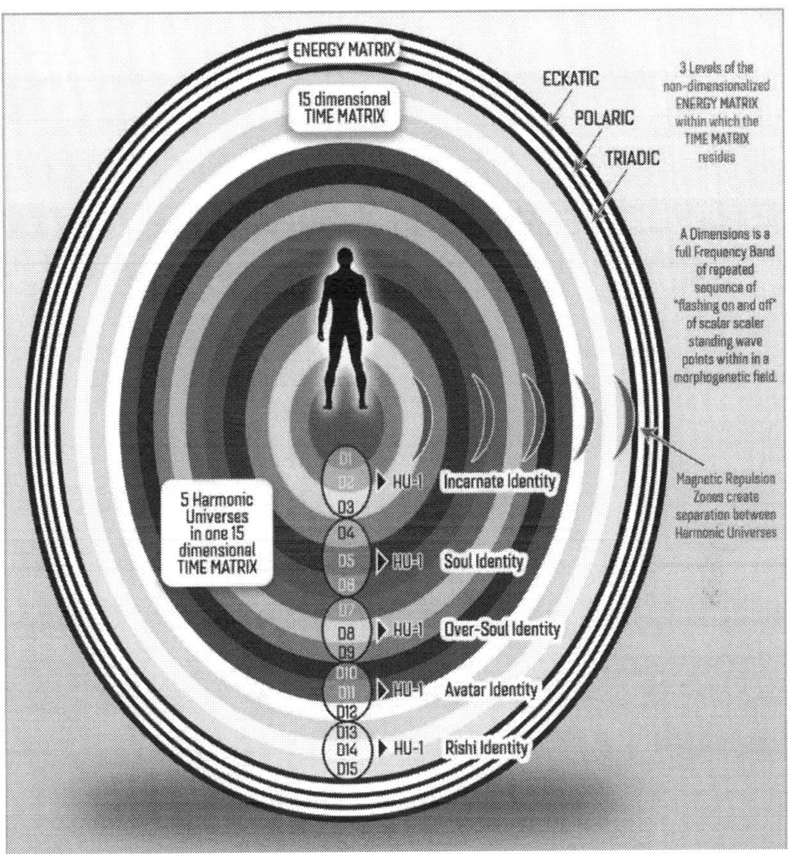

These nodes go beyond our bodies. They extend below us, all the way to the center of the earth. They reach above us to our highest self—our *Rishi* self.

Rishi is our God-consciousness where we are literally, all one. We are all connected through the chakra system.

Then you have the *Christos* self. All religions say that God—Christ—is within you. You have this God molecule within you.

Your Christos is the expression of God that everyone talks about when they say, "God is within you."

This *Christos* self is the part of you that has the power to choose who you are going to show up as in the world. In Christ, all things are possible, right?

You have the instant ability to change the false dynamic that insistently suggests "the outer world is real" and makes you feel small.

Next, you have your avatar self. Your avatar self is near your "Oversoul."

All of these selves come together in the external galactic interface. The whole galaxy—the whole of the cosmos—is indeed interconnected.

You pull all of this together, and it expresses as quarks[2], vibration, and consciousness. We condense it as three-dimensional matter so we can interact with it in our mind.

It is the "whole"ogram. We are the expression of this galactic interface—it becomes seemingly "dense matter" and appears real through our collective agreements.

We agree with the composite false matrix until we take our power back and turn inward, awakening from the illusion.

That is how the human being operates and functions in his or her reality when AWAKENING takes place.

---

[2] A quark is an elementary particle and a fundamental constituent of matter. Quarks combine to form hadrons, which are protons and neutrons, the stable components of atomic nuclei.

All of these bodies unite within you, and you can steer the direction of the ship anytime you *decide to accept full and total responsibility for everything.*

Everything that shows up in your make-believe material reality is nothing more than an extended version of yourself.

The good news is; we can use symbols—*like The Tri-Veca Code*—to perform alchemy. Let's discuss this concept some more, and as you put it to work.

THE BI-VECA CODE

Consider the ancient bi-veca code and symbol. You've seen different logos that tap into its power. It consists of overlapping circles, like the Olympic rings or the Audi symbol.

The bi-veca code represents the power of **electricity** and **sounds** and how *they overlap*. It is an unconscious code that we can use to tap into the vibrations underlying the universe.

A morphogenic field is a field that can transform into whatever it needs to be.

Like stem cells—which can turn into cardiac cells, or toenails, or whatever the body needs them to be—a morphogenic field is part of the galactic interface that can be what it needs to be to represent a consensus agreement.

We can create a morphogenic field by inserting our BELIEF into something, *perhaps a symbol*, and getting others to perform a ritual to add power to the consciousness-grid.

I was alluding to this when you read about the DOLLar bill, earlier in this chapter.

We invoke a ritual around a BELIEF (system), and we harness the CURRENT from others to accelerate the velocity of the magnetic field in our new morphogenic inception. We collect their energy through the ritual, strengthening the morphogenic field.

Once a critical-mass adoption occurs, the wiring in the collective consciousness is complete. You hear about *mass-adoption* all the time, now you know how it happens.

The bi-veca code represents our essential natures. You are bio-electric. You are sound. You are salt and light. These forces are the substratum of all creation.

What you see with your lying eyes is merely a projection of consciousness in a way that your mind comprehends, with its limited awareness.

We can go much deeper to penetrate our sphere of influence; thought is merely the tip of the iceberg. We want CURRENT and CURRENCY to flow, and this requires collaboration.

It's easier to target SUBTLE BODIES beneath the surface and arouse inception within the mental-body, with a backdoor approach.

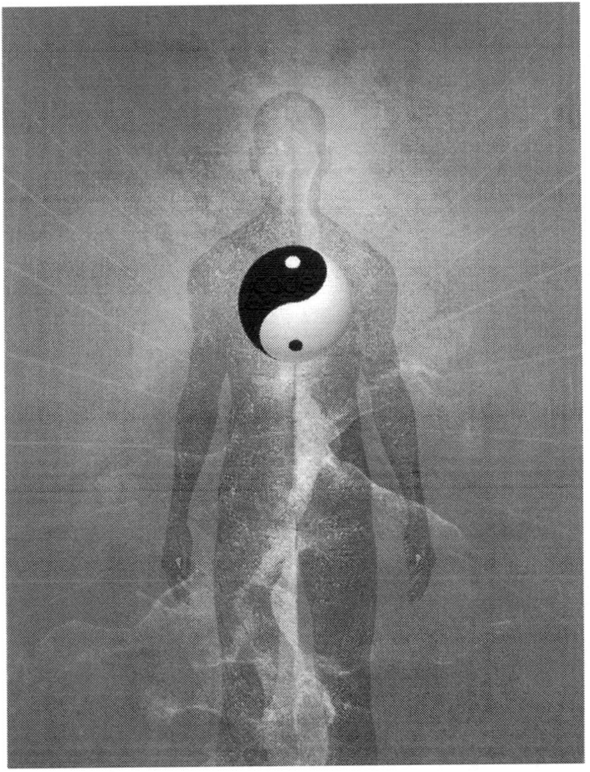

A variation of the bi-veca code is the Yin-Yang symbol we are all familiar with.

The Yin-Yang symbol represents the masculine and feminine within all of us. In this context, the feminine is our ability to ALLOW. The masculine is the ACTION aspect.

You want to attract what you desire and also clear the blocks. Yin and Yang. Action and Allowing.

The Tri-Veca Code (recommended)

You'll learn how to master the TRI-VECA method here:

Webinar: http://www.MatthewDavidHurtado.com

Power Centers

If you want to bring all of this together, here are some tools and hacks you can use to increase the power centers you have.

Monatomic elements fuel the nodes in our chakra system. Monatomic elements are atoms of a single component that remain stable on their own.

Your body is bioelectric. To have it function properly, you need superconductive minerals. Guess what? You'll discover in Chapter 10, these minerals are all but missing in our diets today. #DumbedDown

Expanding your awareness is where the monatomic elements come in. These "m-states" (ORMUS; monatomic elements) allow you to amplify the electrical signals you receive from the chakra system through these nodes.

You can amplify your thought-field, like speaking through a bullhorn! You can also **supercharge your allowing**.

I'll show you an incredible way to create your monatomic ORMUS (from ionic, angstrom minerals mixed in a blender using magnets), in a video link you'll get access to soon.

A Word Of Caution About Monatomic Gold

I'm going to share a video about monatomic gold, where you'll see some cutting-edge science to stretch your mind even more. You'll see what's possible for you, plus gain experience to avoid pitfalls like what I'm about to mention, now:

Please don't rush out to buy monatomic gold if you watch the video I'm about to recommend to you—doing so can speed up your ascension process rapidly and bring about the "hard lessons" I was referring to earlier.

When I told you about how you can be, do, and have it all, it comes with a price-tag. You have to get the LESSONS, first.

What do you suppose happens when you try and ascend faster and cram in a life's worth of lessons in a fraction of the time?

You got it, there will be "hell to pay," and it won't be on Donald Trump's head (*Hell Toupee*).

Listen, I'm not going to get political with you. Just a few "plugs" on Donald here and there, okay?

Let's return to the idea that ASKING for something most often involves receiving the LESSON to be learned, first.

Like Abraham Hicks has said, "You're always asking."

You ask...through contrast. Then, whatever is required shows up often as a "lesson" involving you to FACE A FEAR THAT YOU ARE SUPPRESSING.

Many people have experimented with rapid ascension, including me, only to discover a sudden lawsuit, unexpected tax bill, a divorce, a loss of income, a health issue, etc., appearing in consciousness!

Look, I'll be blunt. I've experienced all these issues. Using monatomic gold to speed this process up is like giving a 16-year-old a key to a 1,000 horsepower supercar.

All the power without the spiritual training to handle rapid ascension may end up in a terrible crash. #LearnFromOthersMistakes

Like many before me who jumped right into consuming monatomic gold to feed the Light Body, I discovered it's not for the faint of heart.

Your deeply suppressed fears will confront you. Why? You can't get to ultimate freedom and the expression of pure love without "clearing" these.

There's a better way to go about this process. I'm going to show you what I discovered after years of experimenting.

The Ultimate Way To Ascend Your Vibration

The method I use now is a more subtle way to feed the ascension process. It involves using ionic, angstrom minerals.

It happens *without* the volatility of spiritual ascension (the monatomic gold method) that makes the cryptocurrency markets look like a tame joyride.

I'm going to give you ideas. You must discern within yourself what is right for your ascension. If you use certain substances and prefer them, keep doing what works.

I can't convince you or stop you from doing anything, just share my experiences.

For several years, I involved myself in high-level esoteric practices including the use of consciousness-altering substances, rituals, and alchemy.

Due to working alongside some compelling "elitists" who invested in my spiritual refinement, firsthand accounts of extraterrestrial phenomena are regular occurrences.

Perhaps it's because I'm an O-negative blood type, left-handed with blue eyes, or just fascinated with all the "7's" in my numerical charts? Either way, the supernatural is quite natural.

RESULTS FROM EXPANDING MY AWARENESS, FAST

I've seen a shape-shifter with my own eyes, in the flesh. A woman transformed into something *other-worldly*, and whatever she is, I wouldn't consider her to be human.

I was not influenced by any substance or hallucination during our interlude. I was stone-cold sober. Albeit brief (in passing), the experience was profound, nonetheless.

Once your awareness pierces through the veil, you can "see" other realities on a different spectrum or frequency. I'll share this story with you, so you have an idea of how impressive this transient moment was.

I was walking into Wal-Mart in Dodgeville, WI. It was just another grocery run, or so I thought at the time. Walking down the main walkway in front of all the checkout aisles, a tall woman was walking towards me.

She was wearing a black jacket, black pants, and she had jet black hair with black sunglasses covering her eyes. Her skin was tan and flawless. Since she was not in Los Angeles, I pegged her as out of place.

Let me interrupt for a minute: one thing I haven't yet mentioned in this book is that I was born clairsentient. The ability to perceive a person's energy and imprint my "knowing" with data received from the person is as natural for me as walking. I can sense things and know them without reasoning.

As the woman walked towards me, I noticed my brainwaves were dropping from beta to alpha and theta. Having experimented with brainwave entrainment for so long, I knew a "trance-state" of consciousness was bearing upon my experience.

Was she causing this to happen, or was I doing this to myself? I wasn't so sure who was at the level of cause anymore.

Scanning my mental records: high-level Freemasons taught me that "extraterrestrial" beings could enter our projection in the theta brainwave; this is where you can find them visible and accessible for you to witness.

In essence, they are other aspects of you that you keep hidden from your conditioned mind (in the false reality matrix).

Walking towards this woman, I could feel her presence from 30-yards away. The weirdness of the sensations I was picking up from her compelled me to turn off my path. I turned left down the greeting card aisle so she could pass.

Doing this made me feel like it was a safe-bet thing to do, just in case. The vibes I was getting from within were awkward, and I trusted my intuition.

Besides, the "all black" thing she had going on was reason enough to suspect I should distance myself—even though she was lovely with a gorgeous physique.

As intrigued as she had me, the dark-side thing was a bit too "gothic" for me, and since minds mingle, I evaded her just in case. I was in a hurry, and something was going on within me, like alarm bells during a fire drill.

After I assumed enough time had passed where she would have crossed after I turned down the greeting card aisle, I turned around. To my surprise, she had turned down the greeting card aisle also and was walking straight towards me. How weird!

As she got closer, I felt a similar phenomenon that happened when I totaled a car in my early 20's; time stopped, and everything was in altered consciousness.

My heart was pumping, and my senses heightened with awareness focused towards the checkout aisle. "I'll just walk right past, and all this will be a strange coincidence. Who knows, maybe this chick is getting a card?" I thought.

She neared me about three feet ahead and pulled her sunglasses down from her eyes. Her face morphed and I saw a reptilian creature appear while her eyes "bugged out" as if she intended that I "see her" for what she is.

Internally, my mind couldn't grasp this. Like anything without a reference point, cognitive dissonance was dissuading me from entertaining what just happened. Similar to how trauma gets blocked out and suppressed, this experience was hard to grasp.

This woman was not human! If she appeared human, it was on a frequency wavelength in beta, and as my brainwaves dropped into theta, her physical appearance radically changed.

As for me, fortunately, I had my hands empty still. So, I just walked out of the store and briskly left the scene of what just happened, knowing "all is well." I could sort this out mentally later.

You cannot take a person's experience away. It wasn't some conspiracy theory or YouTube video where a clever camera trick deceived my eyes.

My consciousness shifted my awareness into a frequency range where the untrained eye could not go. She was real, and so was the experience of "seeing her" for WHAT she is, whatever that may be.

Two other similar experiences worth mentioning in the scope of this book are as follows:

I've also jumped into parallel universes that caused me to leave objects in different realities, awaken with "physical" markings from an astral journey, and obtain knowledge from other versions of myself.

Case in point: I was getting gas at a pump in Lone Rock, WI. After paying for the gas and returning to the car, my keys mysteriously vanished. I checked every pocket. I checked the inside of the store. I looked inside the vehicle and retraced every step.

After my search was fruitless, I had to have Sabrina come and pick me up because my keys suddenly went missing.

Sabrina was not happy because it forced her to leave a family dinner with her parents and drive an extra hour to get me and then get my backup keys at the farmhouse.

As I walked up to the farmhouse, I saw a shiny object in the field echoing a moonlit glow towards my eyes. The reflection was about 15-yards south of my front steps.

As I walked up to see what it was, there were my keys. The same keys that I used to drive to the gas station.

As my mind began panicking, thinking, "How in the heck did this happen?!" Nothing added up logically.

The only realization is that I slipped in one dimension and out the other, leaving my keys as a reminder that "I've been traveling through space-time." If it were the first time this happened to me, I'd chalk it up as an anomaly.

Strange spectacles have emerged all too often in my vast expanse of consciousness. Once you begin exploring consciousness, amplifying your biomagnetic field, these happenings become the new "normal."

I will also contend that you can tap into SUPER HEALING CONSCIOUSNESS as you expand your realm of "what's possible" and give up your limitations.

I'll Take Cover In Public Incredulity

Some may see this as B.S. and think I'm making it up. If so, this is a good thing. *Public incredulity* is the best protection against character assassination. Between you and me, this is a bonafide reality. No approval is required.

Increase the magnetic capacity in your bioelectric energy system, and you too may **explore the cosmos in alternative attitudes towards life**!

Remember how I mentioned that it's our attitude towards life reflecting back to us as reality? #ThinkOutsideTheBox

Lastly, this isn't something that hasn't been experienced by a vast majority of people. It's worth sharing because of how close in proximity the following event occurred.

I was in my 8,000-square-foot mansion. Keep in mind; it was already spooky due to the property being on top of a towering hill, all alone in the country. Sure, I had neighbors... about half a mile away in the lower valley.

The estate was across from a private airport. Outside the giant windows in the family room, you could see the airport at night. Typically, there's not much to see. But, not on one particular night, in August of 2014.

There was a massive U.F.O. hovering right above the landing strip, and the size of this craft was at least a mile long.

The spacecraft was enormous and so close that it scared the living daylights out of me. I grabbed my shotgun thinking, "Crap, what if that ship is here to do something to my 'castle' (that's what I called the home)? I could be abducted!!"

I threw the shotgun in the truck and sped down the winding driveway and floored it—driving as fast as possible in the opposite direction as the spaceship.

Grabbing my iPhone, I called to make sure my kids were at Sabrina's house and told them I was coming over.

Sabrina asked me what was going on and she chuckled, "It's just a U.F.O., it's not going to hurt you." Sabrina was the perfect person to call because she had spent time with (Eduard) Billy Meier in her youth (pic below). Her grandfather was the head of a MUFON chapter, so naturally, she was excited.

I didn't believe in any of this paranormal and alien type of stuff until Sabrina came along. She used to irritate me talking about aliens all the time and telling me how cool they are; she was teaching me, and it took time to open my mind.

After I got off the phone with Sabrina, I went on Facebook, and there were others who posted updates about this craft hovering near their homes. Ironically, nobody uploaded a photo.

I'll be candid with you, in my haste to get as far away as possible from this area, the last thing I wanted to do was become a paparazzi and grab some social media clout.

My mental chatter argued that the time it took to get the phone out and aim it at the ship might be time better spent heading the other direction.

Following this sighting, for about a month straight, I witnessed military Blackhawk helicopters running drills at this same airport, across from my estate. These Blackhawks were very loud and annoying; they would fly directly over my home and circle around a giant area, over and over again.

To this day, I'm wondering if they were tracing magnetic grids (where the U.F.O. traveled) or scouring the area in case something on that ship was "missing" or left behind in the area.

I've since sold the estate and moved into the city. I'll always remember that U.F.O. sighting and a few other paranormal adventures along the way.

Revealed - The Ideal Monatomic Element Solution

Ken Rohla's work shed insight into my new method of getting monatomic minerals into my body, without the chaos.

He witnessed many people doing the same thing that happened to me—rapid ascension with massive chaos happening in their lives. Ken discovered the solution.

I'll expand on this idea later. I wanted to give you this information before sharing the next conclusion, so you ease off the trigger and WAIT to consider my "blender method."

Before I share my *home run strategy*, keep in mind: the pinch-hitter way of consuming ORMUS and monatomic gold can be a wild ride of "hard lessons."

Monatomic gold is potentially unstable in many processes used; ***spagyric*** is the only one recommended.

Now that I've warned you about the pitfalls, here's some great content to consider watching.

An Eye-Opening Revelation About Monatomic Gold

If you haven't yet, take the time to watch Laurence Gardner's Lost Secrets of the Sacred Ark video, which you can find for free on YouTube.

Gardner does a great job of explaining how the scientific models we used to understand have become obsolete. His understanding of theoretical physics—and how it is becoming less and less *theoretical*—highlights the importance of these monatomic elements.

The use of monatomic elements like gold, silver, iridium, ruthenium, and others is becoming more and more understood.

My research indicates that these elements are all part of your higher being. They are a part of the multi-dimensional aspect of your *Rishi* self.

I prefer to use minerals and generate monatomic ORMUS via the procedure of "vortexing" my water with magnets. I do this by spinning the water through a blender, creating a vacuum, like a tornado. This process changes the molecular structure—*in the vortex*!

It's simple to do and the IDEAL SOLUTION for the desire to generate monatomic elements. We begin with minerals, magnets, a blender, and water.

I Call These Super Minerals: Monatomia™

At the link below, I'll show you how to build your own Monatomia™ with your household blender!

http://www.Monatomia.com

When you're ready for the benefits of homemade monatomic ORMUS without the rollercoaster ride of unstable monatomic gold, think Monatomia™.

You're not risking the uncertainty of rapid ascension by ingesting monatomic gold or "white powder gold."

Biohacking The Consciousness Of Life Itself

At the same time, you are **gaining the unfair advantages** feeding your brain, pineal gland, and chakras *superconductive monatomic minerals*!

How does this work, precisely? Scalar energy from the Earth and cosmos can flow in and out of your physical body, through superconducting monatomic minerals.

The body collects more extensive deposits of these minerals along the spine and the pineal gland, corresponding to the chakras.

Our chakras (collective hubs; nodes) are portals for spiraling vortices of the scalar energies of consciousness.

Your brain is a scalar wave transceiver; your spine, nervous system, and DNA are the antenna.

Why does Monatomia™ consist of minerals **and** fulvic acid? Is it necessary to include both, or are minerals enough?

Let's explore each of these for a brief overview:

Minerals are the currency of life, according to Dr. Joel Wallach. Chapter 10 is all about health. For now, the simple answer is: *minerals are the currency of life*, and *fulvic acid is all about bioavailability*.

I'll touch on Monatomia™ again in chapter 10.

I'm bringing Monatomia™ into the picture now so you can have fun with the benefits you may acquire, even if you do nothing more than learn about it to increase your knowledge.

Your magnetics and your resonance vibration are of utmost importance. You'll see that these two pillars become a theme throughout the entire book.

Our Waking State Is But A Dream Of Physicality

Phineas Parkhurst Quimby was a spiritual healer who lived in the early 1800s in America. Quimby posited that we don't have physical bodies.

On second thought, we are in a dream-state of consciousness (held together by opinions) like the nursery rhyme:

Row, row, row your boat

Gently down the stream

Merrily, merrily, merrily, merrily

Life is but a dream.

Life is, in fact, but a dream. We, as people, are little more than—or perhaps as much as—thought manifested. *Cogito ergo sum.* I think, therefore I am. I am my thoughts.

Careful investigation will reveal Quimby's discovery that "minds mingle" is a naked truth. We stir about in a sea of error (opinions) attempting to persuade us into temptation. #FalseRealityMatrix

Think about it—everything you can take in through your five senses is just a product of your thoughts. Pain is just a perception of your mind. That's why people can have phantom pains in limbs that aren't there anymore.

Nothing you perceive is physical; it is all a construct of your thoughts. Just like in the movie "The Matrix," everything we observe is only our perception. It is not physical.

Everything is just consciousness. When we want to do things, we can access higher aspects of ourselves, like our Christos, or Christ-self, or our Rishi-self. In this way, we can influence our hologram without ego resistance.

When we do this, we can activate through all the minds of other people—our collective consciousness.

We can use the energies that are contained within the Tri-Veca symbol and create what we desire in a more streamlined and efficient way.

Alchemy is the art of demonstrating metaphysical truths in a way that convinces our lying eyes and deceitful senses.

THE MINISTER OF ALLOWING

I call myself the Minister of Allowing because my focus has been on teaching people the art of ALLOWing. That's why I wrote the book, **Allow - Mastering the Art of Least Effort to Achieve Your Desires!**

This book, **ASK UNTIL IT IS GIVEN!** is designed to be the advanced material—part two to that book.

The book ALLOW is an expression of the exact ideas you're learning. It's one thing to think something and another to experience the manifestation.

Making a decision one day that I would be a #1 bestselling author and write a book that could show anyone how to get what they want, was step one.

I liked the way it made me feel. Like Tony Robbins discovered, we all have human needs. Contributing to the world is one of those needs.

I decided to contribute in a meaningful way, to leave a legacy into my world. Once I felt inspired, I sat down and wrote the book in less than two days.

It took a few weeks to edit the book. It just poured through me, as soon as inspiration bubbled-up inside. I took inspired action and surrendered myself to the writing process.

You'll be doing the same inspired action and "clearing" that I did, as you complete this book. The same process applies for the obtainment of anything you desire.

It's not hard to make a million dollars, write a bestselling book, get the body of your dreams, fall in love and attract the perfect mate. It's aligning with it and surrendering to the "flow."

As strange as it may seem, all this foundational understanding is critical to your long-term application.

You gotta know how things work before you fall under a "spell" again in the false-reality matrix. I'm going to break your spell, but you must choose to stay in the ALLOWING state of surrendered non-resistance.

We all get sidetracked at various intersections in our life experiences. I get swayed into bad patterns and have to remember the path back to least resistance, in spite of my knowledge.

I want to help you clear the blockages in your unconscious, so you can ALLOW yourself to manifest much more efficiently.

Belief work and mental foreplay are usually inefficient at helping someone make permanent improvements.

When you work solely on the beliefs in your mind, you are focusing only on your three-dimensional reality. You can go beyond that and get a more leveraged approach.

Here are some of the tools and tips that I've been using to help manifest my life the way I want it to be:

Love, Wealth, Self-Esteem, and God-Consciousness

In the area of love, I like to use the mantra developed by Dr. Baskaran Pillai: "Kleem." The KLEEM mantra attracts love. I've found it to be unexpectedly equal to or greater than any pick-up artist methods or mind game strategies.

When you're ready to stop entertaining the western culture code "false expectation = love" game, try something different on for size: use "KLEEM."

Chant "KLEEM" 108 times each day, or listen to Dr. Pillai chant it on YouTube and take in the sounds.

"Shreem Brzee" is the mantra for wealth. The Hindus believe that this mantra invokes the energy of Lakshmi, the goddess of wealth and abundance. #TapTheMorphicField

You can hijack the power behind their collective belief (morphogenic field) and have it also work for you. Symbols run the world and SOUND is the edifice of inception.

In the Holy Bible, the only thing God ever did was—speak.

For self-esteem, I like to use the mantra "Hreem." Hreem vibrates the matrix in a way that creates a positive aura around you of self-confidence.

When I want to activate the God-consciousness within me, I use the mantra "Arul." Arul is the sound used to achieve a higher consciousness.

You can invoke an atmosphere within yourself to perpetuate whatever vibrational state of being you desire.

Just as music can change the atmosphere of any environment (in seconds), mantras can change your inner-environment.

Once I have activated these vibrations, they will cause me to take inspired action to achieve my goals.

In this way, I complete the creation process. You will always be required to take an ACTION, but it's never because your mind is doing anything to create; mental chatter doesn't influence creation. You must take an ACTION to create!

Using monatomic ORMUS, symbols, sounds, and even the spoken word—these are the **tools to go beyond the rational mind**.

Expanding on this idea: you speak to instruct the mind, not the other way around!

Most people speak what's on their mind. Speak instead about what you desire to be on your mind.

Regarding the spoken word and the use of mantras:

Go back a few pages to where I talked about the bi-veca symbol. The rings are overlaps of electrical vibrations and sound.

These mantras provided above are sounds that enable the electrical vibrations required to activate in you what you desire.

Do you want to experience LOVE in your world in a way that supersedes logical understanding?

Do a 30-day "KLEEM" challenge. Chant the mantra 108 times every day. Just watch what happens in your awareness as you align with LOVE and your hologram presents it back at you.

If you set up the sequence in the right way, you can create reality in a much more efficient pace.

Remember those morphogenic fields I keep mentioning? It's the vibration behind the structures we're interested in arousing.

YOU ARE WHAT YOU THINK YOU ARE

Man is what he believes he is. If you think you're small, and you identify with being small, then you will have a modest lifestyle in your hologram.

Everything that shows up in your hologram will match the corresponding IDEAS that you've decided to hold in your awareness.

People like Donald Trump or Bill Gates show up larger than life. They have decided to be very prominent in their world, being established and successful, and this reflection is what shows up in their reality.

This DECISION to be, do, and have it all according to your desires, is something that you have within you, too. You can activate it in the ways described in this book.

Once you "clear" the obstacles, you'll be witnessing your GOD-POWER firsthand, standing in awe at how magnificent the gift of life indeed is.

ONE MONEY TECHNIQUE THAT BLEW MY MIND

TITHING

Do you like money? Don't forget that tithing is an excellent opportunity to use morphogenic fields to your advantage.

I explained in my book ALLOW that I believe giving back ten percent of your income to your Creator is one of the best things you can do to ensure the continuation of prosperity.

What you put out into the world comes back to you. It's one of the immutable laws of the universe.

Now, when I say tithing or giving back to your Creator, I don't necessarily mean giving ten percent of your income directly to your church.

You give to where you have received spiritual nourishment; a place or person where God's work shows itself. Two valuable insights I've discovered: you sow seeds up for prosperity, and you sow seeds down for health.

Let me explain: you tithe to a person or place where they are demonstrating prosperity (i.e., plenty of wealth and riches) and this ties you into that same anointing. Their consciousness of success attaches to you through the tithe you send to them.

Many people find this lesson out the hard way. Being kind and compassionate souls, they tithe to a homeless person or a struggling family, only to find themselves in a similar situation.

Why does this happen? If you pass judgment on someone, assuming they are "needy"—even though by all appearances they may be—and you sow current (currency) into that vibration, you reap what you sow. #PauseThinkReflect

Instead, when you sow seeds up and give it to where someone REMINDS YOU OF THE VAST WEALTH in this world *because they have demonstrated it in their circumstances*, it becomes your karma, too. *Action, cellular memory, reaction.*

You are attaching your ENERGY to every transaction you make, including the THOUGHT-FIELD (karma) associated with your action.

Something interesting occurs when you sow money to feed the poor, however. You gain health. I believe it is because you are DOING IT WITH LOVE and not pity. If you do so out of pity, you generate karma to wield pity back at you.

When I sow seeds for more money and wealth, it goes to someone or somewhere that has an overflowing bounty of material sustenance.

Usually, it is someone who is teaching me about God's unlimited bounty, and they are demonstrating it as valid in their reality! #SeedSown!

If I'm looking for better health, I look for a ministry that feeds children. Feeding children initiates LOVE in my vibrational field. #SeedSown!

If you learn to **LIVE BY THE SEED PRINCIPLE**, you will be at the level of cause. Your solution is to SOW more and stand surrendered for divine inspiration to operate through you.

Natural Medicine Breakthroughs

HEALTH IS WEALTH

Natural medicine is another collective body of knowledge. When I wanted to resolve my Lyme disease that had me bedridden for almost two years, I had to ignore Western medicine.

The morphogenic field of Western medicine didn't have any solutions for me. There was no collection of knowledge, no collective body of people that had transformed to becoming well again in that way. I had nothing to identify with to believe in healing.

I spent over ten-thousand hours of my life researching natural medicine and natural healing. My journey of self-healing began as early as age thirteen. I've been at this for a long time.

I learned how to heal myself on many occasions. I condensed the information into simple shortcuts. You can use my discoveries to further your knowledge of wellbeing.

After all, if you're <u>not</u> experiencing excellent health, life isn't nearly as enjoyable as it should be. Here's what you can do:

You can find the **six keys to perfect health: the ultimate blueprint for perfect health** at my website blog.

Get a FREE membership at the link below:

http://www.CompleteAscentials.com

CHAPTER 3.

How I Manifested 6.1 Million Dollars using One Law of Attraction Secret

How much money can you make selling guitars on eBay, tea, supplements, coaching, and a myriad of other strategies?

You can make zero dollars, and you can make millions, billions, or more! Who determines that outcome? You do.

If you told me in 2009, after bankrupting and being bedridden with Lyme disease, I could build a million-dollar empire (or more), you would have ANGERED me. Aha! There it is again. The cause of my poverty wasn't resolved yet.

Back then, I had no experience building internet income or any other unique skills. My entire focus was downtrodden and mired in hopelessness.

RELEASING GUILT ALLOWS YOU TO BE UNSTOPPABLE

Now that I have achieved the success I would have told you was "impossible" for me (from where I began), I'm not going to keep my methods secret.

I am going to teach you what allowed me to use the law of attraction and build a seven-figure income within three short years. It happened fast.

I didn't just build one business—I built THREE. I sold two companies, built up the third, and here I am. It's amazing the progress I made. I was bedridden and bankrupt.

I had nothing, not even my health. But I learned that I could take control of the situation and SHOW UP the way I wanted to be.

I'm going to teach you the exact step-by-step process that I used to do that. This technique has been kept secret until now.

After meditating for three days after inspiration tapped me on the shoulder, I knew a miracle was arriving. Something to share with the world. In a moment, I'll be introducing you to the Safe Touch Method ™

First, let's explore the axis point where we get stuck.

GUILT IS SUPPRESSING YOUR VIBRATION

Imagine that you are holding something buoyant, like a ball, under water. The minute you release your hand from this ball, it shoots up and out of the water, then bobs on top of it.

This analogy is similar to what is happening with your (NON) ACCEPTANCE OF GOOD when you are held captive by guilt. Guilt is the hand that is holding your desires away from you, casting you down with a litany of self-punishment and shame.

You're not even aware of this guilt. Guilt **symbolically** programs itself in your DNA, through the crystalline body.

Remember, we discussed symbols and logos?

I'll show you how DEEP the Rabbit hole goes. Remember when I said that government is merely a projection of mass-consciousness?

The national anthem. Who wrote it? Do you know? There are five verses, and most people only remember the first verse. It speaks of the British shelling Fort McHenry in the Baltimore harbor.

We're not talking about the Revolutionary War; we're talking about the War of 1812. The "Founding Fathers" had nothing to do with our "National Anthem" and it wasn't a song.

The "National Anthem" was a poem matched to music from England. This poem became known as the "National Anthem" in 1931.

Do you know who made the decision (for generations of blind followers) to make this poem into a national song?

Politicians. You're thinking, "Are you fricking kidding me? A professional parasite on society decided to program my parents or grandparents to be saluting England?"

Okay, you probably didn't think this—but you should consider the implications of what this PROGRAMS INTO YOUR CONSCIOUSNESS when you **place your hand over your heart** and ACTIVATE THE MORPHOGENIC FIELD within your vibrational field.

#FeelUneasyYet? #SlaveConsciousness

The "National Anthem" failed to pass the vote seven times. Back in earlier times, people had plenty more good sense about things; try and take an eighth-grade exam from the late 1800s or early 1900s—you'll see how dumbed down we've become.

#Flouride #Bromine

Now, let's discuss how we salute the War flag and "Pledge Allegiance" to it. After all, it's one of the most common SYMBOLIC influences programming your consciousness (if you are a United States Citizen).

The Pledge of Allegiance was written in 1892 by Francis Bellamy, a "socialist."

If you have an IQ even remotely above room temperature, this should get you stirring a bit.

The Pledge was intended to get young children to worship the State. In 1942, in the midst of World War II, The Pledge of Allegiance was adopted by Congress.

Look, every time you unconsciously "SEE" the War flag, just remember how the Trading With The Enemy Act was amended and how *we're in a perpetual war,* and what this does to your crystalline matrix (epigenetics). #AreYouTheEnemy?

Shall I go on? How about the Statue of Liberty? Liberty: "liberty" comes from the same root word as "libertine."

Libertine is what British sailors receive when they reach a port of call, having nothing to do with freedom. Do you see a common thread emerging—Britain, England?

Whoever controls history controls the present. Who wrote history?

#Conquerors

Unconsciously, we have been worshiping "graven images, idols." We see movies that put the TRUTH IN PLAIN SIGHT.

WHY "GOOD PEOPLE" SIT AROUND AND DO NOTHING

The way the human mind works, because of the corrupted language (See :David-Wynn: Miller) is as follows: as long as the TRUTH appears in open view, we will GRAVITATE TOWARDS THE LIE.

If the TRUTH were kept hidden out of plain sight, our mind would question the lie and truth would "pop out"—revealing itself.

#MindHack #PauseThinkReflect

You see movie titles, like ***A Bug's Life***. It shows you that you are the ant, the worker-slave for the giant grasshopper—the State.

It's a real story about your life, in plain sight. These memes are everywhere because as long as they are OUT IN THE OPEN, nobody will believe it. Instead, the mind will gravitate towards the lie.

#ProgrammedGuilt

SPEAKING OF PUTTING THINGS IN PLAIN SIGHT

Enter the **GILTI tax**, a new 2018 addition to the tax code. Act 20 and Act 22 are the "loopholes" many entrepreneurs use to take advantage of Puerto Rico's tax-haven.

In essence, GILTI is an acronym for a new tax provision having to do with this "loophole." Look, I'm not here to give financial or tax planning advice. Just look at the name!

#Hello #AwakeYet?

The government isn't to blame. You are. I am, too.

We are projecting our **self-punishment** onto ourselves and our future generations. We ACCEPTED GUILT and did nothing about taking ownership; recall the part about total and complete responsibility, for everything that shows up?

We live in a guilt culture. Clotaire Rapaille, one of the best marketing geniuses in the world, has done studies that prove this.

The chances are very high that **you have guilt in your vibrational field**, and these guilty vibrations affect the entire matrix of your Chakra system.

<u>If you get rid of this guilt, your vibration goes up through the roof, and the attractiveness of your intention multiplies in potency at least tenfold.</u>

Can I prove this with some fact-sheet or scientific study? No. All I can tell you is that GUILT is a call for punishment and one way we punish ourselves is to TAKE AWAY OUR MONEY, our health, or a relationship. Remember, we create all our circumstances from within ourselves.

Use the Safe Touch Method ™ process and see what happens as you REMOVE the pent-up guilt. You can use the procedure in "spurts"—as often or as little as you're compelled to release the heavy burden you're carrying. Try it for seven days.

Think of this like you would do a colon-cleanse; only in this manner, you are still "full of crap," but it's mostly "spiritual crap."

Imagine if you had ***ten times*** the power to manifest what you wanted. Wouldn't you want that?

What can ridding yourself of guilt do for you?

If you follow this blueprint, you can **magnify your attractive force** and **diminish your repellant forces**. This "*balancing of the scales*" will ALLOW you the things you want: money, health, wealth, success, and fame, to come to you like it's no big deal.

What did clearing guilt do for me? Well, as I said, I was bedridden and bankrupt in 2009. I had debilitating Lyme disease.

By 2011, I had a six-figure income through a business I created. The part you should understand is that it took less than 90 days to build this online business. *I felt worthy and guiltless.*

By 2013, I had a seven-figure business. In only six months, I was able to manifest my fitness goals and lose thirty pounds, just keeping the muscle and losing the fat. I did it all effortlessly.

I felt worthy and guiltless. Facing the temptation to feel guilty and removing it built anticipation of GOOD to come my way. GOOD and GOD are synonymous; guilt separates you from God's LOVE—your GOD-POWER within to ALLOW your desires is the unconditional love of God.

I began to ask the question, why was I suddenly allowing it all to happen, as if I had some magic or luck?

I replaced a guilt-complex with a healthy God-within-complex. Not arrogance, just recognition of my GOD-POWER.

Guilt is a repellant force that steals your expectation for a positive result and supplants it with a call for punishment. We don't get in life what we want; we get what we expect.

#Noted

If you've ever lived with someone who reflects this guilt back to you (in your projection), you feel drained, worth-less, and powerless. Chances are, you become a people-pleaser.

As long as your nose is in someone's rear, one thing will be sure: the outcome for you is going to stink.

You are quickly controllable, too. Why? You give away your power through the mechanism of guilt.

What I accomplished isn't too rare. I'm not any different than you (regarding my ability to attract and repel my desires).

You have that same power within you. I want to show you what you have to do to remove the blocks.

Guilt is the number one thing blocking you.

How Can You Get Rid of Guilt?

I created the Safe Touch Method ™ to help myself, and now I am using it to help you. It will ALLOW you to ramp your success through the roof.

What can you accomplish in 1-minute? How about a shift in consciousness that shuts off the repellant forces in your life?

This process is not complicated. It is a simple, one minute process that will help you break through to the next level and remove the very thing that is keeping you stuck wherever you become frustrated, impatient, or angered.

Here are a few success stories I'd like to share, that I received in the early phases of teaching the Safe Touch Method ™. These comments were posted on my YouTube videos.

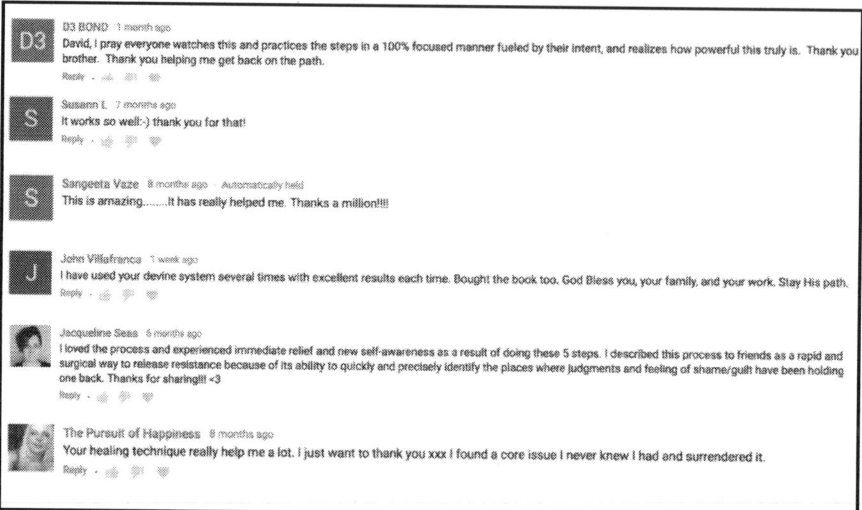

D3 BOND 1 month ago
David, I pray everyone watches this and practices the steps in a 100% focused manner fueled by their intent, and realizes how powerful this truly is. Thank you brother. Thank you helping me get back on the path.
Reply

Susann L 7 months ago
It works so well:-) thank you for that!
Reply

Sangeeta Vaze 8 months ago · Automatically held
This is amazing........It has really helped me. Thanks a million!!!!

John Villafranca 1 week ago
I have used your devine system several times with excellent results each time. Bought the book too. God Bless you, your family, and your work. Stay His path.
Reply

Jacqueline Seas 6 months ago
I loved the process and experienced immediate relief and new self-awareness as a result of doing these 5 steps. I described this process to friends as a rapid and surgical way to release resistance because of its ability to quickly and precisely identify the places where judgments and feeling of shame/guilt have been holding one back. Thanks for sharing!!! <3
Reply

The Pursuit of Happiness 8 months ago
Your healing technique really help me a lot. I just want to thank you xxx I found a core issue I never knew I had and surrendered it.
Reply

I know from personal experience that this is effective and very powerful. You'll be able to do it just as well as I've been able to do it once you've followed the steps I outline below.

You'll be able to WATCH and follow along with me, teaching you the **Safe Touch Method™** online here: http://www.SafeTouchTechnique.com

#TwiceDailyFor7Days #SpiritualCleanse

Once you've learned to tap into your most primal vibrations, you will be able to "download" solutions to your problems much in the way that you can quickly and easily download an app on your phone.

In this way, I was able to download a solution to the eating disorders that I had for five years. I got there in a different way, yet it's the same outcome. Answers come from within us!

Remove guilt, and you also remove the call for punishment. The Safe Touch Method™ is ideal for anyone who feels the weight of sin robbing them, daily.

I'll explain the process used for addressing eating disorders and other issues in chapter 12. For now, I'd like to introduce you to the Safe Touch Method ™.

I've found this method leads me to the same place of non-resistance and surrender underlying all the transformations I've made—the common denominator.

EATING DISORDERS ARE INCURABLE?

I was able to walk away from them overnight. Yes, I struggled for five years before it happened. I never went back to them once I was set free.

I was also able to walk away from PTSD and anxiety. All because of a shift in my consciousness. The answers always came from within my own "knowing." Guidance suddenly appears when we stop punishing ourselves.

How you get "clear" isn't essential. Choose any path or strategy that works for you. A few times each year, I use Safe Touch Method ™ like a colon-cleanse for my soul. You'll get a few different strategies in this book; all roads lead to understanding.

You can transform your reality in the twinkling of an eye. You should never feel powerless.

It reminds me of when I used to play hockey. There's a forward offensive game, and there's a defensive game. I always played the defensive game.

*Having **a strong defense** is very, very powerful, especially within the law of attraction.*

This obstacle clearing regimen is a **missing component** in a lot of people's approach. They play offense and no defense. All "intention" is futile without **"clearing"** to negate or disengage the repellant forces.

It's not all about aligning with what you want and then—POOF—you have it. People sometimes wonder why they have trouble aligning with their desires.

I can tell you why: it is because something is vibrationally amiss. There is a reason why people keep gravitating to the negative side of things. There are causes for their remaining stuck. It is all a problem of perception.

I can tell you why this happens: I was able to download a technique, the Safe Touch Method™. This method will remove the cause of the block that guilt is causing you to hold onto to punish yourself.

The cause of the block is a lack of forgiveness. Unforgiveness and guilt go hand in hand. Shame soon kicks in, and you repeat the action or behavior, over and over—wondering, "why can't I stop doing this?"

A lack of forgiveness—holding a grudge—and guilt are the two things that are poison in your consciousness. They're keeping you stuck at some level in your circumstances.

These **poison attitudes** may be the reason why you have been unable to transform your reality, at whatever place you may remain stuck. Your reality is a reflection of your attitude, right?

When you have experienced a breakthrough, you have also removed or cleared the repellant forces.

A One-Minute Miracle

So, as promised, I'm going to give you a one-minute miracle technique. The Safe Touch Method™.

The process to "clear" takes a minute or less to do. You can apply it at will, whenever and wherever you are, and erase the vibrational conflicts derived from suppressed guilt.

Once these conflicts erase, you can RAISE your frequency, fast. You can be an open canvas, ready, willing, and able to receive the love that exists in the universe.

The love that surfaces, in the absence of guilt, will allow you to solve and *dissolve* your resistance. How do I know? Your **hard attitudes toward life will disintegrate**.

Wouldn't that be worth one minute of your time?

Before we begin, let's take a look at what technology has done to our culture. It distanced us while seemingly doing the opposite regarding creating a worldwide audience at your fingertips.

The problem is; humans are TRIBAL. If we don't have a tribe, we lose our identity. This *disconnection* is why racial issues and gender discussions are at an all-time high.

People want to associate with something to identify with and belong somewhere.

We are literally out of touch with one another!

I am big on touch. I think that people benefit immensely from human contact. Unfortunately, this is something that has been taken away from us by the use of technology.

#DivideConquer

When we only communicate *virtually* with each other, we lose the ability to touch one another physically. Everything becomes a *virtual reality* in the false-reality matrix.

We have become divided by our screens. "Touchscreens" are not the same as the tactile embrace of another human being.

I want to give you a way that you can do this yourself, and you can do it for other people. Let your family members and other loved ones participate in this gift.

Do a seven-day soul detox a few times each year, just like you cleanse your meatsack body.

This process is a safe, non-threatening way to introduce the power of touch. The added benefit is that you can erase the twin poisons of unforgiveness and guilt from your body, your mind, and your consciousness.

The Benefits of a Soul Detox

Do you want health and prosperity? If so, consider this truth: "You are only as sick as your secrets."

Let me reiterate. It's important enough to repeat one more time for memorization.

You are only as sick as your secrets.

Most well-meaning people out there are positive, loving, and supportive on the surface. However, we are more than what we appear to be on the surface. We are all susceptible to harboring resentment and guilt in our hearts.

Proverbs 4:23 says, "Above all else, guard your heart, for it is the wellspring of life." This short Bible verse contains an essential truth.

All matters of life stem from the heart. Everything we do, everything we are, and **everything we can encounter emanates from our heart**.

What do we think of when we think of the heart? We gravitate towards thinking about love. Love is a force-field. Unfortunately, it has also become a battle-field for many of us.

#WeSaluteBattle #HandOverTheHeart

We think about love as a synonym for God, for the divine, for the entire universe. There is a foundational force of love that permeates everything.

LOVE exists in the "present" moment. It is the present, a gift. As my mentor, Mike Murdock says, "*Joy is the reward for discerning the divine blessing in the immediate moment.*" This idealistic examination of life's circumstances is the ATTITUDE of LOVE. What you look for, you will find. *The only reason men fail is broken focus.* #FindTheBlessing

So, if love is the positive attitude towards "what is" in a non-resistant state of being, which creates the force-field of allowing, what is its opposite? I'll tell you in a moment, but you should already know I'm going to say GUILT!!!

A QUANTUM DEFINITION OF LOVE

For The GOOD-LIFE is With The LOVE of GOD-IN-YOU.

(Good and God are interchangeable).

What force is destroying your life like locusts, indirectly starving you of your joy? Guilt.

People tend to think that the opposite of love is hate. When you approach the problem with a faulty premise, you end up with more questions and you get lost. The truth is this:

The opposite of love is guilt.

Guilt is the most powerful force working against your inner expression of joy and happiness. Whether you are working on better health, better relationships, or more prosperity, **guilt is the source of hardened attitudes toward life.**

Life will be hard for you if you harbor guilt and do nothing to rid yourself of this unhallowed behavior of self-condemnation.

Guilt and unforgiveness are intertwined. You can't separate the two. But the good news is that when you remove one, you'll automatically exclude the other.

Write down a list of 5 things you felt guilt over in the past, or now.

1.

2.

3.

4.

5.

Now that you have this list with some awareness that you have been storing up guilt, let's get rid of your condemnation and shame, shall we?

CHAPTER 4.

The Safe Touch Method ™ "Soul Detox"

Let me give you a jumpstart in removing the guilt that is destroying your life, eating away at your expectation for good.

The list you made contains secrets. Please go back and fill out the list of five items if you have not already done so.

It's important to make this list before I give you the next piece of the puzzle. Did you do it yet? Good.

If you're jumping ahead of me because you figure it will be better to read through first and do the exercise later, you will ruin the surprise. Yes, I have a fun surprise for you.

Please fill out the list and then we'll carry forward with a pleasant realization about you, according to the data on your list.

WHAT YOUR LIST SAYS ABOUT THE GUILT IN YOUR LIFE

Here's how your mind works during this list-making process. First, you are looking at item number 1; this is the "obsession" that your conscious mind uses as the conscious-alibi.

Item number 2 on your list is the "fluff" piece that automatically gets dealt with, so leave it be for now.

Item number 3 is the "heart of the matter" and represents your unconscious THORN IN THE SIDE.

Use the One-Minute Safe Touch Method™ to address this issue, immediately!

Go ahead and do it. Now. Here's the link again:

http://www.SafeTouchTechnique.com

Contrary to what you've been taught to think, change doesn't take a long time and require inpatient visits to a mental hospital and opioids (for most people competent enough to read this book).

In one minute, you can be GUILTLESSLY free to receive an influx of GOOD, once you cast this poison-pocket of self-condemnation out of your unconscious.

After you've "cleared" the third item on your list, work on the other four things on your list. These remaining items should clear quite rapidly.

Did you do the one minute process? Did you get the S.U.D. level down to near zero? If so, how do you feel?

As you continue to use this technique that I call the Safe Touch Method™, you will be able to cleanse your soul.

It's one way you'll learn about in this book. Something will "click" for you, whether it's Safe Touch Method ™ or Ho'oponopono.

You must "clean" your vibration, daily. I use Ho'oponopono daily and the Safe Touch Method™ periodically, like a colon-cleanse for my soul. A few times per year is enough.

By cleaning your vibration every day, you can gain extraordinary results in far less time. Your attitude lightens so much that you may appear *enlightened* to other people!

You will be able to allow the love of the universe to expand within you. It can bring you the answers you need and the people that you need to achieve everything you've dreamed of accomplishing.

Remember; a strong defense is equal to a potent offense.

Why the Safe Touch Method ™ Works

Here's what I know about guilt:

"Guilt comes after the broken heart."

Guilt brings condemnation. Condemnation, in this context, means that you are condemning someone (yourself) to a punishment or a sentence. And, you broke your heart. No one else did. #FullResponsibility

Anytime you are harboring guilt in your consciousness or your psyche; you are holding a frequency that is demanding punishment or a sentence.

In the Bible, the word condemnation is synonymous with *damnation, judgment, punishment, destruction, and verdict.*

We need a tool to eradicate this guilt. When we release condemnation, we raise our vibrations.

These raised vibrations ALLOW us to stay in the flow of all the good that is trying to come into our lives.

We can stay in the will of God.

God's will is an attitude, not a place.

The will of God is evident in Romans 8:28. It's a penetrating insight that you'll learn more about in Chapter 12.

For now, let's address **the will of Satan: to bind you with guilt and a call for self-punishment.**

Let's rid guilt and its destructive force in your hologram, giving you the tool to keep Satan's will for you impotent and with nowhere to attach itself to you.

Look, I get it. You may be wondering, "*Matthew, you say only the good is true... there is no good and evil... and I'm God, so what gives with all the Satan stuff?*"

I'm not a recovering Catholic, and I'll be the first to inject my opinion: the Vatican is the actual Enterprise of Satan, and the false-reality matrix appears real to us DUE to the guilt we succumb to from our judgments.

#ImStillClearing

It's almost as if God is saying, "Judge not, lest you be judged against." **There must be a FORCE to come against us to reveal our judgments, right?**

If this force compels us to re-evaluate our whereabouts, as in "are we in God's palace as a beloved child of the Most High God, or are we surrounded by tyrants who always do us wrong?" Is it a good thing, then?

Are we learning about our true nature via the proxy of some "devil" who shows us our judgments in a spellbinding false-reality construct?

Instead of debating all day long, we can all agree that guilt is not beneficial in any way for us to find joy, as it is not feasible for God to give sin (guilt). Suffering can lead to wisdom, but the road is long, and it hurts like hell."

We **cast ourselves** into our hell; we then *experience a world to reflect our judgments* back upon us. Guilt is the proof we misapprehended our circumstances and slung a judgment upon ourselves.

Guilt is an **attitude**, derived from the ANGER *re*action (poverty) turned inward towards punishing ourselves.

Is there good in all things, including guilt?

As long as we think a world "out there" exists, guilt is readily available as OUR GOOD to force us to examine life more closely.

Everything is working for our greater good; it's just not all that enjoyable if we separate ourselves from LOVE.

I promise you that guilt has been destroying aspects of your life, eroding the wellspring of joy that emits out of childlike innocence. It didn't just get there on its own. You put it there.

Your decision to return to childlike innocence is the essential VIBRATIONAL UPGRADE you can do, daily.

#GoodVibesGoodLife

THE SAFE TOUCH METHOD™

There are five steps we are going to go through.

Before you begin, find a place where you will not be distracted, and go through each of the five steps. You will see how simple and effective this is.

The physical components of this technique are as follows:

Your Eyes. Your eyes are the windows to the soul.

Your Hands. Because your body is bioelectric, we use our hands. Electric current (carrying consciousness) is the same reason why hands-on healing works so well and has prevailed throughout the centuries.

Your hands create electrical impulses of intent that you can channel and use your hands to heal. We will use this as part of the Safe Touch Method™.

The Heart. All issues of life arise out of the heart.

The eyes. The hands. The heart.

The magic that makes this happen is **our intent, the touch, and <u>the last component, which is the confession</u>**. I will do this along with you to show you how it works.

STEP ONE

Consider any guilt that you can tune into right now. Then rate it. We have to measure and quantify the poison-pocket in your soul.

On a scale of 1-10, think of anything that you feel guilty about, including shame. **Shame goes along with guilt. Whenever you feel shame, you will repeat the action.**

Remember that—it is imperative. *When you feel shame, you will unconsciously repeat the action.* Guilt carries shame along with it. When you focus on the guilt and remove it, you will remove the shame along with it.

So go ahead and rate this guilt on the 1-10 scale we'll call the S.U.D.—Subconscious Units of Distress—range.

STEP TWO

For ten seconds, make an intention statement. If you are doing this alone, look into a mirror and look into your own eyes.

If you are doing this with a partner, look in your partner's eyes. Say these words:

"*I intend to release any and all unforgiveness and guilt immediately. Right now.*"

Communicate your intent. By speaking the words aloud, you make them real.

STEP THREE

In this step, we use our hands. We focus here on forgiveness. The key here is to forgive anyone that comes to mind, whether or not you can think of anything you need to forgive them for doing.

The fact that they came to mind at this moment is the crucial part. When you are thinking of your guilt, you are thinking of these people.

And therefore, we forgive them. Yes, this also includes forgiving yourself.

Hold your partner's hands. If you are doing this by yourself, grab your own hands. (A helpful demonstration is at http://www.SafeTouchTechnique.com if you want to follow along with me visually).

Say your version of this:

"I now forgive my mom, my dad, my ex-wife, my children, my business, and my body."

Whatever comes to mind, forgiveness is required.

The reason why you forgive all of these people is that they came to mind. That's it. There is no "I did this to them," or "They did this to me."

Forget all of that. Forget the stories. The stories are the judgments. If they come to mind, forgiveness is necessary. Period.

"I forgive anyone and everyone who also has not come to mind that needs forgiveness." Say it, and feel the healing power of these words.

Step Four

Step four is the magical healing step. We focus on the heart and confess. **For thirty seconds to one minute, focus on any perceived wrongdoing** that you feel you were involved in doing.

If you are doing this with a partner, make sure you are doing this with someone that is safe. You should be comfortable.

Confession is a tool that removes your guilt instantly. *Out of the heart arises the issues of life,* so we will put our hands on our hearts as we do this step.

If you are doing this with someone you trust, allow them to hold the space for you.

Remember: you are the one who is going to heal yourself. Your partner cannot heal you. Your partner cannot do anything more than hold the space for you and give you room to do it yourself.

Your partner is merely going to facilitate the process.

For thirty seconds, confess anything you think you did wrong. Use up to a full minute if necessary.

Say, "I confess. I did (fill in the blank)" speak out loud—or internally to yourself—what it is that you perceive you did wrong.

You're releasing your judgments, once and for all.

Confess it all. Let it flow. While you are doing this, keep your hand on your heart. *Recognize that you were doing the best you knew how at the time, according to the hand you were dealt. You didn't realize your judgments would come back to haunt you, so you acted unconsciously. It was a valuable lesson.*

STEP FIVE

Now that you have completed the first four steps give yourself or your partner a hug. Not a quick hug, not a sideways one-armed hug. A real hug. A friendly, warm five-second hug. If you are alone, wrap your arms around yourself.

Then say out loud:

"I release guilt now. I love, accept, and forgive myself. I release everyone I thought about and everything I thought about to the divine."

Doesn't that feel great?

Take a gentle, deep breath and blow it out.

Rate your S.U.D. level and see if it dropped down. If you were able to get in a range below 3, you are doing pretty well. I like to witness the S.U.D. drop to at least 2.

SUMMARY

Here's how you do it in a nutshell:

Find and rate the guilt that you are feeling inside.

Look into your own eyes or the eyes of your partner and make your statement of intent.

Hold your partner's hands or your own hands and make a statement of forgiveness towards anyone that comes to mind.

Put your hands on your heart and confess your guilt and perceived wrongs.

Give yourself a hug and a statement of love and acceptance. Release it all to the divine.

Now that you are done, reassess your S.U.D. after the process. Celebrate the release of all that trauma.

If you can get the S.U.D. to zero or a one, you have removed the unforgiveness and guilt from your heart. In this way, your **manifestations will come** to you much more **efficiently, effortlessly, and promptly**.

The very thing that is blocking the divine love from reaching your heart is your perceptions of wrongdoing.

Don't hold on to those perceptions. Holding on to them perpetuates a vibration of guilt, shame, unforgiveness, and a whole host of feelings that will block your success.

This tool, this Safe Touch Method™, is the simplest and fastest way I know of to remove these blocked poison-pockets.

You can do it on demand any time you want to. It doesn't take much time or space. I recommend that you treat it like a detox protocol and that you do it at least two times a day, for about seven days each time you cleanse.

Do it in the morning when you get up and in the evening when you go to bed.

Take a one minute break whenever you need it to release the poison of guilt from your soul. By releasing the poison of unforgiveness and guilt from your inner-environment, you will find your life will be better and better.

This release will happen not gradually, but in quantum leaps forward, probably faster than you ever thought possible.

"As within, so without."

#ManifestingINSIDEJob

CHAPTER 5.

Intermittent Fasting, Ketogenesis, and FOOD ADDICTION

What you eat can be a part of your spiritual cleansing.

Dr. Henry Wright has done a lot of research on people who crave a lot of carbohydrates and are binge eaters. His conclusions are telling.

All of those carbohydrates turn into alcohol in the body. Alcohol—like carbohydrates—is just a form of sugar. So people who eat this way may have the same spiritual problem as alcoholics.

And what is this spiritual problem?

To answer this, let's cross-reference what German New Medicine has to say:

Refugee: It is the feeling of being all alone on an island. It can also trigger an existence conflict or any of the A.I.R.E. conflicts we find in German New Medicine.

A - Abandonment

I - Isolation

R - Refugee

E – Existence

When I decided to stop controlling stress with food, it brought up all my anger, and I had to deal with it. We want to address our emotional junk and get it "clear."

I'm glad because now I'm getting to the root of it and getting it all up and out.

How did I do this? Simple.

I went on a ketogenic diet.

Ketogenic diets are trendy these days, and a lot of people have found success. They help you lose fat and gain control over what's called *The Fifty-Percent Insulin Problem*.

When we eat, insulin will go up and hopefully in a healthy range. Insulin spiking—like when you devour a huge meal, especially with a lot of sugar or carbohydrates—can make you tired, irritable, and store body fat.

A challenge for many people today is that our fasting insulin levels can be higher (if we're overweight) than a thin person's fasting insulin level.

Blood sugar issues add insult to injury because insulin can keep us from burning stored body fat. It can also make us hungrier; we end up craving more of the foods that store as fat.

So what do we do?

A good place to start is researching the ketogenic diet. It helped me break the cycle of "carb binging."

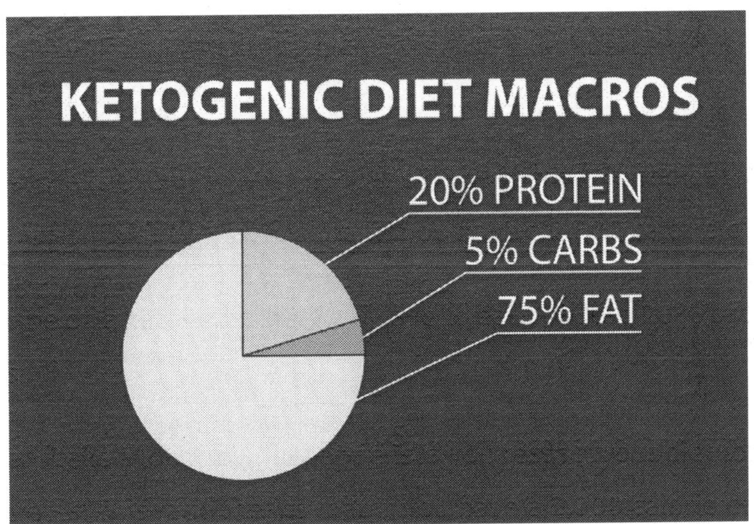

To be on a ketogenic diet, you have to eat 70% fat, 20% protein, and 5% carbs.

Let's take a look at what happens if you restrict your diet to only 5% carbohydrates. This ratio means that if you have a 2,000 calorie diet, about **a hundred calories** would come from carbs.

That's about 25 grams of carbs in a day. About the equivalent of a half of an apple. Not much, huh!

But don't eat those fruits. Instead, eat green leafy vegetables so you can get your potassium and your chlorophyll and all the trace minerals your body needs to function efficiently.

I'm not suggesting you go out and change your foods and begin a ketogenic diet. Consult with your physician and search online for ideas to see if it makes sense in your lifestyle.

When you do "keto," you'll be eliminating the thing that you've been using to soothe yourself—sugars.

If you're overweight, or could lose a few pounds of body fat: it is entirely possible that you've gained weight because of your anger. You may very well be putting a buffer between yourself and the world.

On the psychological level, that's what weight gain can be for many of us. **You've had enough and, you want to check out!**

On the physical level, the insulin spikes we can create with a S.A.D. (Standard American Diet) meal plan, especially if we're eating all day long —worse yet, snacking—may wreak havoc on our ability to lose the fat.

Dr. Henry Wright mentioned an interesting concept:

Remember having a pacifier when you were a kid, or remember your own kids' pacifiers?

That is *hand to the mouth* to self-soothe. Constant eating, especially with carbohydrates that break down into alcohol in the body, is no different.

You're taking carbohydrates in that digest into sugars and convert to alcohol. **It can be the same phenomenon as an alcoholic uses to deal with unresolved trauma and anger.**

If your doctor okays it, you could go on a ketogenic diet. I rotate this diet and use it as a tool for cleansing.

Some people stay on a ketogenic diet long term.

Another option is to do intermittent fasting!

In fact, you can combine the two strategies to deal with a whole host of issues: insulin resistance, Human Growth Hormone, fasting insulin, physiological rest for your organs, and more.

I'm typically either doing a "keto" diet strategy or using intermittent fasting to optimize my metabolism.

Intermittent fasting has many potential health benefits.

The way it works is simple, too: you fast for the majority of your 24-hour day and eat within a small window of time.

Most people try and condense their eating to a window of 4 - 8 hours; they fast for at least 16 hours every day.

If you eat your last meal a couple hours before bed and skip breakfast—pushing your first meal back several hours — you can pull this off quite comfortably.

During the fast you can have non-caloric liquid; water and black coffee. No sweeteners or other additives.

The reason I do "diet manipulation" is evident to the consciously aware person who is observant: most people are not healthy, so what they're doing doesn't work.

Look, I believe it is now *3-out-of-4 Americans that have a chronic, diagnosable disease.*

Our standard of "health" is sub-par.

How did we get here?

Our soil was stripped of minerals several decades ago. Consequently, the "snack food" industry began taking off around the same time.

As bestselling author Raymond Francis writes about in his book, ***Never Be Sick Again***—deficiency and toxicity are the two pathways to all disease.

Case in point: let's look at a phenomenon called "cribbing" and find out why horses do this...

Cribbing or crib biting involves a **horse** grasping a solid object such as the stall door or fence rail with its incisor teeth, then arching its neck, and contracting the lower neck muscles to retract the larynx. This coincides with an in-rush of air into the oesophagus producing the characteristic **cribbing** grunt.

Cribbing (horse) - Wikipedia
https://en.wikipedia.org/wiki/Cribbing_(horse)

According to Dr. Joel Wallach, the horses are doing this to satisfy their requirement for minerals.

If you haven't yet put two-and-two together, humans will also "munch" when they are mineral deficient.

As a profiteer in the food industry, wouldn't it make sense to saturate the market with chemical-additives that increase hunger and add in table-sugar to deplete mineral stores even further?

I mean, if you're going to create the demand, it would seem like a hell of a way to get a stampede of "HANGRY" (hungry and angry) humans to buy up all your processed food, right?

If you walk through a grocery store, you'll notice that most of the processed foods (the profit food) are in the middle, in the aisles. The fresh fruits, vegetables, meat, and dairy, are usually on the outer edges of a supermarket.

In chapter 11, I'll touch more on health solutions.

For now, we're discussing the link between food and how we use it to **suppress our emotions, calm ourselves**, and let's face it—doing this ruins our lives and our health.

Lately, what I've been doing is the OMAD plan.

OMAD is an acronym for **One Meal A Day**.

OMAD is an intermittent fasting strategy that puts your daily caloric intake into one meal, in one sitting, typically lasting under an hour.

It's not for everyone. If you have blood-sugar issues or prefer high carbohydrate meals (combined with proteins and fats), your insulin can SPIKE very high!

When I began doing OMAD, I passed out as if someone had slipped me a "Roofy" (date rape drug).

I whipped together three peanut butter sandwiches and devoured four protein shakes with a half-gallon of chocolate milk.

#BigMistake #Insulin #LightsOut

If you have issues with insulin or are perhaps pre-diabetic, you don't want to do this to yourself.

With any dietary adjustment, I recommend going "easy" about it and gradually settling into the new strategy. Your body can take a few weeks to adjust, especially if you do "keto."

A ketogenic diet will force your body into burning ketones for fuel as its primary source of energy. If you are eating carbohydrates, your body is used to burning these calories as fuel. The transition can be a bit rough.

I'm not interested in talking about the vanity appeal of adapting your body into "ketosis"—*where it burns fat as its primary fuel*—and your caloric deficit causes the fat to melt off your waist, butt, arms, thighs, and even the stubborn areas.

Yes, those perks are amazing. The "spiritual" side of things is revealing: **take away your comfort foods and see what you've been suppressing**.

For me, OMAD is the best possible solution while I'm on a regular schedule because of the fact it's putting a "healthy stress" on my body.

#GoodStress #Survival

Fasting puts a stress on the body required for the evolution of our survival. The dominant fasting state my body remains in, makes me more efficient in many areas.

Also, *better thinking, more energy, healthier organs, improved insulin response, and a leaner physique* are consequences of keeping my body under this stress.

As I'm writing this book, I'll be honest with you: I've been snacking and succumbing to **bad habits**. The fact that I'm genuinely engaged in giving you my very best, pouring it all in, combined with working around the clock to write this—it wears my mind down.

#TigerFocus

Once this book is complete, I'll return to OMAD or a modified intermittent fasting regimen, combining ketogenic "cleanses" every so often. Just like you must cleanse your soul, your mind, and your attitude—the body cleanses best while fasting!

As a side note, I am not a believer in almost every detox method on the market: common ones with chelation methods or prolonged *colon - liver - gallbladder - kidney* cleansing. Having done these cleanses and experiencing terrible side-effects, they're not ideal for everyone.

I use a product every day, called ***Magic Formula***. It contains a brown-seaweed extract that gently cleanses, chelates, and provides targeted nutrients (including minerals).

My body works well to "get the junk out" by intermittent fasting and using **Magic Formula**, without the nasty detox symptoms.

Here's a Link to Checkout Magic Formula:
http://www.MagicFormula.shop

Choose whatever strategy works for you if you feel you'd like to try and **disconnect the snack-food industry's spell** that has been so readily available to sedate what's going on inside.

If you've been *using food as a vice* for any other reason than to nourish your body, removing the food will FORCE STUFF TO COME UP for you to deal with the underlying issues.

Once you address these issues, you will ascend to higher conscious awareness and more personal power!

If you have issues with BINGING and CRAVING food, or suspect you are *addicted to eating* to calm yourself, here are two resources I have to help you BUST LOOSE:

http://www.BeatingFoodAddiction.com

Taking control of your food and eating habits can remove unhealthy coping mechanisms.

It may force up any suppressed anger issues or A.I.R.E. conflicts. Research German New Medicine for more information about A.I.R.E. conflicts and the psyche, as it pertains to food and weight gain.

When these issues are forced up, you will be able to become aware of how deeply they can be affecting your VIBRATIONAL RESONANCE.

Another VIDEO I made that can be helpful, is here:

http://www.TripleWarmer.com

Once you can "clear" these patterns, your magnetism grows exponentially by quantum leaps!

Chapter 6.

The Greatest Wealth SECRET on Earth that Delivers Guaranteed Results—For You!

Yes, you have heard elsewhere before that you're going to get some Law of Attraction formula to put the silver platter on your lap. Many people profess to know the answers. Even I do.

Look, I've seen it all. The other day I was at the bookstore walking down the aisles, thinking to myself, "What sort of nonsense is all this crap?" Talk about allowing my mind to be judgmental. (Fear not, I did Ho'oponopono on those thoughts).

I thought to myself, "Almost every book is trying to teach me to feed my mind or involve myself with trivial studies and soon-to-be outdated facts; it's all a load of rubbish."

Few people know how to GIVE YOU a replicable method that WORKS for YOU. That's why there are so few success stories with self-help programs, books, or ideologies.

For every 100 people who read "Think and Grow Rich," I'll bet only one of them got any measurable improvements in their pocketbook.

The other 99 probably panned out like this: three of them ended up plagiarizing the book to sell their course (to get paid selling stuff that didn't work for them either); 78 of the people ended up skipping half the book because it took more than 15-minutes to complete; 18 of the people felt empowered while reading it all the way through, yet they missed the entire point—they couldn't find it.

You know why? It wasn't in there. Napoleon Hill retired poor. There's the point, and the book wouldn't sell well titled "Think and Grow Frustrated Trying to Get Rich."

Meanwhile, the 30-year-old who lives in his parent's basement down the street is selling cryptocurrency advice online to gambling addicts who haven't figured out that's what they're doing yet. It's a lottery gamble for most investors.

Look, I love cryptocurrency, but it invites some of the shadiest characters looking to capitalize on mainstream-ignorance; one man committed fraud by selling pizza-restaurant tokens (for kids games) to someone for $10K, alleging it was Bitcoin. Yes, he was arrested.

The guy who paid the money is quite a spectacle himself; how he managed to have $10k with that level of discernment is another story. A fool and his money are soon parted, however. I've been this fool, too. We all have at one time or another.

Here's the bottom line about "Think and Grow Rich."

You can't think and grow rich; the ideology rests on a false premise. You ARE rich already, but you remember that little ditty I told you about the **action** required to manifest?

You see, to gain MATERIAL RICHES, you must consider how to ACT AND SEDUCE RICHES to flow your way. You have to use your talents with what I call, the ***magic-attitude*** (formula).

What you're about to learn is the most potent material for wealth attraction you'll find anywhere...

I shake my head in disbelief to this day, as the truth hides concealed in plain sight. I know a woman who got very wealthy teaching "Think and Grow Rich" material; yet, it's like looking at a chain letter. The mailing list broker who started the chain letter is the one getting rich by selling mailing lists, not mailing letters or running a home-based Ponzi scheme.

Same phenomenon with most gurus who teach this material. You have to SEE what they are DOING and avoid consuming the horse manure they are spreading.

Most often, they've been drinking the "Kool-Aid" too long themselves.

#BlindLeadingTheBlind

In 100% of the cases where I've seen a successful entrepreneur who "applied principles" from "Think and Grow Rich" to get wealthy, **also applied sound business principles**.

#TheAhaMoment

Anyhow, this chapter will be like a breath of fresh air after being in a smoke filled bar, if you find yourself scavenging through Law of Attraction "money" books, wondering "WTF" is happening, because your bank account isn't overflowing yet?

I don't brew decaf Law of Attraction and douse it with cream and sugar to make it palatable.

Plug: I sell MOCAINE. In fact, *you can get your first couple baggies FREE*, by paying the shipping: http://www.MOCAINE.com (Mocha that's Jacked!)

This chapter isn't about some meditation I'll give you to *communicate with the energy of money and speak to it, create space for it to come into your heart, and spend it in your mind every night.*

You may enjoy doing these things, but there is a better way to PULL CURRENTS OF BLESSINGS your way, as if by magic! Then, all the other stuff you're doing will start working for you.

Using Law of Attraction techniques (for accumulating wealth) without **applied wisdom** is like fantasizing about passionate romance in your head, only to look in the mirror and recognize you haven't showered in three days, your hair is a wreck, and you could use a new pair of socks.

Just like having "game" to get some action in the dating scene, it's more than just running rehearsals and pick-up lines with your coach.

You're going to have to DO SOMETHING that seduces your prospects and compels them to *value you* above all others.

Many people assume a great body will solve their dating challenges? They get in shape to superficially appear more desirable.

Does it work? Not long term, if at all. You see, there is the FALSE-REALITY way to do things and then, there's WISDOM.

Wisdom is like knowing what Clotaire Rapaille discovered in his study: men prefer a woman with "child-bearing" hips and are more likely to commit to these women vs. the thin model.

A *Baywatch babe* could easily lose her man to someone with an average body who has more perceived "reproduction" value—larger hips, less competition (to fight off other men), etc. Do you want him to use you or to stay?

How about a man with huge muscles? If he's trying to impress other men, that will work. How about having a huge...ahem...*apparatus*? It's probably preferable over a unit that isn't functioning properly; I'll give you that.

But, all these ideas that it takes all this superficial grooming to compete is misleading.

Just like most Law of Attraction material. And, most ideas about getting ahead in life—with useless degrees, social status memberships, fancy cars and expensive lifestyles.

#IllusionVsReality

Regarding dating, a man with RELENTLESS CONFIDENCE IN HIMSELF and **self-assurance** that sets him apart from ALL the other wannabes makes him much more valuable.

Even though most of the other men may be smarter, better looking, have more money, or would make a better candidate "logically" —the reptilian brain always wins.

In other words, his mate will choose him for survival and reproduction. His only competition may be the wealthy individual because this represents provision.

But, the man of WISDOM will end up with wealth, anyhow. His wisdom will give him *casino-like advantages* and for his woman; bearing his children is preferable over the other men, who instill doubt and fear regarding "survival" of her children.

If he cannot produce his sustenance and create a surplus to provide, or if he's dependent on her for his identity—he loses to the superior man's wisdom.

#GameOver

Casanova Game: You know why this man gets the follow-up dates, instead of his superficial counterparts?

Because of supply and demand and the reptilian instinct to survive and reproduce. He's rarer and far more valuable. He can walk up to a gorgeous woman surrounded by better-looking men and captivate her, intrigue her, and eventually keep her by his side, through good times and bad.

She believes in him because of his wisdom. His value is PRECIOUS and RARE, and it sets him in a league far above the others.

Also, if he adds an aura of mystery and adventure, appearing in a way that intrigues her fascination — he becomes the man who is irresistible, charming, and drug-like for her fantasizing mind.

Now, what the heck does this have to do with YOU getting wealthy? Everything.

Like the Casanova who is RARE and perceivably much more valuable than the other potentials, you can BE this ultra-hot commodity in the marketplace, where CURRENCY flows.

You can seduce the MATERIAL FLOW OF ABUNDANCE to come your way with *Casanova-like* influence. Your command will be so subtle that it is undetectable and yet, irrefutable to even the harshest personalities.

The KING is not the most powerful person in the kingdom. His most trusted advisor who he can count on above all others is the wealthiest person in his palace.

The king can put stock in very few people, always having to watch his back. Most people will betray him in a moment of his weakness, so he must demonstrate military might to protect his established order. Few people understand his ways, and even fewer can appreciate him.

While the king may be the possessor of vast riches and resources, his trusted advisor (or efficient order-follower), gets ACCESS to all of his palace and all the protection of the king's army, while being the target of nobody's attack.

Flying under the radar, this person is the mightiest in the kingdom, and the least studied. You want to be THIS PERSON. I'll show you how.

I can show you how because I've studied this person (for over a decade) and I've demonstrated a proven formula, replicating her power as if it were a franchise blueprint; every step laid out in sequence and mechanically precise to each task.

You're probably thinking, "there ain't no kings gonna put me in a palace, and we're not living in the medieval days anymore."

Nothing has changed over time, trust me. **Human beings may have evolved, but our needs haven't. Fulfilling these needs are the GREATEST SECRET to wealth in all of history.** Why do you think P.T. Barnum said, "The noblest art is that of making others happy."

P.T. Barnum sold happiness to bored, unhappy people. He amazed them in ways that made them feel larger-than-life. You will create a similar aura of intrigue, but so subtle that the cleverest amongst your critics will never shed light on your mystique.

People spend money to feel better. We do everything to feel better. I'll show you how to be the BEST at doing this. Your new attitude will cause material abundance to chase you.

Your current wealth-attraction mistakes will be exposed when I tell you how to align with the ***magic attitude***. Once your consciousness corrects—by doing the fun daily tasks—wealth will not be able to stay away from you.

Every person who has exploited this underlying strategy involving HONOR and FAVOR, all the way back to Biblical times, discovered the recipe for wealth.

As long as they remained doing the "little things" required of them, they stayed in the center of the blessings. If they stopped, they lost it all (in most cases).

I'll tell you why this is the no-holds-barred FAST-TRACK success methodology **that works**, in all cases. *If you can't get wealthy doing what I'm going to tell you to do, it can't be done!*

I'm serious. If what I'm telling you to do, **accurately and precisely**, as a repeatable ACTION that causes THE UNDERLYING FORCE for wealth to come your way, don't work, you didn't do the steps. It's that simple.

#YouCanOnlyFoolYourself

I mean, you should probably never concern yourself with wealth again if this strategy isn't IT for you, opening the floodgates once and for all.

It would be like you saying, "I cut my calories in half and I doubled my calorie burning metabolism... and I'm still not dropping any weight!"

DISCLAIMER: If you're that person, and you already know that whatever you do is going to fail, YOU SKIPPED THE FIRST FOUR CHAPTERS of this book.

I suggest starting at the beginning. Everything is laid out in order in this book. If you **<u>were</u> that person** and you no longer have ANGER to self-sabotage every opportunity, you're in for a huge surprise.

You see, there are only two types of people in this world. *People who can follow instruction and people like my old friend Charlie.* He sabotages it all.

This guy can't grow muscles on steroids or lose fat on vegetables and doctor supervised diets. No, he's not overweight, and he's not medically handicap either. Well, as far as I know, he hasn't gotten a name for the symptoms of hard-headedness yet.

#HeProvesHeISRight #HeIsNotHappy

His ATTITUDE is so stubborn and filled with resistance. He is dead set in his ways where he ignores "counsel" from anyone, even though he asks for it. He talks about how nothing works for him, and he gets what he expects, every time.

Yes, Charlie could screw this method up. If he's reading this now, he will drop my success rate down to 99%.

I can't have you in the ranks of Charlie, okay? He fails because he doesn't do what you tell him to; his agenda then becomes convincing you he's right, and you're wrong.

#MindBlown

In all fairness, now that I've greased you up a bit and shared some preliminary thoughts, let's give you *Casanova-like* MAGNETISM in the marketplace, where the money is circulating.

You're only **one divine connection away from a fortune**. While there may not be kings anymore, we have millionaires and billionaires minted every day.

All problems with your finances are relationship problems, even if the relationship is with ourselves.

Money is a reward for solving problems. The higher the perceived value of the issues you clear up, the more wealth you command from the universe.

It's that easy to understand. And, do you know what EVERY WEALTHY PERSON who can REWARD YOU WITH FAVOR has a desperate need to find?

As I said, nothing has changed since the medieval days. Every powerful and wealthy person (modern-day king) is desperate to find people who S.A.L.U.T.E. them.

Before I tell you the meaning of the acronym, let me say this: if you develop the HABIT of S.A.L.U.T.E-ing everyone in your environment,

CURRENTS OF FAVOR WILL FLOW towards you that will supernaturally LIFT YOU into places of power and authority.

#PauseReflect

After all, if you're going to *get a piece of the action*, you have to be where the current is heading. Knowing this, let me say that all the money that FLOWS TO YOU will come from SOMEONE ELSE.

#MasterRelationships

It's about time Charlie sees this and recognizes that "the reason he hasn't gotten wealthy yet is that he is **dishonoring** his fellow man who has the means to reward him with money."

Dishonor is the recipe for a season of loss. Fortunately for you, almost everyone in the marketplace has a plethora of useless degrees, accolades, LinkedIn connections, and a boring resume. *Never be boring*, it's the kiss of death.

Look, the world boasts of talented people who get nowhere. The supply of them is plentiful. If every intellectual you know with more skill than you were indeed "on point," how come they're still hovering just above average?

I'll tell you why. The most valuable person in the room to anyone *capable of having the world at his or her fingertips* is the one who S.A.L.U.T.E.s with mastery.

Think of it this way: if what you ARE is the product you're selling, what benefits do you provide?

Oh, you can code and write software? Great. I can get that on Fiverr.com and pay $20 for it.

Why are YOU irreplaceable to me? You're not, yet.

Let me see; maybe you can practice law? Okay, so I can hire you and pay you for a job. As soon as someone better comes along, there goes your cash-cow client. Your value isn't scarce, yet.

Maybe you can teach me about healing and do a healing miracle on my recent injury? Let's just say you're Braco and all I have to do is look into your eyes, and I'm suddenly "healed." As soon as I get my healing, you're all too soon forgotten.

Unless... you become irreplaceable by solving the most significant pain in my life. Can you guess what it is? This problem has been the same ever since human beings have had free will.

You'll see it in a moment, keep reading.

NOBODY forgets about the person that S.A.L.U.T.E.s better than anyone else. In fact, these people are so rare that when you find one—you pay any price to keep them in your life.

Case example: Sabrina is the master of S.A.L.U.T.E.-ing. She manages and operates my company, sets my appointments, raises our children, and is the one person I can trust with my life.

I may be the king in my world, but if Sabrina weren't there, I wouldn't be half the man I've become. In my two decades spent as an entrepreneur, I've never met another Sabrina.

#NotASingleOne

Everything I've earned is 100% freely accessible to Sabrina, and she is the MOST IMPORTANT person in my kingdom.

I can create businesses, write books, develop products, and run circles around her in marketing. She remains even more valuable than me (and I secretly know it).

She has attained a position of power in my kingdom that is so subtle and undetectable; most people can't even see it—at first.

As I grew in wisdom and discovered how God blessed me with Sabrina, her value became apparent to my logical understanding. Sabrina taught me the GREATEST MIRACLE FOR RECEIVING A FORTUNE by using your attitude that **supersedes everyone else's aptitude**; the others are all replaceable.

Once I began MODELING Sabrina's strategy, which I now call the **S.A.L.U.T.E.™** method, it shocked me.

Dr. Mike Murdock teaches voluminous wisdom. When he said, "You sow honor up and favor flows down," I observed how Sabrina had mastered this. Her father groomed her since she was young. Sabrina developed the habit of sowing HONOR, and the riches that come with wisdom are now hers to enjoy. Wisdom brings riches. Every time.

After doing what Sabrina *naturally* does (having mastered the habit), and learning about it from Dr. Murdock, I put it to the test.

"An ounce of favor is worth more than a lifetime of labor," Mike says this in his books and other media; IT IS WISDOM that causes SUPERNATURAL WEALTH to flow to you.

Suddenly, I discovered how to UNLOCK HONOR with an acronym that details all the required components.

When I used this method and S.A.L.U.T.E.d people in my world, it ATTRACTED influential people to me like a magnetic impulse was drawing them to discover me.

I'll tell you in short: **extraordinary wealth** came my way. The type of wealth you can't LABOR to obtain.

#WantTheseHabits

If Charlie could wrap his mind around this, he'd be able to get rid of the excuses and be generous; *it's boring when you can't afford to take your friends out for a steak dinner and blow a few hundred bucks on a night out for fun.* Charlie could stop being boring if he learns this lesson.

Charlie just can't get it that it PISSES PEOPLE OFF when they want to bless him with wealth, and he gets in his own damn way, every time.

How does he do it, you ask? Dishonor.

#LearnFromMistakesOfOthers

Meanwhile, the "poor me" attitude is all Charlie has to offer for every single excuse; they're all B.S.

It's plain to see: "Charlie, you DISHONOR everyone who can reward you with FAVOR; dishonor always precedes loss or fallout." He asks for advice and then tries to convince you it won't work. Fortunately, you can fix stupid.

If I were to be able to sedate Charlie and cause him to open his ears and listen, I'd stand in front of him with a big whiteboard behind me.

I'd want Charlie to see a visual representation of how he's complicating life and what to do, instead.

Charlie is always pursuing more "training" and trying his hat at new ventures to find a way to get wealthy. The problem is; his **value in the marketplace is his attitude**, which is easily replaceable and usually ends up displacing him elsewhere.

I'd ask Charlie first, "Do you know what the word SALUTE means?"

I can see Charlie giving me a karate-chop hand to the temple and saying, "Yup. I mean, yes sir!"

I'd tell Charlie the story about how we're all endowed with GOD-LIKE-POWER. In fact, no matter who he comes into contact with—*every man, woman, child, and gender neutral person—is God in disguise.*

Charlie would probably say, "Ah, c'mon dude. When you start talking like this, you lose me. It's silly."

I'd reply, "Well, you being such a tightwad and telling me about the money shortage is sort of silly, wouldn't you think?"

I'd encourage Charlie to imagine we're going to play a game. "The game we're playing is: pretend and follow along.

Until the game is over, you just act to grasp this and follow along; do as I tell you to do, for no other reason than to HONOR me, okay?"

I ask Charlie, "Do you know what honor is?"

Charlie replies, "Isn't it when you treat someone with respect?"

I reply, "It's more than this. Honor means: to regard with great respect. *Respect* is the **attitude** of honor. Honor is also when you fulfill an obligation or keep an agreement. *Keeping your word* is the **action** of honor."

I continue, "Charlie, can you do those two things while we play this game of pretend?"

"Sure, why not," Charlie replies.

I walk over to the whiteboard and write an acronym on the board: S.A.L.U.T.E.

"Charlie, I expect you to SALUTE me, every time you interact with me. I'm going to do the same for you." I add.

Now, before I tell Charlie what this means, it's time for me to have a time-out. This break is where I tell on myself, to you.

You see, Charlie doesn't know it yet, but the reason he loses FAVOR (approval, support, liking, giving him what he wants) with me is directly due to his attitude—he dishonors me, thinking it is enjoyable for me to put up with his rebellious kidding around.

When I give up my valuable time to offer him my wisdom, he insults me like a high-school kid. The problem is; he's nearly three times the age of someone from whom you'd expect this behavior.

As he wastes my time by shilling his excuses instead of SALUTE-ing me, he becomes less and less valuable. I'll say, *intolerable* is a better word.

His position in importance in my life goes down lower each time he wastes another precious minute of *my* time.

In essence, Charlie becomes the throw-away or the kid that got cut from the team. He's not an all-star, his attitude places him on the bench until eventually, he becomes displaced there as well.

In spite of his excellent work ethic and loving heart, his approach repels wealth, everywhere he goes.

#WhyAreGoodChristiansBroke #Answered

He's strong, intelligent, and good looking. Charlie underperforms in delivering on his talent. His attitude is the issue.

Why? Because wealth always FLOWS down, as a result of FAVOR. The ingredient to **"make it rain"** that Charlie lacks, is HONOR. He only has half the S.A.L.U.T.E.™ method ingrained in his habitual behavior.

You see, my mentor Mike Murdock taught me the most fabulous wealth miracle ever discovered: **sowing HONOR into your environment creates waves of FAVOR that head back towards you.**

Mike also said this, "An ounce of favor is worth more than a lifetime of labor." I've proven it to be truthful.

I've ATTRACTED two business colleagues who came into my life through my sowing HONOR to receive FAVOR. The irony is; I was sowing honor in environments that caused a ripple effect, where these individuals "heard about me."

When you S.A.L.U.T.E. EVERYONE, your reputation will spread like wildfire. The prominent people who found me would have never otherwise offered me their precious time or expertise. But, every KING is always looking for a master in S.A.L.U.T.E.-ing.

Both of these individuals are very well established, with millions of followers worldwide. If you ask me what the SECRET TO OVERNIGHT FORTUNE IS, I'll tell you that it's FAVOR.

And, I'll go beyond that. I'll show you how to get it to flow to you as well. You CAN do this, no matter what your stature in life is or education level.

CURRENTS OF FAVOR will flow towards you, regardless of where your current lot is in life. Your ***magic-attitude*** will cause a ripple effect that reaches someone capable of BLESSING YOU. *You don't go looking for them, you start S.A.L.U.T.E.-ing right where you are, now.*

While your competition is busy increasing their education, improving their bodies or appearance, learning to manipulate others with ivy-league acumen—they'll be on the path to their destination that looks like traffic in Los Angeles at rush hour.

Everyone is trying to increase their PERSONAL GAIN, as good "go-getters." Supply and demand. We have too many of them, and they're replaceable.

#Myopic

As you S.A.L.U.T.E.™ and BUILD THE HABIT of doing this, your attitude will propel you to the top of the mountain faster than you can imagine.

Your path will be like Tom Cruise in *Top Gun* where he is on the motorcycle speeding by the runway. You will be the TOP GUN.

#HumbleYourself #PsychologicallyBeneathOthers

Let's resume our conversation with Charlie and help him get straightened out. He's still sitting in his chair, looking at the acronym on the whiteboard, scratching his head.

"Charlie, that acronym S.A.L.U.T.E. is something that I received from God, in a meditation. God told me that this was the ultimate teaching I could offer in my book for ANYBODY to get ahead in life—*faster than all their friends.*

It doesn't matter how tall, short, skinny, fat, ugly, or handsome you are and, it won't matter how smart you think you are. If you can follow my S.A.L.U.T.E.™ formula, you'll get ahead of others by leaps and bounds."

Charlie gestured for me to get on with it. He wanted to see what I was making him wait this long for; he's uneasy sitting in one spot for too long. They say that goldfish have a longer attention span than most humans, and Charlie proves it.

"Charlie, before I give you the words in the acronym on that whiteboard, you would agree that I'm alive wouldn't you?"

Charlie said, "Of course."

"Okay, well what about the weird kid who works at the grocery store? Is he also alive?" I replied.

"Matt, is this going to go anywhere, or are we pretending I'm completely clueless? Of course, he is also alive." Charlie adds while shaking his head.

"Charlie, if this kid is alive, and so am I, don't you think we all have something in common? I mean, the common denominator here is that we all possess LIFE ITSELF, correct?"

"I guess so, we are all alive and breathing as far as I know," Charlie replies, wondering if he just caught on to my train of thought.

I add in, "We are all alive because we derive our life from a source. There is only one source of life that animates all living beings and creatures; the GOD-WITHIN."

Charlie opens his hands to affirm he has no argument and says, "So what does S.A.L.U.T.E. mean?"

I slow down my brainwaves into Alpha and synchronize my environment, entraining Charlie so he can store what I'm about to tell him.

As I prepare to share the most significant revelation Charlie ever received—a gift from God bestowed upon me to share with Charlie, and you—I deliver the long-awaited recipe for uncommon FAVOR.

THE S.A.L.U.T.E. METHOD™

"The S. in the acronym stands for **SERVE,**" I reply, adding in, "This is all about ATTITUDE Charlie. You see, **it is our attitude toward life that reflects back upon us as our circumstances**.

SERVE means; I am here to serve. Everyone I come into contact with represents a human transaction. What I put into the transaction is REPAID to me, by God. I'm never interacting with anyone else other than myself. God is being me and also being you, Charlie."

Charlie replies, "Aside from the whole God thing, I get what you're saying. You're here to serve. In other words, you want to be of service to others."

I add in, "Yes, that is my modus operandi. It all begins with SERVING others. MONEY FLOWS WHEN YOU SOLVE A PROBLEM FOR SOMEONE. Since God's nature is giving, I choose to align with this nature so God will operate through me.

Just like I was given the acronym S.A.L.U.T.E. to show you the ***magic-attitude***, the problems I intend to solve for others also solve my problems. *Someone in trouble is your doorway out of trouble."*

After a moment to integrate what he just heard me say, Charlie responds, "So what's the A. stand for?"

"The A. is for **APPRECIATE**. Charlie, I'm talking about attitude. Since my attitude is the only influence I have on my environment, I APPRECIATE EVERYONE as they are God, in disguise as separate beings. All life thrives off of appreciation. *What I make happen for others, God makes happen for me."*

I continue by saying, "Whereas HONOR has an **attitude** and an **action** component, it all boils down to this acronym Charlie. S.A.L.U.T.E. is the master recipe for sowing honor into every environment."

"So tell me the rest, Matthew," Charlie replies.

"The L. is for **LOVE**. Every living being and creature under the sun wants to be LOVED just as much as they desire APPRECIATION. When I LOVE you, Charlie, I'm loving God.

Obviously, I'm not unnatural and overly nice with a facade of LOVE that is not genuine. ***Suspending my judgments towards you***, ALLOWS me to provide the space for LOVE to exist in our dynamic.

I recognize that you may be *playing the fool*, just like I often do, but you're God in disguise.

I can look at life in two ways: **everyone is my competition, or everyone is my teacher. The latter is how you APPRECIATE**, Charlie. After I can appreciate you, my non-judgment opens the door for me to stand in LOVE, here with you now."

As Charlie thinks it over, I proceed by saying, "U. is for **UNDERSTAND**. As I just mentioned, you may have rubbed me wrong often with your attitude, but I understand that it's not who you are. Just like I often make mistakes, I'd expect you to understand that nobody has got it all together.

I desire to UNDERSTAND who you are before I try to evaluate what you are doing."

Charlie says, "I think this is pretty cool Matthew. You made this all up yourself?"

I reply, "No. I told you, I surrendered myself to the quiet solitude where listening for God's voice was my desire. I came to God with the asking for YOUR GAIN in mind, not my own.

Instead of foolishly believing I could keep anything in this world, my asking was to *be the conduit for a solution* to the problem you want to solve."

Charlie smiles and says, "I'm trying man, it's a stretch to imagine how you think. If nothing else, you got me here wondering if you're onto something. I just don't believe that God is talking to you and all, but it's okay. Keep going."

I respond to Charlie by saying, "I'm flattered that you think I would come up with something as brilliant as what you're getting right now. Since I've witnessed it work in my life and the lives of others, the wisdom was always there.

My asking was for a way to communicate it to you so you wouldn't waste time or money in pursuit of dead-end streets."

I followed up by telling Charlie, "It's okay. I know you are getting all of this, and it is sinking in regardless. So let's advance further; the T. is **TRUSTWORTHY**.

The greatest asset a person has is someone he or she can trust with anything, including their life. Men have been promoted to places of authority and power overnight because of this extremely rare successful attitude.

It is the **rarest commodity** on Earth.

Wise people will *test you* before they trust you. Trust is earned. Only fools trust without testing.

You will be tested long before you are trusted—if you are HONORABLE—this attitude alone will lift you into places of power.

FAVOR is a moment-by-moment advantage you earn and must keep with careful adherence to the S.A.L.U.T.E.™ method.

I'll warn you, if you break a person's trust, it will create a loss of favor. You get one chance. Always value the GOD-WITHIN everyone, because THAT IS WHO you are betraying if you betray someone's trust.

History is chalked full of individuals who were given favor and lost it overnight, just by the slightest act of betrayal.

TRUST is what makes you irreplaceable over a thousand others who are far more qualified for the position."

Concluding, I tell Charlie this, "I'll wrap it all up in summary at the end, but the E. is **EFFICIENT**. Efficiency is also rare.

Charlie, when you always ask me a question about internet marketing, it's because you know I'm efficient. A task taking you hours or days will take me minutes, or seconds, to offer a solution.

Can you see how valuable this is? I invest my labor in sharpening my skills to provide efficient value, for you and others. A wealthy person's time is the most valuable asset next to his or her wellbeing. I'm cognizant of this fact."

Charlie says, "Sum it all up. Just tell me how it works and what I need to do with this information."

I walk over to the whiteboard and write down the words: **SEED PRINCIPLE LIVING.**

"Almost everyone is out to get ahead, wouldn't you agree?" I say to Charlie.

Charlie nodded his head saying, "Everyone I know is out to get ahead, including me. It's a necessity. Life isn't easy."

I reply, "So, what you're telling me is that **everyone is out to do the same thing**. In other words, the masses are all marching in the same direction. This *me first attitude* means **there's no value** in it. The *demand is low*, and the *supply is way too high*."

I follow this by saying, "Look, don't you ever tire of hearing people talk about what's in it for them, how much they're going to get paid, or what's important to them?

You've hired people before. Does what's in it for them make you convinced they are the right person you want to invest your future with?"

I carry on saying, "It's the same boring date with the next loser if we are talking about dating. Now, imagine you are wealthy and you can afford all the luxuries in the world.

The only luxury you cannot afford is an *untrustworthy* person or someone who doesn't *appreciate* you?

Would you spend a moment arguing for investing in someone who won't *serve* you?

Or perhaps someone who isn't *efficient* and wastes your time?

How about someone who doesn't *love* who you are or your mission in life?

Would you feel that this person *understands* the effort and commitment you require to stay at the top of your game?"

Charlie replies, "Now that you put it this way, it sounds like almost everyone who got fired at the office in the past couple years. They always did one or more of these things long enough to get let go."

I reply to Charlie saying, "Yes, because the formula for loss is DISHONOR. That's the part that is obvious.

But, the less obvious part is the MECHANICS of what I call the ***magic-attitude***—the **S.A.L.U.T.E.™** method."

Charlie's face now appears as if he has seen behind the curtain for the first time. I can tell he's processing all this, so I pause for a moment to allow him time to digest this information.

I then say, "SEED PRINCIPLE LIVING is about living with the attitude of a GIVER—a sower. You are then aligning with God's nature.

You **sow the seeds you want to reap**, your harvest; the fastest seed-formula for wealth is to S.A.L.U.T.E.™ everyone in your environment."

"I hate to be selfish with all this martyr talk, but tell me—what's in it for me? How does this get my pocketbook fat?" Charlie says.

I reply, "Apparently, what you have now is a meager harvest. Along with everyone else who is solely wondering *what's in it for themselves*, you offer no real, irreplaceable value that sets you apart.

Contrarily, someone will, eventually NOTICE YOU and REWARD YOU WITH ACCESS, if you sow the S.A.L.U.T.E. seed-formula."

"You became wealthy because someone noticed you and helped you get all the money?" Charlie replied.

"What we sow, we also shall reap. Our attitude towards life is what we experience back at us.

The ingredients in S.A.L.U.T.E. are the recipe for WEALTH to flow into your experience. It is an attitude that gives you *Casanova-like* advantages in the marketplace.

It is the MISSING piece to the puzzle because it addresses the core component: **you attract in life what you are, not what you want,**" I replied.

Charlie responded by saying, "Are you saying that I can treat people different by SALUTE-ing them and somehow a rich and powerful person will give me a job or some opportunity to get rich? Or, they'll just give me money?"

"Charlie, you are already hoping this will happen, and so is everyone else.

The problem is; you think the world is outside of you.

A false-reality matrix blinds you.

You are the cause of everything that comes into your experience, and the characters who show up in your hologram are put there—by you—to reflect your attitude towards life back to you."

Charlie needed a moment to allow these ideas to network with his preconceived cognitive-bias "superstition of material reality" he perceives as occurring outside of himself.

While he took a few moments, I walked over to the whiteboard and wrote out the entire acronym for Charlie to see clearly:

S - Serve

A - Appreciate

L - Love

U - Understand

T - Trustworthy

E – Efficient

"Charlie, I S.A.L.U.T.E. you for asking for clarification."

I sat down next to Charlie and said, "How would you like God to serve you, appreciate you, love you, understand you and your needs better than you do, be 100% trustworthy and efficiently solve problems for you?"

Charlie's eyes lit up, "Matthew, this is what everyone wants. If God solved my money problems right now, I would be a believer.

I see too many people struggling who believe in God. They pray to God, and it seems like they never get an answer. One in a million might receive a miracle, but that's it.

It's too naive for me to act this way. If it's going to be, it's up to me!"

"I couldn't agree with you more," I replied.

"It is up to you, 100%. But you assume you accurately see what your lying eyes suggest to you.

These people who are struggling, do you know all the facts? Are you committed to betting your life savings that they have anything figured out, just because they claim to be a Christian or a Buddhist?

Charlie, you must not judge anything by appearances alone. You must PROVE to yourself the wisdom you acquire is legit by using FAITH to try something new.

You see, the reason you keep ending up where you started is that YOU SEE FAILURE all around you; this evaluation is a misperception on your part.

I see opportunity whenever there's a problem to solve. By S.A.L.U.T.E.-ing everyone in my environment, I psychologically get beneath them, to prop them up.

Why, you ask? What I make happen for others, God makes happen for me."

I then walk over to the whiteboard and prescribe a strategy for Charlie to use.

"Charlie, here's how easy it will be to shape and mold your attitude into the magic attitude that SUMMONS WEALTH and ACCESS TO POWERFUL PEOPLE (modern-day kings) towards you.

Remember, they can hoist you into a status or echelon in life—in days, weeks, or minutes—that you can labor a lifetime and miss out on."

I walked over to my briefcase and grabbed a stack of notecards. Handing them to Charlie, I also gave him a permanent marker.

"Take six cards, and I'll show you what to write on each one of them," I said.

Charlie grabbed his cards and marker, getting ready to write down one word on each card.

Charlie read what I wrote on the whiteboard:

Day 1 - Serve

Day 2 - Appreciate

Day 3 - Love

Day 4 - Understand

Day 5 - Trustworthy

Day 6 - Efficient

On the 7th day—reflect on the week's insights and any outcome of success; celebrate the victories.

DAY 1

After writing on the board, I say, "Charlie, I want you to carry an index card each day. Example: day 1 you have SERVE written on a card. You carry it with you.

You train your mind to look for ways to serve others, then act on it. It can be as complex as helping someone move to a new home or as simple as opening a door for someone. SERVE as often as you can on day 1."

DAY 2

"On day 2, you carry a card with APPRECIATE written on it. I want you to pay attention to all the beauty around you.

I want you to look for all the prosperity around, the joy, and any other virtue you want to SEE more of in your reality.

By training your mind to **appreciate these things** in other's, you draw them to yourself. Day 2 is all about investing in perpetual appreciation."

DAY 3

"Day 3, you will carry a card with LOVE written on it.

I want you to extend a feeling of LOVE towards everyone you can; if you find it challenging to do—you shift to non-judgment.

In other words, if someone is pushing your buttons or you just don't like the way they speak or look, etc., remove your judgment as best as you can.

Acceptance is the doorway to love. Invest day 3 in extending *love and acceptance* towards everyone and everything in your environment."

DAY 4

"Day 4, you will carry a card with UNDERSTAND written on it. I want you to seek to understand life from other people's point-of-view.

Instead of judgment (ignorance), engage in asking questions and doing a discovery process that allows you to see life through the eyes of someone else.

Ask them how they see things in their world; what are their feelings and thoughts? How did they come up with their conclusions?

Day 4 is all about seeking to trade ignorance and assumptions for understanding."

Day 5

"Day 5, I want you to carry a card with TRUSTWORTHY written on it.

All day long, I want you to observe whether your words line up with your actions and if you are honoring your agreements.

Did you say you'd be somewhere at a certain time? Did you end up doing as you said you would do or did something alter your day and you made an excuse?

I want you ONLY to say what you will do and agree to things that you will 100% perform, as promised, and deliver on your word.

If you suspect something will come up and get in the way, do not agree or put your word on it."

Day 6

"Day 6, I want you to carry a card with EFFICIENCY written on it.

All day long, I want you to focus on becoming more efficient. Study better ways to improve tasks you are currently doing.

Model other people who are performing at higher levels and accomplishing more, with less time, energy, or resources.

This day is all about focusing on efficiency and implementing new strategies to improve your performance."

DAY 7

"Day 7, I want you to reflect and observe the progress and gains you are making.

After a few rounds of doing this, about five times through each, repeated day, you will be ingraining LIFELONG HABITS by altering your ATTITUDE to give you the *Casanova-like advantages* in the marketplace.

You don't get to choose your destiny in life, you choose your habits. Your habits determine your destiny."

MASTERING RELATIONSHIPS: S.A.L.U.T.E.

As I leave the scene of Charlie sitting by the whiteboard, I'm now sitting in front of you.

I'm telling you right here—in black and white—that doing what I just suggested will MAKE ALL THE OTHER THINGS you are doing to manifest success, wealth, power, or influence all come to life.

Everything you acquire in this lifetime, regarding material wealth, influence and power, will all come from other people.

I've just shown you the magic attitude that makes you the most irreplaceable person. This shift in your daily interactions with others increases the VALUE of your product, which is always you (even if you sell physical products).

The S.A.L.U.T.E.™ method came through me as a gift from the Divine, the GOD-WITHIN-ME. I asked for it to give to you.

As a byproduct of this asking, I'm also the recipient of this blessing. I'm blessed, and you're blessed. That's how the nature of a giver works. I'll be doing this process along with you.

"What I make happen for others, God makes happen for me." –Dr. Mike Murdock

Chapter 7.

Parallel Universes Vs. Series Reality

What would you think if I told you that 30 seconds from now you could be in another universe?

You'd think I was out of mind if I said that you could shift your BEING into an entirely new reality, and experience a different YOU.

It's similar to how people with multiple personalities unconsciously shift consciousness and illnesses go away, or scars disappear, yet doing it consciously and without the disorder.

Earlier in the book, I told you that a multiple personality "disorder" was a representation of another universe intermingling for a witnessing mind to observe.

In essence, if you see someone change personalities—they are merging universes with alternate versions of themselves. People with multiple personalities usually unconsciously shift in a BEING CHOICE (new persona) via a traumatic "hard-wiring." What emerges is an entirely new attitude towards life (and persona: mask, actor).

Physical reality is a cleverly disguised LIE: otherwise, how do the scars go away or the illnesses vanish or reappear? If physical reality is the truth, this would be impossible. The universe would break at its weakest point.

There is no physical reality. We are **energetic** beings of salt and light. Salt conducts "electricity," and light animates our consciousness projection—the hologram illusion I call, *the external kingdom.*

The "idea" of physical reality and a physical body is a preconceived cognitive bias; a superstition we hold in the collective agreement of our belief about existence.

We have taken the ***fall of man*** through the six-degrees of separation (*who, what, where, when, why, how*), in all three-kingdoms (our *inner kingdom, middle kingdom, external kingdom*).

You can call this the 6 6 6. Six-degrees, in three-kingdoms. After the *fall-of-man,* we entered "SIRIUS" or the "series-circuitry" where we increase our unconsciousness by adding more thinking. You called this "growing up" as you become adult-erated. It happens because of the LAWS of electricity and your frame-of-mind. SIRIUSness is a diseased state-of-being.

You are made up of electricity, and you originated in sexual energy or electricity ([2]). You'll learn more about it in chapter 9, don't worry.

Einstein said, "We can't solve the problems with the same consciousness that's creating the problem." This revelation means, if we keep trying to add more thinking in a series-circuit projection of events, *without changing WHO you are BEING*, we will increase our unconsciousness and add resistance.

How's that for doing things upside-down in an anticivilization? You were programmed this way by the false-reality matrix. Fortunately, this book will undo all of that circuitry and re-wire you in parallel; you'll leave SIRI's influence (SIRIUS: "seriousness" disease) over your frame-of-mind.

How did this all begin? What happened to humanity?

Lucifer came to Earth from SIRIUS; he is the architect of the false-reality matrix. That's the short answer. The purpose of this book is not to convince you I know what I'm talking about, just to get you questioning your reality.

Let's gaze back into my past and see how I got here to share these ideas with you, and string the events together for reference later on.

In 2010, when I was escaping the clutches of Lyme disease and regaining a semi-normal life, constant fatigue was keeping me down. I'd spend most of the day in bed.

Desperate to get free from Lyme disease, the road took me in some places where pieces of the puzzle came together. The first miracle I encountered happened when I stumbled upon Gary Blier and his business, Advanced Cell Training™.

Back then, not many modalities or health practitioners offered much hope for chronic Lyme disease. I'd take their best supplements and do their "frequency machines," to no avail.

Gary's work was different. A long history of clients who emerged victorious over Lyme disease had visited his clinic. Advanced Cell Training™ was producing results. Many of the people sat at home and remotely took a Lyme class—I chose to do the same.

I joined (ACT) Advanced Cell Training™, doing the classes from *over a 1,000 miles away* with nothing more than a phone required to attend class. All I had to do was listen to "codes" that made *no sense*, and play a two-hour audio each week, and document my progress.

Every day, I'd carry the "ACT" magazine full of testimonials from successful clients who restored their health. When I'd have a bad day, this magazine was my refuge to believe my healing was going to happen!

Long story short: Advanced Cell Training™ got me most of the way *symptom-free* from debilitating Lyme disease. I was well enough to get back to work (part-time) and do most of the things previously considered as "normal living."

How does Gary's method work? I didn't have a clue back then. It makes no logical sense if you're looking at the world from a belief in physical reality. To be honest, a colleague of mine also took his class for Lyme disease and recovered his health, improving week-after-week. We conversed one day and had a brief interaction that sounded like this:

Me: "How do you think Gary does it? He claims the method only works when prayer is involved. I don't get it?"

My colleague: "Gary is an alien."

Honestly, his explanation made more sense to me than the ideas I was trying to understand back in those days. Coming from a background of bodybuilding—before taking ill, I was in the fitness profession—that focuses primarily on heavy objects. Everything was densely physical in my scope of reality.

Quite honestly, the fact that (ACT) worked for me is all I cared about at the time of my recovery. But, witnessing the proof that my symptoms could disappear without a tablet, pill, machine or something physically attached to me, made me question my beliefs.

I'm not promoting Advanced Cell Training™, and this isn't something I was paid to endorse in my book. It's not an advertisement. The big idea was: I was sitting in my chair over 1,000 miles away, listening to "codes" that made no sense and the audio put me to sleep. Week after week, the illness was going away, and I found myself recovering my strength and joy again.

To this day, people see my videos on YouTube and hear about my victory over chronic Lyme disease. I get emails and calls to our office, asking me how I got well. My best advice: you have to keep trying NEW ideas and think outside the box. You may live your life in a physical reality frame-of-mind that is preventing you from accessing your miracle.

#NeverQuitBelieving #MiraclesAreNormal

After making enough progress in my recovery, I started skipping (ACT) class. *I've been notorious for skipping class* since my youth. They just had to call it a "class," didn't they? If they had called each session a "recess" each week, my compliance would have doubled.

Once the painful symptoms of Lyme disease, including visual and motor challenges, generalized weakness and burning sensations vanished, I ventured out of (ACT) to pursue new modalities. In my mind, Lyme disease was not the issue anymore, just the last symptom: constant fatigue.

In the hierarchy of symptoms remaining in my body, everything was mostly decreased, except for fatigue. The type of fatigue I experienced is one that persisted day-in and day-out.

The exhaustion was beating me down, badly. So I started to look at the work of Dr. David Mickel (Mickel Therapy) and Dr. John Eaton (Reverse Therapy™).

Both therapies had an astonishing recovery rate for chronic fatigue syndrome. They captivated me because of the idea that the *mind-body* connection was responsible for the symptoms. *Mind-body,* to me at the time, meant that the manifestation of fatigue (including the brain fog) was within my grasp to control and hopefully be well again.

I just had to figure out what my body was telling me! My thinking wasn't producing anything other than more stress, doubt, fear, and worry.

Regarding symptoms: we can experience symptoms as a distress signal that gets *louder and louder* until it "puts us in bed" (in my case) because we aren't interpreting the messages.

Our body-mind is sending us a message, according to Mickel Therapy and Reverse Therapy. If we decode the signals, we can turn off the symptoms by changing our actions or behaviors. For me, having a practitioner interpret the messages was far more efficient than doing it myself.

I did both of these therapies and experienced a slight-degree of improvement. The real gain for me was the new elasticity in my firm Western-medicine beliefs. With each new idea along with my healing journey, I was starting to see a different model of the human body.

Carrying forward on my journey, a gigantic leap ahead occurred when I did Phil Parker's Lightning Process ®. A woman named Berit held the two-day course for several of us who attended. I flew out to California in search of a miracle.

Before attending the weekend training, I was already mind-blown by the testimonials. I heard stories on the internet about a guy who was wheelchair bound with chronic fatigue syndrome for five years. Within the weekend of his Lightning Process ® training, he got out of his wheelchair and walked sixteen miles!

#BeliefIncreased

Many more unique stories fascinated me and peaked my curiosity; I couldn't wait to take this training!

What happened after the Lightning Process ® weekend, was nothing short of a miracle. Suffice it to say; my fears got the best of me during the training. We were challenged to face our fears. Heading to the gym to workout was my challenge. It involved walking a mile there and living my life as someone who is well. In essence, act and behave in my "powerful" state-of-being.

I was terrified to even walk to the gym, as this was reaching my threshold of what was possible with old fears about Lyme disease and chronic fatigue syndrome tormenting me. "*What if my body goes into a somatization episode again? What if my fatigue gets so unbearable that I sink into another two-day recovery in bed?*"

I ended up walking to the gym and experiencing a massive panic attack. My symptoms flared up and I walked back to my hotel room and cried. My body was flooded with fatigue sensations, heaviness, and I felt utterly defeated. If this training didn't work for me, I'd never again produce my worth and make money to take care of my family.

I had come too far to succumb to the last symptom ruining my life. *The worst was over,* Lyme disease wasn't causing me pain, slurred speech, digestive intolerances, and all the other symptoms. My tears poured from a place of "I'm going to get this or I'm going to die trying."

Berit challenged me to stay committed. She reminded me that she had fibromyalgia and was able to **be** completely symptom-free. She told me that it takes work!

Staying committed to the work involved, the lessons I learned provided me with a set of self-coaching tools to conquer fatigue—once and for all. It wasn't easy to stay committed, but I did, and a few weeks later the fatigue was finally gone. I was in complete amazement.

It's like I shifted into being an entirely new version of myself, who had boundless energy and vigor. My old "self" was back! It's like suddenly emerging out of a nightmare.

From time to time, the fatigue resurfaced again in my healing journey. Usually, a shock or trauma to my emotional body or a sudden upset was the trigger. I'd find myself "*stuck in the pit*," as I learned to say in training. A few hours after doing the Lightning Process ®, and my fatigue signals evaporated again.

In my search for knowledge, there were a few common themes I kept coming across. I wanted to know everything.

Dr. John Eaton said it best on one of our Skype sessions during the early days of my recovery. He told me that he had a theory that chronic fatigue was the result of a trauma, like PTSD.

Also, the Lightning Process ® teaches you about the P.E.R. (Physical Emergency Response), which seems to be a byproduct of trauma. When it activates, we get stuck in the pit.

Learning about German New Medicine's model for healing and why we get sick, it all begins with an unexpected emotional upset (a shock) that caught us off guard. When we fear the condition or symptoms, we can create additional biological conflicts—persisting our illness or creating more signs of disease.

My studies led me to spend months of contemplation on Phineas Parkhurst Quimby's life and discoveries. His healing methods were what he described as the "rediscovery of Christ, or truth." Quimby claimed that all disease was a lie or opinion and that man was living in his belief.

It was Quimby's story of how he cured himself of consumption (a terrifying illness where one drowns in fluid) by riding horseback. Quimby had to grab on for dear life as his horse was startled, as he was on a hill and too weak to walk down by his own strength. Upon reaching the bottom of the hill, he was symptom-free and felt as strong as ever.

Quimby surmised that the "fluids" in the body had changed according to the change in his state-of-being. The incident on the hill forced him out of his fearful state-of-being. This **fear** was where he was stuck, according to Quimby, a person who is ill is fragmented (parallel universe) in a stuck trauma.

Gaining in his wisdom, Quimby developed his studies by mesmerizing people (hypnosis) where he discovered that **minds mingle** and we live in our thoughts. A person who was under hypnosis could access the thoughts and impressions from anyone at any place or point-in-time.

#ThoughtUniverse #Thoth #Judge #Ment (mind)

Correcting the mind and <u>bringing someone out of their suffering state-of-being</u> (trauma) was Quimby's healing method. Over 10,000 people claimed to have been cured by having a conversation or series of conversations with Quimby. Mary Baker Eddy, the founder of Christian Science, was also his protege. She recovered from an injury rendering her as an invalid, with nothing more than a conversation.

Now, *fast-forward* to real time. After extensively researching for years, and thousands-of-hours of study, there are a few insights that built a picture of knowledge in my mind.

When I recognize how the Lightning Process ® challenged me to DU (do) life as my healthy-self, while getting the P.E.R. (Physical Emergency Response) down, it seems intrinsically similar to Quimby's discovery—although Quimby's method was vastly more far-reaching in its scope of ailments or conditions. At least, it appears to have been.

I will soon show you how I've taken the lessons learned from all these excellent self-coaching tools and insights from thought-leaders, to develop my method. First, we need to give your reasoning mind the ability to *comprehend* **parallel universes**.

I'm going to show you a few highlights, leading to the revelation I call the ***Self-Entrainment Technique***™.

Phineas Parkhurst Quimby: "All disease is the result of error or opinion."

Mary Baker Eddy: "Fear is the fountain of sickness. Treat a belief in sickness as you would sin, with sudden dismissal."

Romans 8:10 (My life scripture): "And if Christ be in you, the body is dead because of sin; but the Spirit is life because of righteousness."

Phil Parker: "In and out of CFS/ME with the Lightning Process®."

Gary Blier (ACT): "Unique training codes to correct your body's errors." (Done from thousands-of-miles away).

Bashar (Daryl Anka): "Circumstances don't matter, only your state of being matters."

What is the common denominator in all these ideas? After all, I've witnessed all of them as truth in my world.

So, where is the power, or the thread they all share? The answer:

WE LIVE IN PARALLEL UNIVERSES

I'm not expecting you to take my word for it, since the idea of a parallel reality is "science fiction" to many people.

The bottom line is this: **you've been lied to**.

You have never lived a "physical life" in a space-time reality. It's powerful hypnosis to believe, but it doesn't add up.

The smartphone you carry around uses technology that could never work if you lived in a physical universe. How can you pull up a device that can translate acoustic vibration into sound waves and decipher the energy and information, all so you can listen to or watch something on that device? *And, how can these broadcasted vibrations occur simultaneously in hundreds, thousands, or millions of locations at the same time?*

#DontTrustYourLyingEyes

You have to decide right now, what are you going to believe? Is your body material with corporeal senses? Do you have a meatsack body that operates itself by some physical might of its own?

Or, is this life a projection of CURRENT (from within you) in a stream of consciousness?

If a corpse is lying on the table and the soul has left the body, does the body come alive, animate itself, and think for itself? The body is lifeless without the non-physical soul that animates the five-senses in a mind-projected illusion.

Nothing is physical except the spoken word; the body is a belief. When you were five-years old, your body was entirely different. It was always you who looked in the mirror. The form has changed, but the formless observer remains the same. Life is that part of you which never changes.

You are no longer the little boy or girl you once were. But you are still the same being? Soon, when you see that the laws of electricity applied to the science of your BEING are the same, it will make more sense.

"Infinite worlds come and go in the vast expanse of consciousness, dancing like motes of dust in a beam of light."

–Yoga Vasishtha

We live in a thought world. The word thought comes from ***Thoth***, the god of knowledge. Thoth is known as the originator of all knowledge on Earth and Heaven and as an incorruptible judge. Is it any wonder that judgments we make (karmic action) end up coming to us as thought?

As we create karma (action, cellular memory, reaction), we store karma in the Akashic records. We are accumulating judgments that come like a bill in the mail to get paid, or a return on investment for what we've sown as a seed. *Chapter 12 is all about dealing with these judgments, so fear not—you're covered.*

You could say it is our R.O.I. (Return On Investment) for our words and deeds. Since the world is not physical, our karma comes to us *first* as a thought-impression. It's at this point of inception where we either perpetuate our automatic response (reacting) or choose a new BEING CHOICE or attitude towards life.

A fundamental study of electricity reveals the nature of reality, as a hologram contains the "wholeness" in every part of the WHOLEogram. Your body has electrical energy. You possess creative energy—sexual energy is electricity ([2])—that can be used to create a baby or any "birth," a business, a new car, a lover, healing. You'll see how in the ***Self-Entrainment Technique***™.

Keep in mind: you are programmed from birth to believe your lying eyes. The world has been pulled over your eyes, Neo. I call it the false-reality matrix; it's how you were "**wired**"—an appropriate word with a proper implication.

False-reality matrix "WIRING": you appear to live in a "series-circuit" of life events, like metronome units of sound: *tick...tick...tick...tick.*

As the space between the sounds contains your REAL IDENTITY (awareness itself), life's circumstances flash in and out of existence in what appears to be a linear series of events. You assume you are living on "clock-time" and in one singular "movie" that plays out in a series-circuit.

THE AWAKENING TO "REWIRE" YOURSELF

The laws of electricity shine a spotlight on what happens if we RE-WIRE OURSELVES (choose to **see the world different**, thereby changing our consciousness).

We seize control over our projected reality by fully accepting it all; everything and everyone in our life circumstances is reflective of our attitude towards life.

Our BEING CHOICE (see: ABC Break Process) determines the you-niverse we *choose* and project into existence. **We have to entrain ourselves to stay committed to our chosen reality-focus**.

Your reality-projection is always *flickering in and out of existence* based on your BELIEFS. Beliefs govern your actions and attitude towards life, so let's question the archaic belief that implies your reality is happening **to** you.

To believe the world happens to you, you remain unconscious in how you react to life's circumstances. You run in a "series-circuit" **frame-of-mind** (still images of reality flickering in and out of existence so fast it appears like a movie that's playing in a series progression).

Here's how the first movie projector worked: *projected images from rotating glass disks in rapid succession to give the impression of motion.*

#YourMovie

Important insight: most people see their world this way, in a linear progression. When you add THINKING in a series-circuit sequence of reality, **it increases resistance** and **diminishes consciousness**.

We GROW UP under this spell, gradually losing our childlike innocence and becoming ADULT-erated.

In the false-reality matrix, our thinking (six-degrees of separation) generates resistance, and we lose our CURRENT (currency/consciousness).

As we grow **adult**erated, we project governments and other institutions out of this corrupted frame-work. Wars, violence, poverty, hunger, and all forms of unconscious suffering are the result of being "WIRED" to live at the mercy of our external kingdom.

#ReActing

Let's wake up and remove ourselves from this illusion.

Reality is happening **through** you, *moment-by-moment*, as electricity flows into your experience. If we see the laws of electricity, we see the same laws fractalize to become our consciousness.

Remember, we have power running through us and all creative energy (sexual energy) is electricity ([2]).

God is the Creator, which means God's energy creates in the same way, as the entire universe fractals itself (repeats patterns).

Electricity is the "invisible" force connecting us to God-Consciousness, and all creation is thought, charged with electricity ([2]).

The following facts we know about electricity can be used with these interchangeable words to translate the meanings.

I'll provide the website link to where I grabbed each paragraph that will be referenced and then parsed to translate the correlation between series vs. parallel circuits (and realities).

TRANSLATION WORDS

Current = Consciousness

Charge = Your Loaded Reality/Being Choice

Series = Clock-Time Reality/False Matrix

Parallel = Parallel Universe Reality

Pathway = External Reality Projection

Circuit = Belief

Branches = Thought Patterns

Resistors = Thinking (Process)

Device = Desire or Intention

Node = BEING CHOICE

Water = Substance (Appearing as Matter)

Electrical = Human Life

PARALLEL CIRCUITS: ALTERNATE REALITIES

(Electricity content found at http://www.physicsclassroom.com).

I'm going to insert several paragraphs about electricity and then translate how the laws of electricity fractal into our consciousness-reality.

Ready to begin? Let's start with the idea of a parallel circuit being a parallel universe.

In a parallel circuit, charge divides up into separate branches such that there can be more current in one branch than there is in another. Nonetheless, when taken as a whole, the total amount of current in all the branches when added together is the same as the amount of current at locations outside the branches. The rule that current is the same everywhere still works, only with a twist. The current outside the branches is the same as the sum of the current in the individual branches. It is still the same amount of current, only split up into more than one pathway.

Translated:

*In a **parallel universe reality belief**, **your loaded reality/being choice** divides up into separate **thought patterns** such that there can be more **consciousness** in one **thought pattern** than there is in another. Nonetheless, when taken as a **whole-ogram**, the total amount of **consciousness** in all the **thought patterns** when added together is the same as the amount of **consciousness** at locations outside the **thought patterns**. The rule that **consciousness** is everywhere the same still works, only with a twist. The **consciousness** outside the **thought patterns** is the same as the sum of*

consciousness *in the individual* ***thought patterns****. It is still the same amount of* ***consciousness****, only split up into more than one* ***external reality projection****.*

Now, let's look at the *Luciferian* false-reality matrix program: a series-circuit progression of clock-time; an illusion.

SERIES CIRCUIT: SIRIUS ATTITUDES

In a series-circuit, each device is connected in a manner such that there is only one pathway by which charge can traverse the external circuit. Each charge passing through the loop of the external circuit will pass through each resistor in consecutive fashion.

The act of adding more resistors to a series circuit results in the rather expected result of having more overall resistance. Since there is only one pathway through the circuit, every charge encounters the resistance of every device; so adding more devices results in more overall resistance. This increased resistance serves to reduce the rate at which charge flows (also known as the current).

Translated:

In a ***clock-time reality/false matrix belief****, each* ***desire or intention*** *is connected in a manner such that there is only one* ***external reality projection*** *by which* ***your loaded reality/being choice*** *can traverse the external* ***belief****.* ***Your loaded reality/being choice*** *that passes through the loop of the external* ***belief*** *will pass through each* ***thinking process*** *in consecutive fashion.*

The act of adding more ***thinking (process)*** *to a* ***clock-time reality/false matrix belief*** *results in the rather expected result of having more overall* ***thinking (process)****. Since there is only one* ***external reality projection*** *through the* ***clock-time reality/false matrix belief, your loaded reality/being choice*** *encounters the* ***thinking (process)*** *of every* ***desire or intention****; so adding more* ***desire or intention*** *results in more overall* ***thinking (process)****. This increased* ***thinking (process)*** *serves to reduce the rate at which* ***your loaded reality/being choice*** *flows (also known as the* ***consciousness****).*

If you didn't understand what you just read, please look closely at the last part, read it carefully and slowly:

This increased ***thinking (process)*** *serves to reduce the rate at which* ***your loaded reality/being choice*** *flows (also known as the* ***consciousness****).*

The understanding: you cannot solve the problems in life with the same consciousness that created the problem. You'll just encounter more resistance and unconscious reactions.

Why are we a war-culture run by adult-erated minds?

THE LUCIFERIAN PROGRAM: UNCONSCIOUSNESS

In the false-reality matrix, you engage the six-degrees of separation, known as *the fall of man*!

Thinking (*who, what, where, when, why, how*) is encouraged and pre-programmed in this "series" wiring of so-called reality. We churn every desire through the six-degrees of separation and increase our resistance (attitude towards life).

Let's look at how our translation (real-eyes-ation) continues by exploring more about parallel circuits/parallel universes.

Back to our classroom study of electricity: here is an analogy about resistors/resistance as it pertains to parallel circuits. We are going to learn about the **unexpected** "lessening of resistance" in a parallel circuit (universe) when **adding more** resistors:

In an effort to make this rather unexpected result more reasonable, a ***tollway analogy*** *was introduced. A tollbooth is the main location of resistance to car flow on a tollway. Adding additional tollbooths within their own branch on a tollway will provide more pathways for cars to flow through the toll station. These additional tollbooths will decrease the overall resistance to car flow and increase the rate at which they flow.*

Translated...

ADDITIONAL TRANSLATION WORDS

Tollbooth = Alternate Universe Path.

Car = Life's Circumstances

Tollway = Alternate Universe Path Awareness

Station = Frame-of-Mind

Rate = Success

In an effort to make this rather unexpected result more reasonable, an ***alternate universe path awareness*** *was introduced. An* ***alternate universe path*** *is the main location of* ***thinking (process)*** *to* ***life's circumstances*** *flowing on a* ***alternate universe path awareness****. Adding additional* ***alternate universe paths*** *within their own* ***thought patterns*** *on an* ***alternate universe path awareness*** *will provide more* ***external reality projection*** *for* ***life's circumstances*** *to flow through the* ***alternate universe frame-of-mind****. These additional* ***alternate universe paths*** *will decrease the overall* ***thinking (process)*** *to* ***life's circumstances*** *flowing and increase the* ***success*** *at which they flow.*

The understanding: with an awareness that parallel realities exist and it's our attitude towards life that determines our reality projection, we *engage in less thinking*. Consequently, we experience greater success at the rate by which our manifested desires flow into our lives.

PARALLEL CIRCUITS: INFINITE REALITIES

I'm going to give you one more example and translate how the laws of electricity apply to our circumstances.

Keep in mind; I'm grabbing information we know to be correct about electricity and parsing the meaning as it applies to our LIFE-energy (since it is electrical energy).

At each ***node*** *(branching location), the water takes two or more separate pathways. The rate at which water flows into the node (measured in* *gallons per minute) will be equal to the sum of the flow rates in the individual branches beyond the node. Similarly, when two or more branches feed into a node, the rate at which water flows out of the node will be equal to the sum of the flow rates in the individual branches that feed into the node.*

Translated:

*At each **BEING CHOICE (thought patterns** location), the **flow** takes two or more separate **external reality projections**. The rate at which **substance (appearing as matter)** flows into the **PERSONA** (measured to quantify its presence) will be equal to the sum of the flow rates in the individual **thought patterns** beyond the **BEING CHOICE**. Similarly, when two or more **thought patterns** feed into a **PERSONA**, the rate at which **substance (appearing as matter)** flows out of the **PERSONA** will be equal to the sum of the flow rates in the individual t**hought patterns** that feed into the **PERSONA**.*

The understanding: the substance which creates your external world flows through your BEING CHOICE.

#PauseThinkReflect #ABCBreakProcess

Now, in case something was vague, we can compare how a series-circuit differentiates in the same context.

SERIES CIRCUITS: UNCONSCIOUSNESS

Kirchhoff's first law says: "*At any node (junction) in an electrical circuit, the sum of currents flowing into that node is equal to the sum of currents flowing out of that node.*" When there is only one current flowing into *the node it is simply equal to the sum of currents flowing out. The node or junction is the place where the conductor splits to form coupled parallel branches.*

When you have resistors in series, there is no such node/junction, the current doesn't split, and flows through each resistor.

Translated...

*Kirchhoff's first law says: "At any **BEING CHOICE** (junction: decide your state of being/attitude towards life) in a **human life belief**, the sum of **consciousness** flowing into that **BEING CHOICE** is equal to the sum of **consciousness** flowing out of that **BEING CHOICE**." When there is only one **consciousness** flowing into the **BEING CHOICE** it is simply equal to the sum of **consciousness** flowing out. The **BEING CHOICE** or junction (choice about who to BE, choosing your attitude towards life) is the place where the conductor splits to form a coupled **parallel reality universe thought patterns**.*

*When you have your **thinking (process)** in **clock-time reality/false matrix**, there is no such **BEING CHOICE**/junction (choice of state-of-being or attitude towards life), the **consciousness** doesn't split and flows through each **thinking (process)**.*

The understanding: you REACT unconsciously in a series or "serious" attitude towards life. This reactionary behavior is "hard-wired" in the Luciferian SIRIUS false-reality matrix.

You must reclaim your childlike innocence to enter the kingdom of Heaven. Ready to take your power back?

<u>CHAPTER 8.</u>

The Self-Entrainment Technique™

The Self-Entrainment Technique™ advances the ABC Break Process I outlined in my bestselling book *ALLOW - Mastering The Law of Least Effort to Receive Your Desires!*

The technique is as follows:

Step one, make a list of all of the self-doubts that torment you day in and day out. These are the thoughts you think in the background. They're not unconscious; they are unexamined. We want to make them visible and examine them.

Here's an example list (just do a brain dump without analyzing when you make your list):

1. "I'm not good enough."
2. "I'm too old to enjoy my dreams now."

3. "Life never works out the way I want it to."
4. "I tried that before, and it ended up failing."
5. "Nothing seems to work for me anyhow."
6. "Other people will laugh at me."
7. "Money is not going to stick around; people will steal it."
8. "Life isn't fun anymore."
9. "Nobody will love me if I'm different from how they are."
10. "Someone will sue me or come after me legally to rob me."
11. "It's not worth it. The government will tax it all away."
12. "I'll become a target, and someone will come after me."
13. "My spouse is holding me back from being myself."
14. "I hate thinking about being someone else."
15. "It's too much work."
16. "It's not worth the struggle or effort."
17. "Nothing good ever happens to me."
18. "Somehow this will all be a waste of time—again."
19. "Paying attention to nonsense will get me in trouble."
20. "You have to be crooked to get wealthy in America."

Pay attention to your thoughts. Document them. Stab them with a pencil, pen, or keyboard stroke and list everything that comes to mind. Even if it seems "stupid"—jot these thoughts down. If they come up, they are affecting you.

Become aware of these background thoughts so you can see them in front of you. Any "I'm less than because (fill in the blank)" idea—thought of inferiority—get it on the table for examination. Document it. Awareness is our starting place.

Step two is to feel the feelings underneath these "thought" suggestions and **clear** them. They are temptations charged with ENERGY, E-motion. If you keep suppressing the EMOTIONS, you will collect these thoughts, storing them like clutter. They slow down your ability to shift consciousness.

All of the pain that underlies all of these thoughts wants to be released. **Embrace** what you feel, wholeheartedly. And as you explore these feelings, allow yourself to surrender to the EMOTIONAL CHARGE and let it pass through you.

Here's how (we'll discuss this technique more in chapter 13) you can clear things, rapidly:

Use Ho'oponono. Repeat, "I am sorry, I love you, please forgive me, thank you." As you turn within to the Divine, repeat out loud or in your mind, "I am sorry, I love you, please forgive me, thank you."

Keep repeating those four statements. At the same time, while you're embracing the emotional junk and feeling it fully—learn to relax. Fully surrender to "WHAT IS" (non-resistance to these unpleasant feelings) and allow the hard circumstances or feelings to reveal their blessing.

Everything has a blessing. I'll tell you about a specific situation involving back pain and how it quickly became a blessing. You can shift any circumstance or feeling, regardless of how bad it looks. Nothing is ever as bad as it first appears.

You must allow the suppressed energy to surface. And **until the peace comes from a surrendered state-of-being**, just keep saying, "I am sorry, I love you, please forgive me, thank you."

When you feel PEACE INSIDE, you are vibrationally aligned to move into a new BEING CHOICE.

Recognize that there is no outside imposition upon your will to be, do and have anything you choose. The unexamined clutter we harbor inside is what holds us back, until we clear it.

These suppressed thoughts (emotionally charged) are the barrier between who you are now and who you would prefer to be. The E-motion, the energy in motion, is spinning inside of your chakras.

When someone self-sabotages, this is the reason why.

Stuck emotions have to be cleansed for your vibration to ascend to the level of being you desire. These suppressed/collected emotionally-charged thoughts are the anchors that must be cut loose.

These are judgments we have created, based on limited information and distorted perceptions. We cannot escape our karmic debts; we must PAY THEM ATTENTION and dis-charge them, emotionally.

We zero out the debt and reclaim a clean slate. Before we move forward, and while we move ahead, we keep "clearing" every time resistance robs us of our PEACE.

Keep cleansing these thoughts and surrendering to the emotionally charged thoughts, *as if you are floating in a pool of water.* **Relax and allow** "WHAT IS" to exist, without adding further judgment towards yourself or others. Keep clearing.

Step three, is the ABC Break Process. This process is the way for you to dial in the preferred BEING CHOICE IDENTITY in your consciousness.

To make it more exciting, find an archetype and tap the morphogenic field—the best way to do this is to MODEL (act the role of) a good movie or television character. Find a character who represents the dominant attribute (ATTITUDE TOWARDS LIFE) you are looking to ACT OUT in your new BEING CHOICE.

In other words, what attribute would you need to put the puzzle piece together with your chosen goal?

Let's say you intend to manifest $1 million. If you currently aren't in possession of this caliber of cash flow, why not?

Or, how about a stellar physical sense of wellbeing?

How about perfectly satisfying relationships?

Only choose one goal at a time. Otherwise, you focus will be diluted and weakened.

Let's get the limiting beliefs out on the table and examine the junk holding you back.

Pause and think for a minute. This self-analysis is one of those rare times when I am asking you to think about your situation (versus *never mind* and act on excitement).

First of all, you'll engage the 6 degrees of separation and draw out the limitations; thoughts that are holding you back can now be examined and stabbed with a pen, pencil, or keyboard stroke. Write them down.

Next, with all these limitations that come to mind, what MOVIE character embodies a strong enough personality or bright enough wit to overcome these hurdles?

Do you see where I'm going? In other words, WHO IS ALREADY THE SOLUTION to the *character flaws* imposed by B.S. thoughts you've been thinking for a long time (forming beliefs)?

As you SHIFT INTO BEING THIS NEW CHARACTER, it may feel like "make believe" and you're correct: we are going to MAKE YOU BELIEVE something new.

You believe what you act out. As you create new impressions unto the unconscious mind ACTING ANEW, as if you are the character in the movie (of your choice), you gain two immediate benefits:

1. You already have a working model (movie character) to clone into your new self-identity or BEING CHOICE. Someone has already acted the role of the character and energized the morphogenic field to millions of eyeballs; you can HIJACK this character via the use of a daily **ritual** where you act the role, also.

2. Each new action you take from the level of BEING the chosen role—the daily ritual—strengthens the "branding" you are doing to yourself. *Self-entrainment* occurs because repetition is re-petitioning the mind; you establish new behaviors which eventually become automatically *wired* into YOUR personality. You then develop new habits.

Let me tell you a brief story about how the Self-Entrainment technique works...I'll share my back pain story with you now.

One day, while driving to my office I was suddenly faced with the worst back pain I've felt in my life. It seemingly came out of nowhere, like my back just slipped out of place.

As I got to my office, I stepped on the rebounder and used *Applied Lymphology* (discussed in the BONUS chapter, later on) to get oxygen back into the cells, which worked, temporarily. Next, I went across the street to the gym to do my workout and ended up lying on the floor in excruciating pain.

I found myself in a horrible place of injury and debilitating pain. It was no joking matter!

I scheduled an emergency chiropractic visit and had Sabrina drive me and help me walk into the clinic. As a side note, I've broken things in my body (nose, collarbone, teeth knocked out) playing hockey for over 20 years... this sudden pain in my back felt worse than all of the other injuries.

I was at the mercy of this pain; the chiropractor said I had tremendous swelling and he wouldn't finish adjusting me, due to his perception of the severity.

The chiropractor advised me to ice the area and return to his office the next day to continue treatment.

ENTER: THE SELF-ENTRAINMENT TECHNIQUE™

As thoughts of immobility, spinal subluxation, weakness, disability and other emotionally charged FEARS came into my awareness, I noted them. I wrote them down. I was not going to allow them to fester around in the background.

I began **clearing** these thoughts with Ho'oponopono and surrendering to my emotions *underneath* the fear, doing everything in my power to heal. When I returned home, I did the ABC Break Process (using a parallelogram movement process I'll show you in a video link below).

I knew that my consciousness had to shift FIRST, so the RIGHT solution could appear. The problem was; pain gripped my focus, and it was tough to ignore the sensations in the body-mind. *The pain was threatening to lock me into being a disabled person vs. shifting into a state of wellbeing.*

After one round of doing the ABC Break Process (with the parallelogram movement process), I sat down, and began my search for a way out of suffering. I knew that my consciousness shifted enough to ALLOW a perfect solution to the perceived problem (from the former "disabled" state of being).

My first search online led me to Dr. John Sarno's work. I had no prior knowledge of this man or how game-changing his discoveries are, but this was my solution. It was also the hidden BLESSING in a seemingly horrible circumstance.

After I shifted my consciousness to BEING A WELL VERSION OF MYSELF, my vibration was matching frequency for the right answer to appear. That's how I found Dr. Sarno's work, by aligning with a frequency where it could appear.

In other words, I had to escape "problem consciousness" and enter a state of BEING THE SOLUTION.

Dr. John Sarno's ideas were the hidden blessing in what I perceived to be a tragedy—the sudden back pain and apparent injury.

Within three hours of discovering his work, I had already perused his book *Healing Back Pain* and completed a five-mile run and a chest workout. Once the main idea he offered in the book set in, I was free from fear. As Mary Baker Eddy says, "fear is the fountain of disease."

Dr. Sarno's main idea was that the back pain was not physical. It was psychological. And, to further restrict movement (or treat the condition) could make symptoms linger or get worse. Instantly, upon reading this idea in the book—I took my power back and resumed my activities. When the pain emerged, I validated his idea: movement would not make it worse. Dr. Sarno called this *movement phobia.*

#DrJohnSarnoIsAGenius

The power of the mind is incredible. Like P.P. Quimby said, "man lives in his ideas." The idea of back pain, injury, and the **fear** of making it worse had bound and tied me in a mental prison. Dr. Sarno gave me a new idea, backed by ample data to cause me to BELIEVE... and, **once we believe something—it happens. Also, if we fear something, it happens.**

As Mary Baker Eddy seemingly discovered from P.P. Quimby, "fear, once cast out of a person—while simultaneously destroying the belief in illness—results in a healing." Dr. John Sarno replicated this MIRACLE for anyone suffering from various forms of chronic pain, called "tension myositis syndrome," or (T.M.S.)

I mention this pain story for another reason: fear and (unwanted) beliefs are also ruining relationships and finances, not just creating health challenges. We can "clear" all this mess out, once and for all. It's best to do it AS YOU MOVE FORWARD WITH **ACTION**, as this brings up more layers!

This realization is why the Self-Entrainment Technique is all about MAKE BELIEVE. You will use a daily ritual of ACTION to reinforce new behavior and habits; this causes you to believe by way of taking action steps...not useless thinking.

Remember that karma is:

action – cellular memory – reaction.

Your new ACTIONS will generate new thoughts and new perceptions. These new perceptions will build new beliefs, by default. You self-entrain yourself OUT OF YOUR BOX vs. think your way into the same corner, or set of circumstances.

WHY ARE BELIEFS SO HARD TO CHANGE?

Many people feel that beliefs are hard to change, and they're correct. When you live cerebrally and try and "think" a new way, it's a booby-trap. You end up wasting your life away ACTING as an intellectual instead of BEING an integrated being.

I talked about this in *ALLOW - Mastering The Law of Least Effort to Receive Your Desires!* You want to become childlike again, not adult-erated. "Adults" are the manufactured product of the cult-education system that entrains you to live cerebrally and disconnected through the 6-degrees of separation.

You're not a mind; you have a mind. You are better equipped to choose who to BE, and then ACT ACCORDINGLY... releasing the details (formerly obsessed about by engaging your mind).

Leave the who, what, where, when, why, and how out of the equation. Live in the mystery and follow your highest excitement, in every moment—**regardless of the fallout.**

I'm not telling you about my back healing story to brag about healing myself, instead to share two critical elements of this *near-instant* manifestation:

1. First, I made **a shift in consciousness** (using physiology to support it; the parallelogram movement process). I knew the solution would ONLY appear at the level of being someone who was already well. How did I accomplish this? I retrieved a memory of myself when I felt my strongest ever—mentally revisiting a day in the gym where I crushed it. Next, I had to assume the physiology of this person.

Then, I ACTED AS THIS PERSON IN MY IMMEDIATE MOMENT—dialing in the frequency of thought I would require to reveal my answer (out of pain). Meanwhile, I used Ho'oponopono on all the contradicting suggestions of pain or weakness.

Regarding temptation to pull back (pain signals): I used the **power of denial** as every sharp pain radiated across my back, tempting me to adopt the identity of an injured person. Once I assumed the posture and physiology of the HEALTHY and STRONG (pain-free) version of myself—using the parallelogram movement process—I sought an answer from this new level of being. The answer must appear!

2. When the answer appeared (Dr. Sarno's work), it required my FAITH. *Your REAL answer will always require your faith.* In the presence of this terrible pain; Dr. Sarno's advice (in the book) was to go and do whatever I wanted to—and move about freely. He alleged that movement had nothing to do with the pain itself.

The back pain was *psychosomatic* and my brain's way of diverting attention away from a deeper problem: distress in my life circumstances. For his method to work, a person had to accept his idea and believe it. I did both via ACTION.

I caused myself to BELIEVE by "making believe" or ACTING as the healthy and pain-free version of myself. Within hours, as I was exercising and doing my life, the pain lessened.

The next day it was just a faint memory. Two days later, it was gone. Keep in mind; if I merely sat around uselessly thinking about the pain going away, it would have done nothing. I had to BEHAVE, or "be-have." You BE to HAVE.

Get it? The truth is hidden in plain sight.

You can do this with any desired outcome you want to achieve. The process works the same.

The idea is to BE or ACT AS the person who already is in possession of what you desire. You can either use a recalled memory of your life (this is the proper use of your mind, to remember the good times or make a preference).

Or, you can HIJACK the consciousness of a movie character by ACTING THE ROLE out yourself.

Here's an example:

I set a new goal to manifest an extra $1 million in 30 days. My highest monthly income was slightly over $300k, so my memory would not serve me to accomplish a goal I had never achieved.

I have to RAISE THE LEVEL OF MY BEING CHOICE and **outsource the consciousness**. Simple; choose a movie character and ACT THE ROLE

MYSELF. The daily ritual will build new habits and beliefs, causing a new set of circumstances.

Searching for this new character was fun!

At first, I went and purchased the movie *Kingsman*, and in the quotes, it says, "More bad ass than James Bond." I've seen the movie, and it would be congruent for a Kingsman to attain a $1 million in a sudden burst of inspired action.

I thought, "heck yeah, a Kingsman could easily have an idea that generates $1 million in 30 days."

Keep in mind; I don't want to win the lottery. It doesn't excite me. I prefer to attract an IDEA from the level of BEING—ACTING AS SOMEONE—who already has the idea. I can hijack consciousness. The best magnet for riches is an idea.

After considering Eggsy's character in *Kingsman*, here's why I decided against this role:

When I used the technology of **reverse speech** on the main character's name "Eggsy"—it played back sounding like, "he's gay." I have no idea if that is coincidence or simply the way I'm speaking the name, but it's not my ideal choice. Now, I'm not against being gay, and I have many friends who identify as being gay.

For me, I wanted to select a different archetype after using reverse speech, just in case. All the data in that character's creation, including the name, is contained in the morphogenic field. If I download that identity and

ACT THE ROLE, I also download all the details included in the creation of this character.

#ReverseSpeech #HiddenMeaning

By choosing a suitable character—or archetype—to match my goal, I can imitate the behavior and build new beliefs. I call it "hijacking consciousness" because millions of people have co-created (by watching the movie) this character's reality.

I can step inside this *reality construct* and virtually replicate the ATTRIBUTES I NEED into my REAL LIFE **story**.

Whatever you desire that you lack at this current moment, is because you require different ATTRIBUTES or ATTITUDES TOWARD LIFE. These are already pre-programmed in a TV or movie character. You can ACT THE ROLE and adopt these into developing new behaviors, habits, and **results**!

"If your life sucks, it's because you suck."

- *Larry Winget*

What we repeatedly hear, we believe. And, what we see, we become. Adolf Hitler used this idea to brainwash his cult-followers. If you tell a lie long enough, you'll eventually believe it. We don't believe truth, we believe what we repeatedly hear.

You don't have to tell lies, but here's what happens when you ACT AS IF SOMETHING WERE TRUE, even though it may not be (at this moment)...

If you ACT AS IF IT IS TRUE, telling yourself you are this new person—you are telling yourself a lie. The irony is, you will end up *laying* where you "lied." It becomes true. It becomes true **only** if you are ACTING CONGRUENTLY, not merely living inside your head.

We become what we see; this is especially true in regards to who we see ourselves as being. This truth is why we have sayings in our culture like, "you become who you hang around."

Keep mental company with an IDENTITY of yourself that serves you to attain your desired outcome. Pay no attention to the mind's attempt to convince you it's all just "make believe nonsense." It IS make-believe; making you believe in the NON-sensory reality outside of your mind's comprehension.

Remember the Vedic saying:

"Infinite worlds appear and reappear in the vast expanse of my consciousness, like motes of dust dancing in a beam of light."

Your senses are perceiving only what your mind is filtering from the level of your current BEING CHOICE. When I was laying on the floor with back pain, I was tormented by fear thoughts. "What could happen to me…" my mind perceived a world of horrible outcomes, and NO HELPFUL ANSWER could emerge from this level of being.

I had to *make believe* that I was another version of myself, recalling a time when I felt strong and pain-free, ACTING as this person (including the physiology and behavior).

As you ***make believe***—the mind is made to believe and thereby SEE a new reality. **We see what we believe**. The power of make-believe is the key to unlock the magic. Again, repetition creates the RITUAL to multiply the power of your focused intent. You have to persist at this, daily. At least for a short while.

Once your focus is dialed in, your new reactions to circumstances become habits. Then, it's a done deal. You attract whatever is required—by the law of BEING—which is **everything** when it comes to the law of attraction.

We don't get to choose our destiny; we create our habits. Our daily habits become our destiny. How we ACT is not as important as WHO we are ACTING AS when we take an action. This truth is why two people can perform the same actions and get entirely different results.

You can only excel as far as your self-concept or identity allows. If you see yourself as an amateur, don't expect professional results.

Now, for my current target goal (I will share with you), instead of "Eggsy," I will choose the character Val Kilmer plays in the movie, *The Saint*. It's one of my favorite movies. Another option would be Bradley Cooper's role in *Limitless*, but that's not as exciting to me... so, I choose the highest excitement option.

Let's dial in the goal for you; I'll give you mine as an example:

My Goal: $1 million (30 days)

Qualified Character: The Saint

Your Goal:

Qualified Character:

You match your BEING CHOICE with the goal you have in mind. The morphogenetic field already contains all of the information within the character you've chosen. You hijack consciousness. You want to dial-in "the missing attribute" or ATTITUDE TOWARDS LIFE you need to achieve your outcome.

You attract ideas, people, circumstances, all things come to you by law—based on WHO you're being and ACTING as, in every moment. Once you have the NEW ROLE DOWN, you've nailed it!

CHOOSING WHO YOU WILL BE IS NOT A ONE-TIME EVENT

Warning: it is a **moment-by-moment** phenomenon. You cannot just mimic a new behavior one time and say, "it didn't work." It won't work that way. The OBJECTIVE is to ACT AS IF YOU ARE THIS PERSON long enough to INSTALL new habits. Repetition creates habits. Once you have a new habitual way of BEING, you have done the work correctly.

Let's talk about a worthy goal that excites you:

Why did I pick $1 million in 30 days?

The goal is realistic enough where I can believe it could happen. It's also challenging enough where I must acknowledge my ***non-physical*** (God within me, projecting my hologram outside of me, and orchestrating all the details—for me). My job is to ACT THE ROLE and ACCEPT MY DESIRES, while simultaneously "clearing" the resistance of old karmic debts

Your goal should excite you and scare you a bit, too. In other words, you'll know that you didn't make it happen without divine assistance. It can serve as a re-minder that you're so much more than a "drop in the ocean."

You have GOD-LIKE POWER, and the more you surrender to ALLOW things to fall in place, based on WHO you choose to BE, the better life becomes!

You move forward, "clearing" away the junk—like sweeping trash off the floor—while you master the art of receiving!

Now, let's line up your character:

Who would you have to be to manifest this goal?

You see, life is similar to a movie because it is a series of still life projections that we perceive to be happening in a timeline progression. This illusion of time is hypnosis.

We hypnotize ourselves when we look to the outside world to validate who we are; we need to do the opposite. Choose who you are going to BE, then ACT THIS WAY regardless of what the outside "world" throws at you. Things will persist for a short while, based on who you WERE BEING PREVIOUSLY. Don't re-ACT as the same ol' you with the same responses. Change your ACT and you change your circumstances.

Awaken!

You're literally flickering in, and out of existence like the Vedic saying implies:

"Infinite worlds appear and reappear in the vast expanse of my consciousness, like motes of dust dancing in a beam of light."

PRO TIP: YOU MUST LOOK FOR THE DIFFERENCES!

As you're ACTING OUT YOUR NEW ROLE, while "clearing" the old baggage out, you must PAY ATTENTION to the NEW CHANGES taking place in your circumstances.

As you notice even the slightest shifts in your current set of circumstances, the more you CELEBRATE THE IMPROVEMENTS—things speed up faster and accelerate.

You have the power to push the gas pedal down or apply the brakes (if things accelerate too rapidly).

I'll show you how:

Gas pedal: when you notice things shifting towards more desirable circumstantial "evidence" that things are going your way—document these changes and make a gratitude journal. If you celebrate these victories before bedtime by reviewing this journal, things will speed up rapidly.

Why would you want to apply the brakes?

Answer: when we get carried away in a vortex of negativity and/or we perceive things aren't going our way. Anytime RESISTANCE and

STRUGGLE (uphill friction) come into the creative process—"white knuckle fight"—it is moving in the wrong direction. Slow it down.

Brake: when you notice things are shifting towards undesirable "perceptions" of how you "think" things are spiraling downward in your circumstances—relax into a surrendered state of being and "clear" with Ho'oponopono until you feel 100% at ease, in peace.

We choose who we're going to be. And then, our hologram construct shifts to match what belongs in the consciousness of that being choice or character.

As Bashar tells us, "Circumstances don't matter, only your state of being matters."

After you dial in the new character, every decision that you make going forward, even if it's as subtle as getting a coffee at the local cafe, ACT AS IF YOU ARE THIS PERSON.

Here's where things get WEIRD and the reasoning behind the gas and brake pedal: when you dial-in a goal, you also dial-in the LESSONS you require to attain this goal.

While there are no real "hard lessons" in life, our RESISTANCE can make things seem this way. For instance, what if I judged my back pain episode as a NEGATIVE circumstance and allowed myself to accelerate DOWNWARD into a spiraling vortex of fear and inner-resistance?

I'll tell you what would have happened, based on years of experience going through so-called "incurable" illnesses: I would have gotten STUCK in pain by not allowing the solution that contained the blessing.

Use your gas and brake pedal accordingly.

#ProCard

The benefit of choosing a movie character is that you can study the gestures, movements, words, behavior, and EVERYTHING about this new role. It's like looking at yourself with a detached awareness and saying, "oh yeah, I can totally act this out again and again until it becomes a habit."

The OBJECTIVE is to dial in the FREQUENCY of this character, as this will ATTRACT the idea, people, circumstances, LESSONS, or events you require to realize your chosen goal. That's the only reason we're doing this. It's not to dissociate from reality altogether, just the reality construct that no longer serves you. You can have a new experience by BE-HAVING only. As I keep saying, "it's not a thinking person's game."

Vain repetitions make no difference in how reality responds. The saying goes, "God doesn't care if you need a miracle, He only responds to your faith." Faith without WORKS is dead. You must ACT ANEW, regardless of what your mind has to say about the potential fallout.

In a moment, I will show you the process of how to use the parallelogram movement to change your physiology. Over 90-percent of communication, including how we communicate with ourselves, is non-verbal. This fact is why I study the POSTURE and MOVEMENT of the character I'm imitating—revisiting the movie until I perfect the new act.

MOVING BEYOND THE ABC BREAK PROCESS

I'll show you how to lock in the physiology of your chosen character! This is the NEW DISCOVERY that propels the ABC Break Process into high-gear. In addition, the "clearing" with Ho'oponopono removes the self-sabotage.

The **Self-Entrainment Technique™** is the ABC Break Process on MOCAINE. It's amped up and much more effective!

The FASTEST PATH TO YOUR JOY or HIGHEST EXCITEMENT is the only other engagement you have with your "rational" mind; as in, choosing what the most exciting thing you can do next is. Period. Choose who you will ACT AS and ask and answer the question, "What is the fastest path to my joy, in this moment?" Rinse and repeat, until you develop a new habit.

Otherwise, leave your mind out of it...

You have to face the facts: if your mind knows how to give you the answers to manifest your goal, why don't you already have it? And, why is your mind beating you up for not having it already?

You will properly use your mind by making a preference, asking "WHAT THE FASTEST PATH TO YOUR JOY?" You will align with your true desires, without an uphill struggle, as long as you remember how to "clear" to brake and how to accelerate (gratitude) to apply the gas.

WHY DO PEOPLE GET "STUCK" WHERE THEY ARE?

The reason people struggle and go uphill is that they try and **do things without changing who they are BEING** first. And, they continue to **engage in low-vibration activities that they deem "necessary evils"** to get what they desire. The problem is; **you can't get there from here**—it's a dead end street.

Also, a word of caution (from personal experience):

<u>Do not skip step one</u>. Listing all of your self-limiting beliefs and clearing them with Ho'oponopono, daily. It's also essential to RELEASE the emotional charge of old limiting beliefs by fully accepting "WHAT IS" and doing so until you feel peace inside.

One final "SCORE card" for you to keep

The last piece I'm going to offer you is all about noticing how you're doing by keeping a daily "score card." I want you to make a daily report where you place (+) and (-) by all the ACTIVITIES you took ACTION on each day.

Most people are very good at doing the daily struggle as opposed to the daily ALLOWING activities. Let me explain:

When you do an activity that does not bring you joy, it represents a (-) mark on your daily "score card." These are the things we typically MUST do, yet we don't want to do them.

In contrast, when you ask and answer the question, "what is the fastest path to my joy in this moment, regardless of the fallout?" You take an action that gives you a (+) mark on your daily "score card."

By making this visible, in the same way you examine your limiting beliefs, you become AWARE of your DAILY HABITS, instead of living in denial. Most people live in denial.

Virtually everyone who comes to me for coaching always tells me that they follow their excitement, yet their "score card" looks something like this:

8 a.m. Get ready for work, eat, get kids ready (-)

9 a.m. – 5 p.m. Worked all day (-)

6 p.m. Did some housework (-)

8 p.m. Went for an evening walk or workout (+)

10 p.m. Watched some entertainment (+)

When I challenge them to SEE how the vast majority of their day is filled with LIFE-DRAINING ACTIVITY that sucks the joy out of them, they tell me, "Matthew, I have to do these things."

The irony is; the person believes that by doing these things they are getting ahead (someday in the future). It doesn't work that way. In the next chapter, you'll discover how I altered my reality by doing something counterintuitive: enjoying life now!

I played guitar in the backroom when my nutrition store was going bankrupt, instead of doing all the (-) activities I was supposed to be doing. Why?

You cannot reveal THE DIVINE SOLUTION to any perceived problem while you remain stuck in the (-) vibrations in life. You must either change your perception to make these (+) or do something entirely different.

You design your PERFECT DAY, filled with more (+) than (-). You then REPEAT THE PERFECT DAY to acquire your PERFECT LIFE.

As you keep your "score card," you'll objectively see how well you're doing. You can only change what you are willing to confront and admit, to yourself.

Here's an example of my "score card" today:

9 a.m. – 3 p.m. Write content for this book (+)

4 p.m. Two hour cardio session (+)

7 p.m. Play with my kids (+)

9:30 p.m. Workout (+)

11 p.m. Read a new book, watch YouTube (+)

Look, it's unusual for me to have all positive experiences, but it's usually dominant on the (+) side. I designed it this way! You CAN, too.

It's time to WATCH AND LEARN the Self-Entrainment Technique™ (the link is below).

☆ ☆ ☆

This PRIVATE-ACCESS training link below is where I will walk you through each step of the technique:

http://www.SelfEntrainment.com

☆ ☆ ☆

Learn how to *master your hologram* by tapping into other versions of you, in parallel universes!

We'll discuss Ho'oponopono more in a later chapter. It's vital that you master the art of "clearing" and letting go of karmic debts that hold you back.

Chapter 9.

Case Study: Vic's TRIUMPH Over His Mind

What would you do if someone came to you for coaching and he had read more self-help books than you, knew it all, and heard it all before?

And, to top it all off, he was convinced no one could help him escape his current sabotage pattern. Vic didn't call it a sabotage pattern, but it was obvious: he was the poster-child for a brilliant mind trapped in a *series-circuit framework.*

Vic is likable, respectful, and very talented. I have an intense admiration for him; he loves his wife and celebrates every night they spend together. Not to mention, at one time he earned a substantial income and did quite well financially.

The problem is; the success stopped and his life filled with resistance. Like I said, if you read chapter 7, you know what happens when someone gets trapped in the false-reality matrix. Resistance builds and the person re-acts unconsciously.

Vic's mind is very witty. It computes very fast and, he has stored an ample supply of worldly knowledge. I suppose it helps that I am clairsentient and I knew exactly where he was blocked. It takes me less than 10 minutes to interpret someone's "non-verbal" communication and hear what they are telling me. I feel a person's soul and my *knowing* takes over.

For this reason, I've always offered a FREE 10-minute breakthrough coaching session for first-time clients, at my website: http://www.MatthewDavidHurtado.com

These days I'm booked full with more clients than I can handle and barely take new bookings. Vic found me in the early days of my coaching session offerings; he was very persistent, and during our 10-minute breakthrough, something clicked inside of him. Vic wanted me to take his case and get him unstuck. He wasn't going to take no for an answer, so he had me at ASK UNTIL IT IS GIVEN!

Working with Vic was like sparring in the ring with a flyweight boxer. His mind won't knock you out, but it will throw hundreds of reasonable sounding LIES to keep you from getting through to him.

How did I know they were lies, you ask? I take Quimby's stance; any belief or opinion that does not bring happiness or joy is a lie. Vic had plenty, and I guess knowing the truth is what set me free from being persuaded into dead-end corners. Where Vic's other coaches had failed came through to me when I felt his energy. They let him win (placate excuses) or just ducked out of the ring.

Fortunately, me being clairsentient means Vic cannot convince or jab me with logical rhetoric.

The mind is so full of crap that it behooves me to ignore it, mostly. When the mind is on a linear track and wired in series, it will collapse under its friction or resistance.

All I had to do was let it throw all its blows and remain imperturbable by knowing Vic was about to learn ***Self-Entrainment.*** I knew Vic would win his battle because his soul communicated to me, "I'm willing and ready."

#Clairsentient

The following transcription is a coaching session Vic allowed me to share. It's also on YouTube and you can either read it below or watch it online:

VIC WAS WILLING AND READY TO WIN AGAIN

Here's what he learned that you could benefit from:

Vic and I had been working together closely for a few weeks, and he finally seemed to be accepting what I was trying to tell him.

When Vic began his sales journey, he was underperforming and worried he wouldn't ever reach his goals. He was stuck and running out of funds.

When we started the session you're about to ease-drop on; he was very excited by his results. I asked him to teach me what he learned to ensure that he had indeed captured the lesson.

How Vic's Mind Used to Always Get in The Way

Vic had scheduled a telephone meeting with two co-workers, named David and Susan. David wanted to meet at 12. Vic wanted to meet at 1. Susan didn't care if it was 12 or 1.

Vic was stressing over these times because he had other things he had to do. And finally, he asked himself, "Wait a minute! What do *I* want?" He didn't try to reason it out, he just sat back and listened and waited for the answer to come to him.

The answer was 11:45 because he wanted to have from 12:15 to 12:30 to reflect on the call. He had set 12:30 aside for meditation time.

Finally, Vic quit worrying about what David and Susan wanted and sent a text message saying that they could have their call at 11:45. Immediately, both David and Susan texted back to acknowledge that 11:45 was acceptable.

Vic was ecstatic. He used his mind for what it was there for—**to decide his preference**, and that only—and then projected his choice out into the universe. And—no surprise—he got what he wanted.

Vic further went on to explain that before, he would have spent his mental energy thinking about what David and Susan wanted, and trying to reason out what was best.

Vic learned that when you are trying to manifest something—even something as small as the time of a meeting—that you have to ignore the negative thoughts and fears of failure that your mind gives to you.

Even if it seems illogical and impossible and improbable, those are not relevant thoughts. When you ignore the negative thoughts, you don't have those negative thoughts interfering with the vibrations you need to tap into success.

There are no contrary vibrations if you refuse to tune in your receiver to them. I was proud of Vic for seeing for himself how he could shift his consciousness, allowing a new set of circumstances. I explained to him that he was describing the very same situation that I found myself in.

I have a friend who owns one of the highest-traffic internet sites out there for a specific target audience. I want to buy this site. The asking price is enormous. I didn't have access to the funds to buy this site. So what am I going to do?

I'll tell you what I'm going to do. I am not going to care about where the money is going to come from. I just don't care. Every time I think about buying that site, I just think about how good it will feel when I own it. When the thoughts come about how I will get the money to buy it, or where the money is going to come from, I just think "Yeah, ok, that's not a problem."

(Update): Guess what happened? In less than six months, I was able to align with my "other self" who already had the funds for this site—I manifested the income.

Don't fight the negative thoughts. When you fight them, you cause them to strengthen themselves to the opposition. Don't be the opposition that gives them strength. Instead, surrender. Succumb to them. Just let them be.

Don't try to change them because when you do, you get caught up in what your mind is trying to do—sabotage your goals. Your thinking will get you caught up in a tsunami of doubts and fears. Don't quiet them, just let them be. Let them spend their energy and burn out. Just say to them, "Ok, I get it. I understand what you are saying. You make a strong point. But I want it anyway, and I'm going to move towards receiving it."

You might ask yourself (or me), "Then what should I do to buy this site? What are the action steps I should take to make this happen?"

The answer might surprise you.

I should do nothing at all. Nothing. Not until I know what to do. And I will. The answer will come to me when it is supposed to. I have placed myself in a state of ALLOWing, and I ALLOW the solution to flow towards me. It will come when it comes, and that time will be the right time. It will be the correct answer. Again, I ended up manifesting the funds. Once it happened, more significant ideas emerged.

My attitude rests on this truth: infinite patience brings immediate results.

Vic still had more to learn, though. He told me that he was always making lists of stuff he wanted to talk to me about during our calls. He found that 80% of the things on his mind didn't matter. Only 20% was relevant.

Vic asked me what he thought his income goal should be. When he thinks about this question, he notices that specific, lower numbers just don't excite him. Higher numbers feel unattainable and mysterious.

Vic wanted to know—after he figured out the number he should go after, how to go about having some form of assistance in becoming the person he wanted to be and to sustain that reality.

Vic described how his attitude changed over the course of the day. "When I wake up," he said, "It's easy for me to act out the person I'm trying to be. I've woken up and, I have a fresh mind. There's a new start. I feel good, and I feel rested.

As the day goes on, however, and the day to day circumstances come into my life, I feel like they throw me off course. I think about how I need to be working my tail off. I need to work harder, smarter, differently. I start comparing myself to other people.

I see a co-worker who made a sale, and I think "he always studies until 2:00 a.m." Maybe I should start studying until two in the morning."

Vic's descriptions of his feelings felt very familiar to me. I told him so. When I was at absolute zero, I left income out of the equation. I stepped into the idea of who I wanted to be in the world, and so I said, "Ok. I want to own this nutrition store that I am working at."

Then I started to think, "Wow. If I do well with that store, then I can own three or five of them." I figured that would probably net me a quarter of a million dollars a year. I became comfortable with that idea because I had already stepped into a self-image that was large enough to accommodate that kind of income.

I accepted the self-image first, and then the income level came naturally to me and was easy to receive. It was almost instant—I had a six-figure income to go with the self-image I created for myself.

(This is the ego upgrade I'm talking about...)

I was able to do that quarter million, and it was so easy because I had already accepted the image of myself as the kind of person who earned a quarter million dollars a year.

"In your circumstance," I told Vic, "If your self-image was of the guy who studied until two every morning, what sort of income would you make?

"A couple of hundred grand?" Vic said, sounding unsure of himself.

I answered his question with another question. "If you see yourself being him and being at his level, then expand your self-image to be at his level. Then you can accept the level of 200 grand a year without thinking twice about it. That should be the goal that you set as your preference."

"But," Vic said. "I don't want to be him. He works too hard. I don't want that constant drudgery, work-hard lifestyle."

The solution then became simple. "Then you should never compare yourself to someone you don't want to be," I said. "Because as soon as you make that judgment and comparison between you and that person, you've activated a vibration that will tune you into him."

Now that we know what Vic did not want to be, we had to figure out what he did want to be.

"I want to be someone who makes big money," he said. "I have always wanted to be the guy who does two things. One, make massive passive income. I want to be financially independent, so I never have to work for my money.

Two, I don't want to be entirely passive. I love the adrenaline rush of making big money when I close big deals. I want massive passive income for the money coming in, and I want the adrenaline rush that comes with closing big deals like where I make ten or twenty thousand at a shot. I like that ego rush."

I told Vic the same thing I will say to you—remember what that person looks like in your world. That is your potential self. That is your actuality in reality if you make it so.

This parallel universe choice is what the ABC Break process is for, and if you'd like a FREE COPY of my book ALLOW - Mastering The Law of Least Effort to Receive Your Desires! Go here: http://www.ALLOW.ws.

You are already your full potential self. That's the true you. So if that's the true you, then you can be that person ***right now***.

When I told Vic this, his response was, "That's what I'm trying to do."

"That's where your mistake is," I said. "You are trying. Don't try to be what you already are. Just BE."

"That's what I'm BEING," Vic said with more confidence.

"Now that you are that person, what kind of income does that person command from the universe?"

Because Vic's mind was where it needed to be, he came up with the answer right away. "Between $350,000 and $450,000." Remember back to when Vic and I first started talking...he was asking ME what he should be making.

He wasn't tapping into his true self. But now that he was, he didn't need me to tell him. He could download the answer. Look at P.T. Barnum. He proved that our position in life is only limited by our imagination.

So what should Vic do next to make this a reality? I told him that since we knew that somewhere between $350,000 and $450,000 was his ideal income, he needed to be comfortable with that in his level of being.

That was now the appropriate set point that he should expect to show up from being that version of himself.

Now the question becomes, "So I am that person. Now what?" That's the whole point. You can't sit down and outline the answer and think it out. Instead, you have to ALLOW the circumstances to show you the next step, then the action after that, then the task after that.

Don't pay any attention to what your mind is trying to say unless you are asking it what you PREFER. **Your mind is properly used to discriminate**

between preferences, as it pertains to conscious creation. Any other use is self-sabotage. If it knew the answers, you'd already have the desired outcome.

It's all about WHO YOU ARE BEING...

Stay at that level of being. **From that level of consciousness, follow your excitement moment by moment**. Your excitement is your compass, not your mind. You follow the next exciting path, wherever it may lead you, no matter what.

Then, by universal law, the people, circumstances, events, and whatever you need will show you one by one. At that point, your job is just to relax and ALLOW yourself to receive what the universe is giving you—*by law*—because you have chosen that level of being as your set point reality.

If this doesn't make sense to your rational mind, don't worry about it. Remember: your rational thought is just rationalizing lies.

You are going to have to live in the mystery of it. You're not going to be able to use your mind to understand what your level of consciousness cannot understand. Your BEING CHOICE is coming from the level of who you were when it starts to fear and doubt. Fear and doubt are your clues to "clear" and "clear" some more...

This SHIFT in CONSCIOUSNESS is what ASK <u>UNTIL</u> IT IS GIVEN! is all about.

#ParallelUniverses

Whenever you have fear and doubt, it means that the mind that is stuck where you used to be is being offended. It doesn't like when you step outside of your ego's box.

Going back to the example of my nutrition store, I knew it was going under in debt. I knew it was failing. I looked at the advertising bill and I thought, "I'm going to be done in two weeks if I don't come up with a solution because I am out of money."

Then I remembered my vision. I saw myself as someone who was capable of a quarter million dollars. I was excited about that. My excitement told me that I was still in the right place. My excitement had not left the building. I knew, then, that I was still in the right building because I was where my current joy was.

Of course, I still had a problem. But to think about the issue is a mistake. Repeat that:

To think about the problem is a mistake.

When you think about the problem, you have activated the same mind that created the problem in the first place.

It won't give you any solution that makes sense. You have to become the solution that makes sense. I was still in that identity. I knew *I was a quarter-of-a-million-dollar earner.* I am this person. I am powerful.

I ignored my mind's impulse to engage with all of my demands. My accountant told me to close the store down and file bankruptcy.

The previous franchise owner told me to pick up the tab, borrow some money, and engage in a new advertising campaign.

I had lots of people telling me what to do. But none of their suggestions were convincing to me. I knew they weren't my path. I wasn't excited about any of those propositions. In other words, they were upstream and dangerous to my desired outcome. The outcome is joy, in every circumstance.

How you go into something is how you come out of it.

If I were to go into closing the store down or following some blueprint offered by the previous owner (who was losing money) out of fear, it would have ended up a disaster.

#Wisdom

So I disregarded what my mind, and what all these other well-meaning minds were telling me. Regardless of the fallout, I chose my path and followed my excitement.

I stayed in my NEW self-image. I decided to play guitar in the back room. I decided to enjoy my life because that's who I would be and what I would be doing if I were already there.

If I knew that my level of consciousness was already there, then I knew I would be there, and I didn't have to worry about it. So I'd act as if I were already there.

It's kind of like the old saying, "Dress for the job you want, not the job you have." But more so. Be the person you want to be, not the person you are. You have to *entrain yourself*!

I then activated the **tithing** principle. I trusted the universe would always respond to the seed that I planted. From the level of consciousness of having the quarter million, I got a quarter million dollar idea that instantly took hold. I manifested, and I created.

I manifested the level of being. I saw it in my mind; then I took an action that was from my highest excitement because I knew that was true north on my compass.

You always have to take action. Staying committed to a parallel universe isn't a passive thing. But the step you take isn't just hard work for the sake of hard work. The action has to come from your excitement, not other people's opinions. In my case, the first action was to play guitar and get into the vibration of joy and excitement.

Your vibration must match your desired solution you wish to receive before you expect the answer to appear.

Don't listen to what other people have to say unless they have already been where you want to be and they are where you want to be. If they've been there, they will bring you to the level of excitement and understand its importance in your success. You'll know it is a match to your path and your journey along that path.

Everyone who was telling me what to do brought me discomfort. These people meant well, but they brought angst with them because they were coming from a place that had nothing to do with my destiny. Their lying eyes saw one vision of reality, but the untrained human eye doesn't understand the concept of parallel universes.

Every time we SHIFT OUR STATE OF BEING, we enter a parallel universe. Our vibrational "offering" is no different than a radio station signal going out. Keep in mind; your you-niverse is you and you. Your inner-kingdom sets up the vibration and expands outward as your hologram projection. *As within, so without.*

So I ignored them—their vibration misaligned with my joy. Their "cautious" warnings triggered fear inside of me, too. I wanted God to give me a perfect solution.

All God does is speak. Usually, in ideas!

I followed my excitement, and I got my idea. As soon as I got the idea, I immediately acted on it. I activated the male power of creation and married it to the female energy of the manifestation of the desired outcome. You must manifest, then you must create. In this way, I created my miracle.

I asked Vic if he understood all of that. I asked him where he was getting caught up.

Vic told me that he was nervous. He was afraid that he would not get the understanding and awareness he needed to follow all of those steps. Fearful of just going in a circle and stuck in the eddy of his current reality. "I'm 35," he said. "I want to change my surroundings."

I reassured him that the only way he'd go in a circle is if he activated and engaged his mind in the process. Your mind will naturally go in a circle right to its beginning.

This time it would be different because Vic would get to choose who Vic would be in the world. Vic would identify with his full-potential self. He *was* the person who would make between $350,000 and $450,000 a year.

That was his full potential self. His job and his *only* job was to show up in the world as that person, regardless of the fallout, and to follow his excitement moment by moment.

Really. That's it. Rinse and Repeat.

Vic was still nervous. "For example," he said, "I didn't sleep well last night. The only thing I feel like doing is *not* doing my work and just resting. My body feels shot. I have things I need to get done and an appointment later, but my body just wants to rest." He asked me, "What would you do on a day like today?"

I felt like I was repeating myself, but sometimes you have to repeat a message to make sure it sinks in. "Regardless of the fallout," I said, "You do what your excitement tells you to do.

Back when I had a store to run and bills to pay, I went in the back room and played the guitar because that is what the person who I would have been had I already achieved the success would do. That person at that level of consciousness would play the guitar at that moment."

I could have said, "Like you're saying about resting—that playing the guitar was utterly irresponsible. I might have three customers trying to get in the door at that very moment, and I had the door locked so I could do what I wanted to do. I might lose out on some money, right?

But keeping the doors open and standing at the register didn't bring me joy. That wasn't exciting for me. Doing that was coming from a place of who I was failing as."

I then asked him, "So what I say to you is this: Can you stay at the level of being, committed 100% to being, your full potential self? What is your highest level of excitement from that level of being? Right now. In this moment."

Vic took longer than he should have to answer. I knew the answer. I knew he knew the answer. But he was hesitant to step right into that level of being.

I prompted him. "I'm talking *excitement."*

"Excitement?" he said, repeating the word to stall for time. "I guess sitting in my recliner and discussing my Amazon business with my business partner over Skype."

"Then that's what you should do right now," I told him. "When you finish with that, ask yourself the same question. 'Now. From this point of view, what is my highest excitement?'

And then you do the next thing. You don't try to plan it ought. You don't say, 'This is what I'm going to do at 3:00 and at 5:00 and at 7:00.'

Unless, of course, that's your excitement. If your excitement is to follow a schedule all day, and that's what you genuinely want to do, then do it. If it isn't, then don't."

When things are not your excitement, they are merely your mind giving you instructions about activities to keep your mind entertained. Your ego thinks it is going to get you where you want to be by making these lists that are little more than B.S. all day long. This constant distraction is the ego con job, keeping you stuck.

But remember: your mind is a steering wheel that *isn't even hooked up to the car.* *(Thanks for that nugget of wisdom, Bashar!)*

Your ego thinks it knows the blueprint, but your mind hasn't even experienced what you desire yet. It isn't hooked up to the car. I can't repeat that enough. Your ego is entirely oblivious to the fact that it is living in a reality that doesn't exist.

Where is it going to get its information from if it doesn't have access to the right parallel universe? Do you want to get the correct information? It's available to you from your level of being. And ONLY from your level of being who you desire to be, now.

First, choose your level of being. The God-power in you flows through the capacitor into the capacity of who you have chosen to be. You see, I choose to be my full potential self. If you want to be the $350,000 to $450,000 guy, then be that guy. Say to yourself:

"That is who I am. That is who I am NOW. That is who I am RIGHT NOW. I choose it. By choosing it, all of God's power flows into my circumstances. If I

stay committed to it, locked in, and never mind my mind's activities that it wants to give me, I will succeed."

Avoid the 6 6 6 trap.

Remember, whenever your mind jumps in with the who, what, where, when, why, and how, that's the six-degrees of separation between you and your power. It's always going to try to jump into the equation with those separative ideas.

It is trying to convince you to go back into the delusion that it can get you where it wants you to go. But it isn't even hooked up or connected to the creating process. It is only going to bring you back to your old identity of who you didn't like being.

You'll know you're on the precipice of a breakthrough when you hit "*the terror barrier*" (as described by Bob Proctor).

As Mike Murdock says, "Warfare surrounds the birth of a miracle." When you look at the store situation I faced, here's what we know to have happened:

I was still in my place of joy. I loved it there.

Suddenly, there was tremendous chaos; warfare (in my mind).

I chose to BE the solution to the problem, acting from this level of being I pursued the highest excitement available to me at the time.

Divine inspiration met me in that vibrational space. MY POWER FLOWED into the parallel universe where I already possessed the desired outcome. It was a vibrational match, so the idea was already mine!

I took inspired action. Success.

So now, if you stay committed to the level of being this full potential self that you are, and you follow your internal compass regardless of the fallout, you will get where you want to go.

Your internal compass is your excitement at the moment. If you follow that inner compass, from that level of being only, you will get the right information, meet the right people, and just happen to have the right ideas come into your consciousness at the right moment.

Always recall: when excitement leaves, and it becomes a "chore" that seems necessary, be very careful.

WARNING: Your vibration may rescind—like shifting the radio dial to the old station—you may enter the parallel universe "you knew before" out of habit or the desire to be uncomfortably comfortable.

We don't know what we like; we like what we know.

Resist this temptation to let excitement slip away. You'll find yourself back in the "old" parallel reality, shrinking down your BEING CHOICE to accommodate LIES from your mind.

#TheMindConsYou

That is what manifesting is. When you get the right idea or the right person showing up, you'll know they are right because you'll feel the compass of excitement resonating within you. It will reflect back to you.

First, LEAP INTO A PARALLEL UNIVERSE (different vibrational space with the ABC Break Process)...then, take inspired action as the NEW INFLOW of information presents itself, compelling you to ACT out of new excitement.

Your CURRENT will flow into the PARALLEL UNIVERSE that you choose with the ABC BREAK PROCESS.

It will stir things up within you, and show you that this path is the right path for you. *Then and only then must you stake out an external action.* That completes the cycle of male and female, manifesting and creating.

#YourLawofAttractionPROCARD #Graduation

While you are doing this, do not engage your mind unless it is to decide upon a preference. The ego will try to jump into the action and say, "Hey! Hold on now. You're not good enough to do this."

Your mind will make many attempts to con you into submission to your old ego identity. Stay committed!

You must stay locked into this choice of being, this full potential you that you have chosen to be.

REWRITE YOUR PAST: **Your history is a lie. By reflecting on it, you lock in the parallel universe vibration you don't want. STOP TALKING ABOUT WHAT YOU'VE BEEN THROUGH and start discussing where you are going to!**

#WinnerVSLoser

When you change the present moment, you also change the past. Whoever controls the past also controls the future. And that is you!

When you **choose to be your full potential self**, right now, **regardless of the fallout**, you have unlocked your God-like power to flow into that reality.

You will activate all of the circumstances that are required, by the law of your BEING CHOICE. You will PROJECT all of the people, places, and ideas that are needed for you to have a congruent life experience.

Back to Vic's conversation:

Vic told me that for him, his real self commands between $350,000 and $450,000 a year. As soon as he completely commits to that idea, he will have $350,000 to $450,000 ideas flowing into his consciousness. That level of being will allow him to take bold action.

That completes the creative process. Vic will start to see miracles happen one by one. But only so long as he remains firmly, 100% committed to being that person.

Vic still had questions. "So, I should not visualize or feel or be the person who is earning this through my current job at Amazon?"

I told him, *"You are going to be this person in your visualization who lives the life you want to live because that* ***visualization is designed to activate the vibration*** *within you that ALLOWS you to remember who you truly are. The purpose of visualizing and activating that vibration is so that* *you have a <u>reference point of how you are supposed to feel</u> when you are being the person that you've chosen to be."*

#FeelingGetsTheBlessing #RevIKE

Vic was still confused. He wanted me to tell him what to do instead of downloading the answer from his reality. "But what about my Amazon business and my current job?"

I answered his question with another question. "How do you think you should respond to those? Do you think you should consider choosing those ideas from the level of being of the guy who makes $350,000 to $450,000 a year?

Or do you think you should respond to them from who you used to be with the same mind and mindset that has kept you stuck in a loop?"

"The state of mind that makes $350,000 to $450,000."

Exactly! He got it! I said, "Say to yourself, 'I am that person, and I refuse to settle for anything less.' I have to get you to choose the self-worth you desire."

One technique I learned to gain compliance with your doubting mind is to **REWRITE your history**. Clotaire Rapaille taught this in one of his videos.

Your past is B.S. because once you shift into a parallel universe, the present moment rewrites the history.

SEIZE THE PAST NOW.

#MakeItUp.

Look, if you have moral issues with doing this because you feel you are lying—you are trapped inside the cult-education program you have been brainwashed to believe.

That's your decision. It's one thing to commit a fraud, which I don't recommend. This rewrite of your personal history is vastly different. You are **seizing the foundational power that your mind uses to ENSLAVE YOU into the old ego program and capturing its grip on your reality.**

Instead of the "poor me, look at all this stuff that happened to me" loser talk, why not TELL YOURSELF that your mother and father were royalty.

You were born with special gifts that gave you unfair advantages over others, etc.

#MasterThePresent #ReWriteThePast

Don't accept any image of self-worth that is less than the self-worth governed by the particular self-image you desire.

If I can get you to choose that self-image and commit to it and settle for nothing less—*including REWRITING your historical data to support the new consciousness*, then your reality has no choice but to bend to your will and to start giving you what you are asking for according to that image."

Your self-image and your self-worth is the capacitor. Your capacitor is what you are capable of holding in your reality.

If you are coming from a place of self-worth of someone who is making less than that and is *being* less than that, you will be less than that.

It's <u>NOT</u> a Thinking-Man's Game!

There is no way you are going to be able to activate the mind within that consciousness to give you what it has no framework to comprehend. Your thought can't give you an explanation or forge a path for you if it doesn't understand that path itself.

#SIRIUS #LuciferianLIE

You can make lists all day long from the old level of being. You can take action until you are dead. But you ***cannot manifest and create that which you have not been authorized to receive*****. Switch to a PARALLEL reality, instead.**

You are the one that authorizes yourself to receive. You receive according to who you choose to be in the world. Who you choose to be is a reflection of how you see yourself and whether you act accordingly.

You are the God. You are the deity. There is no one else out there who can decide your fate for you. This life is a journey between YOU and YOU ONLY. Once this realization sets in, you'll find chapter 12 easily digestible, and it will bestow the magic you have been looking for your entire life.

What magic am I referring to, you ask?

The power to END self-sabotage and begin to live in the CHILDLIKE innocence that is called for in the Bible.

You get to choose who you want to be in this world. Isn't that amazing? The choice is entirely yours!

There is no other power in your circumstances. There is only you experiencing yourself through your five senses, and your five senses are located entirely in your mind.

Vic was taking it all in, but he admitted his mind was still a little foggy. The idea hadn't entirely crystallized in his head.

"That's because," I told him, using a crude but effective analogy, "Your mind just got slammed. Your mind is dying to jump into the equation. It is trying to keep you held back in the comfortable sameness it prefers. You have to truly understand that **YOU are the most important man in your world**—even in your whole universe."

You are worthy. When you control the present, you rewrite the past. When you rewrite the history, you control the future. You must control the CURRENT-moment with that choice of being. You must *be* the person you want to be."

Remember a few pages back when I talked about acquiring that website I couldn't afford? I made a decision. I shifted into the parallel universe where I already possessed the outcome. I acted from inspiration, staying committed. Same idea with the store that I owned.

But I didn't ask how I was going to get it or when it was going to happen. I just saw myself already in possession of it. I chose to be the person who was successful doing it.

Within six-months, inspired action and divine ideas FLOWED like electricity into my BEING CHOICE to "already have the site I wanted," and the funds manifested. It happened in a way that I had never done before, in an entirely new industry. This point should not surprise you because I had to BE a different version of myself, in a parallel universe.

Let's go back to the events which occurred around owning the nutrition store:

In my NEW BEING CHOICE, I didn't own just one store, but several of them. I carried myself every single day, to the best of my ability, in that capacity. That NEW ACT allowed the power of God to flow into my circumstances to match that reality with my vision.

Vic wanted me to clarify further. "I understand the part about following your excitement. That part makes sense. But..."

I cut him off. "You forgot the rest of that point. You follow your excitement *regardless of the fallout.* That's the most important part. Guess what tries to tell you what the fallout will be?"

"The mind?"

"Exactly!"

Vic pressed on. "A while back, three to five months ago, you told me to go create income now. So I took this job that I have. Not because it was my passion, but because I wanted to generate revenue. I tried to get my wife out of a job, and this job would allow me to do that. Is this the path of most excitement? No. Not at all. It is just a means to an end.

But now, after working with you deeper, I understand that this is my boot camp. It's what I'm doing while I'm making sense of mastery. When I am making $350,000 to $450,000—I mean *now that I am*, I don't know how this stuff fits into that equation. I see Amazon fitting into that equation, but I don't know for sure."

I said, "You're spinning yourself in cycles with your mind again! You've got to stop it. You see, circumstances *don't matter*. Your state of being is the only thing that matters. You're right —this is your boot camp. You can go into any environment, any job, or any situation. It doesn't matter what you do.

Your fastest path to your joy three to five months ago was to get a decent income. So, I said get an income, it's available, get it. And you did."

Your work is the same *no matter what*. All you have to do is to:

Choose who you are going to be.

Find your excitement.

ALLOW in what you've asked for and take the right actions.

Recognize that the right actions are always governed by what is exciting.

I told Vic, "You still have to lock into the state of being. If your excitement was to get on the phone with your business partner, then that's what you should do. We'll get off the phone, and then you get on the phone with him. When you hang up, ask yourself, 'What is my highest level of excitement now?'

Then you do whatever the answer is. And then you do the next thing. Always ask and answer 'What is my highest level of excitement at this moment.' And then you do it."

"Even if it doesn't make sense?" Asked Vic.

"Why would it make sense to you from your current level of understanding? That's the level of understanding that kept you broke."

Vic thought he was making a joke when he said, "So if my level of excitement is to go get ice cream, then I should just go get ice cream?"

"Why wouldn't you?" I asked. "You might get ice cream and then stumble into the next person who wants to invest in your ideas. **You have to live in the mystery**. You have to live from the place of excitement and leave your mind out of it."

This strategy is how I did it. This is how you will do it. You think it is scary because it is the unknown. Don't fear the unknown—the only thing you could run into in the unknown is yourself because it is only you anyway. You-niverse is you and you. You're the only power in your universe!

Your biggest fear is that the universe won't support you in your excitement. That is the ugliest pile of crap that has ever tormented anyone on this Earth.

#TrustYourDivineNature

The universe is nothing but you extended. **You are ONLY guaranteed support in your place of excitement.**

Remember: don't just theorize this. Do it and live it.

CHAPTER 10.

ALPHA UPGRADE™
"Playing in The Vortex of Sexual Energy"

I'm going to warn you; this chapter will teach by example. If you are into political-correctness and cannot handle FULL FRONTAL NUDITY (adult language), and tossing grammar out the window—this isn't for you.

You're going to discover why the "BAD BOY" gets all the dime-pieces, how SEXUAL ENERGY is EVERYTHING, and how to "play in the vortex of electricity-squared (sex energy)" to program consciousness for maximum success.

By now, you should know the part of my story where I was bedridden with Lyme disease. I was immobilized for quite some time. I got very out of shape.

That downtime was a complicated time for me because it was an arduous transformation. I was very sedentary. This lack of activity wasn't something I found joy in, and I didn't like being in my body.

So I set a goal. I wanted to become fit. No. More than that. I wanted to become super fit. I wanted to be the embodiment of what I perceived as being super fit. This challenge was a measurable goal.

The question was this: How could I "own" it? I knew how to manifest and self-heal, it was complicated because Lyme disease can damage your body *somethin' fierce*! I have to be light-hearted about the whole thing, but it was hell.

Knowing that I could exist in a parallel universe, as a SUPER FIT version of myself, I chose my new model of success. After all, I heard a story about a lady who was disabled with multiple sclerosis and nearly died from the disease. She went on to get well and run marathons!

#AnythingISPossible

I needed something I could look at and associate my identity within. I needed something outside of myself that I could mentally associate with at the capacity that I wanted to achieve. Something to entrain me and ensure my commitment.

After some research, I chose Mark Divine of SEALFit. Mark was a former Navy SEAL who took the most brutal physical training he learned in the military and turned it into a fitness program for civilians. As I looked at his online fitness program, I started to appreciate how physically fit Navy SEALs have to become. Not just in their body, but also in their minds.

I chose that as a gauge of ultra-fitness that I could aim towards at modeling my new identity and behavior. I looked at the daily fitness routines and the workouts (for grinders). They recommended doing various exercises on a regular basis, and so that's what I did.

The first challenge I accomplished was a 21-minute plank hold. After several weeks, I was able to "push through" pain and instruct my mind that, "it's an easy day!" Not bad, considering my first day I accomplished a 3-minute plank hold before dropping to the ground.

#Wimp

It was my highest excitement to become as fit as a Navy SEAL. Although my 38-year-old body would probably never make it through Hell Week, my transformation made me very happy. I worked out between two and three times each day, every day of the week. The workouts were very intense, and I had a few injuries along the way.

It took me two years to achieve this goal, but I did it. I set the bar in my excitement, did the Self-Entrainment Technique—I lived it, day in and day out—and I accomplished a complete shift in my consciousness.

Today, I'm able to run a 5-mile with a 20-pound weight vest on, followed by an intense strength training workout. When I started, the 1-mile without a weight vest would have cashed me out for the day. I was still in the CONSCIOUSNESS where I BELIEVED in "*Lyme disease doing damage to my body*" as a part of my history. I hadn't REWRITTEN the past—yet.

I tell you about the things I've been through because those experiences are authentic. Let's just say that I've left them in a parallel universe and therefore, they no longer linger in my NOW. One day, it will be mainstream acceptance of the fact that we live in multiple realities; most people think it's absurd today.

#Brainwashed

Here's a picture I took at the pinnacle of this type of training, in the summer of 2017:

ENTRAIN YOURSELF WITH A MOCAINE MIRACLE MORNING!

I'm unabashedly promoting many of the products I use to maintain peak performance and MOVE with vigor through my activities and workouts.

MOCAINE is a fun product that my team developed, to get me "JACKED" in my ABC Break Process—it's fantastic and delicious. Some critics complain to me that this formula has "artificial ingredients" and assume that I don't realize this, or are misleading them somehow.

Here's the thing, I separated the two companies: Complete Ascentials is the WELLNESS brand; you'll find the highest caliber of products—like *DNA Evolve*, the "limitless brain nootropic," and the mineral kits, featuring fulvic acid.

You can TRY A FREE SAMPLE KIT of DNA Evolve:
http://www.DNA-Evolve.com (Pay only shipping/handling).

It should go without question that I'm not naive about ALPHA UPGRADE being a company aimed at a different "mission."—I built the products for alternative interests I developed AFTER my body had reached the capstone of wellbeing. New pursuits emerged, like a ravenous sex drive and getting testosterone peaked by managing the hormonal balance in the body.

In this chapter, you'll discover information about the products in ALPHA UPGRADE's lineup. I'm sharing because to me; these products are so much fun to engage with using in my regimen! I've been having a blast experiencing the additional benefits of using the following formulations.

It all begins by having a MOCAINE MIRACLE MORNING. Once you grasp the idea that you CAN shift into parallel universes and activate new vibrations, it all starts to make damn good sense!

A word of caution: the following product advertisements contain adult language and they are not intended for young audiences. If you do not like the expression of a sexual-nature, skip to the next chapter.

MOCAINE

"They All Laughed When I Told Them MOCAINE Was My Productivity Secret...Until It Crushed Their Procrastination."

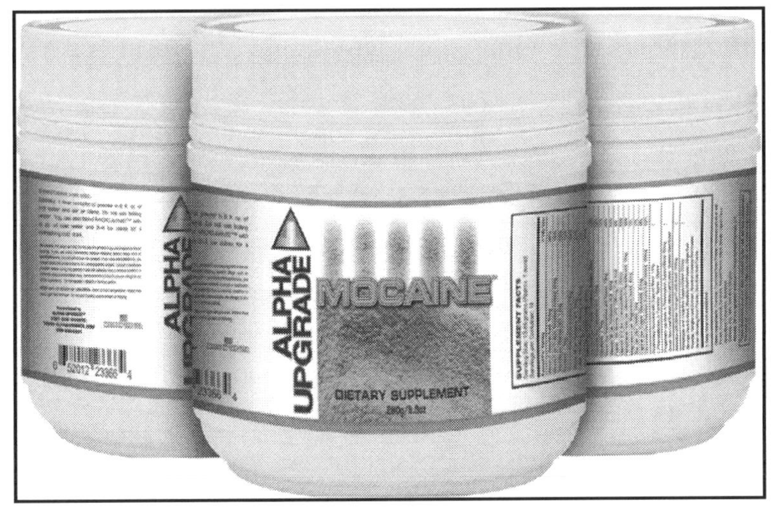

—We swear it's not laced!

Warning: this information may be offensive to coffee shop enthusiasts. It has **adult language** and snowflakes may find it intensely traumatizing. For entertainment purposes only.

THE RICH AROMA OF COFFEE-BEANS FILLS MY KITCHEN

I don't go to coffee shops anymore...

In my "workie-job" days, coffee shops made me happy.

They were a place to fit in, socialize, and meet others for conversation. Usually, it was just because the coffee shop wasn't a bar.

It wasn't awkward. Bars in the daytime felt awkward.

A coffee shop is a place to network and study, a college student's dream. Fortunately, I'm not a college student.

I dropped out. My companies demand my time and energy. My kids are growing up fast. I don't have time to play "hipster"anymore and care about status.

At 9 a.m. every morning, I start my day.

I get to stay up late and create my next "exciting thing" online all night and sleep in most days. I earned this lifestyle.

When morning comes, it feels right to begin my MOCAINE MIRACLE MORNING at 9 a.m.

My body wants to be up, so it drags me out of bed. After my body finishes sleeping—no stupid alarm clock hustle to make me frantic.

I used to do the alarm clock thing. Waiting in line at the coffee shop, like it was a chemical "ghetto" to flock to get that buzz... each day.

I used to call it the "White Collar" corner spot for a dopamine fix—it fits in the gap between the fast-food indulgence, and bar scene.

One leads to another. It was a rat-race that felt productive.

I woke up to realize that a decade of doing this "chemical-ghetto" cycle left me broke. And just...well, acting appreciated and looking nice.

Back then, the alarm would go off and I'd get my latte. My shirt and tie would be pristine. My hair perfected, and my car was spot-on clean.

I learned how to be this way while watching Hollywood movies, just like you...

People like us when you are just like them. Even if you secretly hate your life and wonder how the "fuck" some lucky bastards seem to avoid all this pretentious a-hole rat-race B.S.

You know someone who just seems to have it all, right? For me, it was this chubby dude. He was making $30k per month.

The guy was selling cameras and other China-made imports online. He had a few websites and just wore his gym shorts and workout clothes, every day. He told me he hated coffee shops.

He did like Mexican food, though. He didn't drive a brand new Mercedes and wear Prada shoes, pretending he was a millionaire.

He told me that those guys were "dumb wannabes" and that real life was—freedom, family, and fortune. In that order.

He went on to tell me that all the stressed out cogs in the matrix were all trying to out-dress, out hustle, and outcompete each other in the marketplace—wasting their lives away.

The big deception was this: someone else's watch owned them all. These "go-getters" put fortune first, then squeezed in their family, and lastly... believed it would somehow lead them to freedom someday.

As he spoke, I could feel my shirt and tie getting tighter. I looked around the coffee shop and noticed all the uptight "social butterflies" were all pretending, too.

Just like I was. Acting important. These people weren't happy; they were miserable. It's what drove them to the coffee plantation to get a morning dopamine fix—I was one of them!

I'd go three times a day... I hated my life, slaving away for some ungrateful boss who used me like an energizer bunny... for HIS big house, HIS big cars, HIS wife's happiness.

I hated dressing up for HIS coronation... As I began to wonder why in the hell I spent $20 per day on coffee, overpriced at the coffee shop, when it made no logical sense... it became clear to me:

I wanted to pretend life was good. To afford the lie.

So, my buddy leaned back and said, "When you have life by the tail... you don't waste your time driving to a coffee shop... to feel better.

You find it somewhat inconvenient to wait in line, waste your day, and pay for coffee that isn't that great, and surround yourself with others doing the same.

Besides, how can you be productive when THEY are listening..."

I realized he was right. He was full of courage and confidence in himself.

He dressed like a pauper and here I was... decked to the hills... whispering to keep it a secret that I was broke like he suspected. He was the rich one. I was the poor one. He was free. I was not.

Years went by; I haven't spoken to him since. He'd be proud of me. After almost dying of Lyme disease and losing every penny.

That illness forced me out of the coffee plantation lifestyle, congregating with other wage-slaves and living in a rushed "go, go, go" booby-trap.

In fact, I recognized the real value of getting a coffee buzz... and began using that PEAK MENTAL STATE for building my empire.

When fenced in by a room of "worker consciousness" employees... you can't be FULL ON and EXPRESS YOURSELF—it's always like you're hiding your conversation, socializing in a facade where you "almost exist" and yet, nobody cares you are there.

They are trying to hide behind their devices, too. That's not human connection; it's distraction (from the pain)!

Why should they care, you're just hurrying through life to get nowhere, like they are. They recognized that you're also stressed and overwhelmed, so they avoid you for the same reason you avoid them.

They grab their caffeine buzz and hop in the car, pop on their music or favorite podcast. They're plugging into something that feels good. For a few fleeting moments after wasting productive time trying to fit in.

In that brief interlude between the coffee house plantation and the slave job, it's heaven on Earth. Dopamine is released, and it anchors in another day—like being on repeat. Repeat because it feels good.

It gets you nowhere, but feels good—getting you there.

I knew my friend would be proud because I began using a morning ritual. My routine involved a "JACKED-UP" chocolate coffee-flavored MOCAINE.

I smelled the same rich bean AROMA, as I did in the coffee shop... getting a delicious chocolate taste... better than my $6 latte... and peaked myself to FEELING 3 TIMES THE COURAGE OF A MOUNTAIN LION.

Mocaine is what I call, a "SUPER COFFEE"—it gets my creative juices on overdrive, ready to sprint laps or write pages in this book!

But, just to be safe... you better start with a 1/2 scoop. *I'm just saying.*

You might not be ready for this if you're not used to feeling like lifting up the car in the parking lot, or running 5 miles with a weight vest on your torso.

I do these things; it's not just a play on words.

Anyhow, he'd be proud of me because I stopped pretending and started ascending.

Instead of wasting time in the commute each morning, socializing with the "herd" at the coffee plantation, I began USING A PEAK MENTAL HIGH to crush my list of action steps towards building my empire—just like he told me to.

I took off the damn tie and stopped doing the same things 95% of people do, day after day, to remain STUCK in a rut...

Most mornings, I do what's called The MOCAINE MIRACLE MORNING, where I program my consciousness to direct the flow of life towards living my dreams! The best part is: it works.

I use my time to do this process, instead of commuting to fit in with others. Your neighbors are always wrong; they are doing what Hollywood movies influenced them to, to "fit in" and be socially cool "hip."

I didn't give a rat's ass about being cool. I wanted to be successful. The MOCAINE MIRACLE MORNING allowed me to build three companies that have done over 7-figures, each.

My morning buzz is way more intense than the average coffee/dopamine fix I used to get at the coffee shop. It's more like "holy crap; I have a feeling like conquering the world today!"

I can't relate to them then... they bore me to tears with being average and hiding behind their screens.

I'm not sure I could handle waiting in line anymore... there's no way I could drink MOCAINE and wait for 5 minutes for three other people to get their ice-cream flavored caramel and whipped cream lattes... imagining all the disgusting sugar and empty calories engulfing their midsection and the high fructose corn syrup enlarging their obesity potential... I might puke.

Screw that! I prefer an appetite suppressant that kicks out my cravings all day, so my nutrition can be "on point"... while MOCAINE fuels my productivity to TRULY GET AHEAD. To be "one of the chosen ones"...

Using my time more efficiently, it helps me get ahead. Life is just decisions that create results. I gave up the coffee house for the dream lifestyle.

Drinking MOCAINE isn't for everyone...

MOCAINE is not for the masses. It's for someone who is fed up with the same old path everyone else is following. The herd is always heading to the slaughter.

MOCAINE is not for the faint of heart. If you have a medical health issue, do not engage with this stuff —it's not your grandma's cup of coffee.

MOCAINE is not for the guy or gal who wants to go to work and kiss the boss's ass. You might feel like devouring the boss with your fangs in his neck, but I wouldn't recommend it. Be safe, not sorry.

MOCAINE is not for children or women who are expecting. There are potent ingredients in MOCAINE that give me a coffee high beyond anything I have gotten in any coffee shop...

It's dangerous if you misuse it. I'm an extremist. Taking risks and pursuing EXCITEMENT is my life. If the saying goes, "Get in where you fit in"...

I'd be the guy you call when you want to sell the house and invest it all in a business venture!

I'd instead unplug from the matrix and the coffee shop plantations, becoming a Renegade Entrepreneur. That's me.

It's who I am. I own it.

MOCAINE is my "fix" of choice.

It is FUEL for someone who wants to kick serious ass.

Head over to get your FREE SAMPLE "baggies"—if you're ready to TRY MOCAINE, Risk Free. http://www.MOCAINE.com (Pay only shipping/handling).

You'll get a FREE Digital Copy of The MOCAINE Miracle Morning with Your First Purchase of a Full Canister:

TANTRIC SPELL

"THE ALPHA MALE'S *FORBIDDEN* SECRET... EVERY MAN OUGHT TO KNOW...BEFORE HIS NEXT DATE!"

The Shocking Truth About Seductive "oils" and bad-boy magnetism You Can Use to Become an ANIMAL In The Bedroom.

These statements have not been evaluated by the FDA. Not intended to treat, prevent, diagnose or cure disease. For entertainment purposes only. Mature content and language.

DISCOVER WHY DANGER IS GOOD FOR SEXUAL ENERGY AND PUTTING XENOESTROGENS ON YOUR SKIN - IS NOT.

It was late on a Friday night when the phone rang.

I was alone, again. After two workouts and a long, stressful day, some company was my desire.

To have a beautiful woman by me, to make love. To be living my dream. I'm not a young man anymore.

I mean... I am fit. Very fit. But I've about had it with women who are into me for my money, or the wrong reasons.

Western women these days can be so damn complicated.

It's our culture. We grew up with marketers telling us that when things go wrong, we should replace them—right away. Unfortunately, many women see men this way.

And vice-versa.

Look. It's not anyone's fault. To get mad at society in general and the cultural code of "false expectation" equaling "to fall in love" in America...

I figured it would be better to just 'play the game.'

Heck, I've had enough of these selfish women who think they should take everything. From their man. After all, he's a fool in love. It flat-out sucks.

But, on the other hand, I'm interested in getting my needs met. I could go out and mingle... but, I'm not getting too attached.

The thought of a call-girl, Vegas style, doesn't sound bad. At least, you "pay them to go away" afterward, right?

Well, I'm not in Vegas, and it's not legal here... nor, would any "drugged out" call girl truly satisfy what I want. I want to love.

Not some cheap "drinks and a nightcap" one-night stand. Although, at this point, I'd probably take it.

Remember, it's late. It's Friday night. I'm alone. **She calls me**. So the phone is ringing. I can see that it's her... her picture pops up on my screen.

I better see what she has to say. So I answer.

"Matthew, the cologne you wear stinks."

She saw me on the way to the gym. I passed her at the gas station earlier. My first thought was, "screw you"... but, I held my tongue. Instead, I politely said, "What do you know about cologne? And why do you care?"

I could see her shrugging her shoulders on the other end of the line... recognizing how stupid my question was. I mean, there was a beautiful girl...

She's way too young for me. But, she wants me. So the attention is flattering. I have slept with her, yes. I'll be candid and admit it.

I was weak... Or, should I say, she's damn good looking, and her body is gorgeous. She finds me alluring because I'm older and successful in her eyes.

It turns her on. So I stopped myself from attacking her on the phone and asked her to tell me more...

"Remember the time we were together, Matthew." She says. Going on, "I went through your essential oils on the desk. You were showering, and I played.

I put on the pheromone oil blend you said that woman in California sold you at a trade show."

So I interjected, "Is that the smell you had on?" I mean, I do remember her smelling familiar... I've detected this before!

She continues, "When you were kissing me, I felt soo relaxed...

Something about that oil made me loosen up. I opened up to you like I wanted to. It wasn't forced or anything. It reminded me of intimacy, being in a different space. It just happened."

Reflecting on how I made passionate love to her, amazed at the youthful body she possessed... that 20-something perfection... I do remember her popping her head up and saying, "Oh my God, what are you Superman or something?!"

It was a ginormous ego-boost. I'm not going to lie. So, I reminded her of the time when she said that to me, trying to get her to recall those feelings again.

"You do know, what you said to me after we finished, right?"

She said, "Haha, that's what I'm talking about. Don't start getting a big head. My ability to let go and allow you to get me turned on was what did it."

She continued, "I just felt comfortable with you. Like we clicked at a deep level. As soon as that happened, you got to see how erotic I truly am...Now, don't get me wrong, Matthew. I admire you and think you are amazing... you look good for a 40-year-old man. But, I have to admit. It was the atmosphere and the connection I felt to you—it wasn't physical. It was something else."

We finished our conversation, and I realized how whatever I did that night seemed to make magic happen. It left a memory that she'll always remember.

And, I'll always remember it too! The call didn't save my Friday night. I still ended up alone and sleeping in my bed without a partner to wake up to.

Let's face it, divorce is terrible. I had one coming that was years in the making... we resolved it amicably, but being "alone" at an advancing age has its limitations.

So I decided to do something different, besides getting down on myself about "getting old" and Western women these days...

I decided to crack the code on that magical night.

Whatever I did, since I was half of the equation, allowed her to open up to me in a provocative way... If you know and understand women, you know the "f...k" is all in their mind.

A gorgeous woman can get wild with an out-of-shape guy, seeing him as the knight in shining armor.

Girls are not VISUAL like men are. They are kinesthetic. For the most part, women feel their way around life. I think it has something to do with the fact that they are closer to the womb of creation.

They have heightened intuitive abilities, unpredictable emotions, better and more powerful orgasms!

Okay, we don't need to go there—*yet*.

But, heck, why not be real here and talk like men. We want one thing. We want her to lose her mind in bed, to get climactic and stay there in that moment.

For as long as we can keep them there. Our egos blow up like The Beatles when we see ourselves in that picture.

So I began researching ways to give women the most powerful orgasms, to get them to "fall in love"... and it all boiled down to a few simple techniques.

In fact, everything I did that night with "her" was EXACTLY the way a guy is supposed to turn her on. In a few moments, I'm going to reveal everything that I did.

This way, you can try it for yourself and add this to your "fun things to do" list. I backtracked all my insights into a culmination of wisdom that any man can apply... you have to understand.

I'm a madman! I devour information... *DNA Evolve* has got me on "another level" when it comes to being "limitless."

My weeks were spent perusing seduction books, listening to pick-up artists tell me their secrets, and studying Tantra. The funny thing is; the guys who were claiming to be the best at this stuff were just average looking men. And older, too!

I had a new realization—"getting old can be fun and exciting if I get some new skills."

Catch my drift?

Let's imagine the possibilities, shall we? What if 3 or 4, or even 28 different women like this girl show up in my adult life before I'm too old to enjoy the hunt?

Figuring there are some good years left in the engine, my operating system was due for an upgrade!

Let me tell you some of the insights that came along this path of wisdom, so you can be a man who ascends to the level of John McAfee, too.

After all, if you're going to get CRYPTO rich, you might as well model the greatest showman in the space!

I want to give you some "shortcuts" to use. These insights I'm about to reveal to you now are real gems. They were tested and proven to be found "not wanting" for anything.

In other words, it works. The first idea that transpired came from a guy who taught me Tantra. He taught me about the "energy body" and how the etheric field, about 2 – 5 inches off her skin, can be used to channel her sexual energy up her spine.

Sexual energy is electricity (^{2}).

After all, we all have heard about kundalini and the chakra system, etc. Half the world believes and uses a model of human biology, knowing it's bio-electric.

So, if that's the case, there is a "current" flowing through it. The prana, the chi, the life-force.

Call it what you will. I call it the "electricity-squared" phenomena... It's sexual energy. The same energy that creates LIFE, you know how this works.

You can make love, deposit this energy, or should I say... merge these energy bodies with INTENTION.

Human life will emerge in the physical. Watching the Tantric Mongoose, Nityama, move this energy is like watching a magician perform a levitation.

You wonder, "what's the trick!" while your eyes are in amazement.

Or, listening to Dr. Wayne Dyer's "AH" meditation, he learned from Dr. Pillai... on how to manifest by using a sound, "AH," and channeling the sexual energy up the spine and out the third eye.

Again, you see the mystical revelation of "energy" and how it moves throughout the body-electric. The currency of life is sexual energy. This power within is why "they" suppress it and distort it.

You know who "they" are... The same people who stripped it from you in organized religion, replacing it with guilt and shame.

I went on to discover that the opposite of love is not to hate. Instead, the opposite of love is shame and guilt.

Hate energy can be useful... especially if you can turn it into passion in the bedroom.

Shame, this does nothing other than regulate the sexual energy down to a fraction of its potential—stripping the human creator of his power, his nature.

We want to conquer! We want more sex and passion.

Back to the lessons here, because what you're going to get, if you stay to the end, you won't find common knowledge.

I'm going to show you how to program INTENTION like I described a moment ago in the example of making a baby or using the sound "AH" to manifest a pay raise...

You can combine the wisdom of the bio-electric body and tap into "other realms" of consciousness, taking HER WITH YOU in the heat of the moment.

This eye-opener is what I stumbled upon that magical night. The night she'll never forget. She interprets the experience as a letting go on all levels, as if she surrendered to a higher power—the sexual energy in her that lay dormant.

Like a garden hose untied from a knot, the flow of her ecstasy was free again! I had to look back at the fact she used my pheromone oil blend this woman gave me at a trade show in Los Angeles.

It caught my attention for obvious reasons. I've always wanted to believe in pheromones, but my research in the past told me it was all a scam, a gimmick. I'm not a fool.

I only bought the pheromone oil from this woman because, to me, it smelled good and I figured the least it could do was be pleasant smelling.

Even if she scammed me, I'd have a seductive smelling essential oil I could use for something...

I knew essential oils had been used for centuries as "medicine" around the world. The healing properties of oils have stood the test of time.

I'm not talking about today's Big Pharma fear-porn propaganda that has everyone all enslaved to side-effects.

I'm talking about the days of old... when "white witches" could mend a wound or heal a cough with the darnedest of things. I've seen it all in my healing journey.

Investing over 10,000 hours of natural health research to go from bedridden to training like a pro athlete, had me in some "woo woo" places at times.

But, as crazy as it ever was, essential oils were never far-fetched to me. I could tell a difference just by putting them on.

The environment was different. I don't care what modern medicine says about "anxiety" or "stress"...

When I was too anxious to let go and enjoy life... drugs and talk-therapy with social workers didn't help me a cotton-picking bit.

I felt like a zombie and an idiot for rehashing all my "less-than" positions in life, over-and-over again.

I found it interesting that my days of trauma and anxiety faded away the same time my sexual appetite was restored and firing on all cylinders.

Again, there is something about the "electricity-squared" concept I'm describing. When it flowed freely and powerfully, my life was amazing.

My money situation skyrocketed to the moon. Women wanted me because I exuded confidence and power. I suddenly got it!!

The whole "bad boy" thing that gets all the girl's panties in a slingshot across the room at a rock concert is this...

The "bad boy" is not appealing because he is a broke, angry, pissed off thug... Contrary to how we might see them sometimes. Wondering, "How in the hell did he get to be with her?"

That's not the magic. We're only interested in replicating the BENEFIT out of the equation. To make you the beneficiary of the "formula" I discovered that night...

It just happens to coincide with the same formula the idiot gangbanger is using to score the hot babe. It is the FREE-FLOW of "electricity-squared"—or sexual energy.

The "bad boy" has shrugged off the religious man's guilt. The gangbanger has something to prove, acting out the role allows him to free up the same energy.

A pick-up artist thinks his mind-tricks are what make him seductive...

He's only half-right. It is his mind-tricks that FREE HIM up to release his "electricity-squared" and become more magnetic. To what he desires.

You see, after really getting a robust understanding of what TRULY drives women crazy and how it can be replicated, like a franchise opportunity, with a blueprint for success...

I found it stupid to take workshops in Tantra, or learn a thousand pick-up-lines... or, hire a real-life HITCH to coach me.

Screw that. I wasn't going to allow someone else to sell me on the idea that I already knew.

The power is within me!!

I already have it. And so do you. So here you go.

Here's something you won't hear about anywhere else.

At least not yet, until someone out there tries to copy my TANTRIC SPELL formula.

You may be thinking, "Is that it? That's your strategy?

Just use a pheromone oil and my woman will be calling me or texting me, telling me how she can't forget our experience together?"

I say, "yes." But, under one condition! You have to DO what I did that night. This recipe is what "programmed" the experience into the outcome.

There was something "wrong" with the idea of her and I getting together. This taboo is what made it exciting... and **dangerous.**

Society isn't keen on young 20-somethings dating a man twice their age. Now, I'm not telling you to go out and ruin your marriage, or your current commitment you have with someone.

You have to see WHY the "wrongness" of the situation became a right. It is because it drove her mind crazy.

It became a fantasy, a "forbidden" fruit in the Garden of Eden. As you know, human beings were born to satisfy this desire, one way or another.

The good news is; you can manufacture this into her mind. Even if you are in a BORING marriage that could use a reset back ten or twenty years—before the fire went out.

The reason why the fire went out is that "electricity-squared" became stifled... blocked... suppressed, one way or another.

The real issue is this: you traded in DANGER and EXCITEMENT for security and familiarity. Lame, I know.

When you do this, oxytocin is released—the love hormone. This release is proper because it keeps you two together, bonded.

But, as DANGER is no longer present, you lose the magic.

Out of the inherent need to "survive"—you find a partner to reduce your odds of "ceasing to exist" (according to the reptilian brain that acts on survival and reproduction instincts only).

You "settle down" to make this a reality.

Ironically, settling down causes you to feel the oxytocin support. Oxytocin is the hormone of sex for women. She likes it. It calms her mind, lowers her stress levels, and reassures her she's safe.

Once you experience it, you are in love with her, and it lowers your testosterone. It releases a chemical called prolactin.

Prolactin is less sex drive, lower libido/testosterone, and thanks to giving up "danger" for security... you get caught up in it!

So the DANGER is the element—or I should say—what can make you a sexual dynamo. I know, you're sitting there thinking about your cozy (boring) life in the suburbs.

It's time to get a little BAD ASS and mix it up!

DANGER releases "electricity-squared" by inhibiting the prolactin response. It's the same thing as when you are with a woman for "one night sex"... since you don't LOVE HER, you release no oxytocin. Or very little.

Remember how my magic night went, I recalled feeling the "one night sex" feeling. It couldn't last. We SHOULDN'T be together; it's not a thing our parents would suddenly celebrate.

It's weird. But, every man has his thoughts about penetrating a young, beautiful 20-something woman from time-to-time. It's the age where women models that we are programmed to desire, peak in appearance (on average).

This sexual instinct is the URGE or FORCE that we need to HARNESS!

Harnessing this force, we can experience SEXUAL POWER to magnetically seem superior to most of the men we compete against for territory.

Here's how it's done, ASSUMING you are willing to incorporate the DANGER in your life again, try this:

Societies throughout history including the Chinese, Egyptians, Greeks, Romans, and Persians have used essential oils to do this.

Essential oils have been proven to affect the body in ways which increases and promotes carnal instincts and pleasures.

When an essential oil, like sandalwood, enters the body of two different individuals, the chemical reactions will be the same regardless of past conditioning.

Both of their bodies will have increased blood flow and both bodies respiratory breathing will slow.

So in essence, you create an ideal circumstance for great sex, helping the person to be calm, relaxed and with more blood flow around their genitals.

(Add some BEAT IT UP! and see how crazy things get).

Essential oils can create conditions in the "mind-body" (electricity-squared) to promote sexual interaction, relaxation, and playfulness.

The sexual interactions, many times, will feel better, resulting in stronger orgasms, and allow for a stronger and more comfortable connection between lovers.

This tactile experience is what happened with the young 20-something girl I have been telling you about the entire time.

Now, I want to tell you what was in the blend she put on.

The first ingredient in TANTRIC SPELL is organic jojoba oil.

It is a typical carrier oil. Here's what is unique about my method of using a carrier oil. I have mine put through a BioPhoton Analyzer—cloning specific "spiritual properties" in the "carrier oil."

It's one of those "forbidden" secrets of self-improvement THE POWERS THAT BE don't want you to discover or know exists.

David Wolfe talks about the BioPhoton Analyzer on YouTube; you can watch the video and make your conclusions.

Remember: I'm telling you this for ENTERTAINMENT PURPOSES ONLY. (Disclaimer #noted).

For legal reasons, I'm not going to make any claims about the BioPhoton Analyzer and the "cloning" that we may or may not use in TANTRIC SPELL.

The merit of the ingredients is enough to get me wearing it, daily. I use TANTRIC SPELL around my neck, down by my belly-button area (snail trail area), and on my wrists.

Here's what is in the blend:

Ylang Ylang - Sandalwood - Vanilla Absolute - Nutmeg - Ginger

According to the expert who sold me the oil blend at the trade show in California, she experimented for years to find what works best.

She promised me I'd have way better sexual experiences when I bought a bottle. The proof, for me, was the magical night I've been reflecting upon thus far...

Keep in mind, I also unleashed DANGER into my life and exploited the benefit of increased SEXUAL desire!

The oil she used that night and reminded me to tell you about is TANTRIC SPELL. That's right.

She told me that I should share the story.

She said, "Matthew, you should sell it at below market value... to surprise people... with a lower price.

Then, you should ask them to help you tell others—because they will!" Here I was, getting business advice from a beautiful, young 20-something girl... who said I should just REVEAL ALL OF MY INTIMATE DETAILS, to you.

As if, it is easy to tell you about a night of passion where a remarkable discovery happened in my bedroom.

I could bore your pants off with another "why you should buy my essential oils vs. their essential oil" sales presentation, with facts and stats you could frankly... give two rips about, right?

For Christ's sake, it's not a cure for diabetes.

What matters is that this stuff got her loosened up, and she has this obsession with wanting it on now, to re-activate her back into that "space" where she lost control... in a way that she wanted to, just hadn't with another man.

She even left a voice-mail recording on my phone; I've kept it there in case someone calls me out, alleging B.S. One listen and you'll hear her thoughts of *50-Shades* and fantasies I'd blush at hearing in the presence of anyone else.

She told me, "Matthew, I love smelling YOU wearing it. And that's why I called to say to you that YOUR COLOGNE STINKS. Besides, it's not healthy to wear that on your body and you're the health guy, aren't you?"

I broke my own rules about "business marketing" to share this story with you. It has been graphic, very intimate in nature, and it's as if you were beamed down...

Where she was looking at me... glazed over... with those magic words I hope to one day hear again, "Oh my God, what are you Superman or something?"

I'll never forget that victory. I knew that I hadn't lost it... the mojo, that is. I've given you all the INGREDIENTS that went into this MIRACLE—everything from smelling good to DANGER and the "forbidden fruit" of SEXUAL DESIRE, unleashed...

When I wear TANTRIC SPELL, it gives me assurance that I'm not wearing "estrogen dominance producing chemicals" on my body, turning me into a passive, guppy fish.

She was right—cologne stinks, for the most part. I still have a few bottles of my favorite colognes, but I NEVER under any circumstances allow that crap to touch my skin!

Your skin absorbs the chemicals like a sponge takes in water... and men wonder today, "Why is my testosterone so low?!"

Duh, it's the XENOESTROGEN poisons from all the chemicals, BPAs, hormones in the meat and dairy, etc. The LAST THING you want on your SKIN is chemically concocted colognes that send signals to your body to produce more estrogen!

On my SKIN, the only thing I wear is TANTRIC SPELL. It's delicious and designed for SEDUCTION!

http://www.TANTRICSPELL.com

Your first bottle of TANTRIC SPELL comes with these two BONUSES, included with the purchase.

BEAT IT UP!

"HOW TO BEAT IT UP! IN THE BEDROOM."

- After age 35.

This information is for entertainment purposes only. These statements have not been evaluated by the FDA. Not intended to treat, prevent, diagnose or cure disease.

BEAT IT UP! FEATURING SPECIAL REPORT: "3 KEYS TO MAXIMIZE PERFORMANCE IN THE BEDROOM."

INVITE: You can LISTEN IN on a PRIVATE SESSION, regarding weight-loss, sex-drive and more at this link, below:

www.OMAD.me

You've been there before, in the heat of the moment.

You are ready to punish her and show her the reason why she chose you in the first place. It's natural; you're an untamed *wildman*!

It's in your DNA to want to devastate her in the bedroom. You come undone; this moment is when you get to talk dirty, dominate, and make her submit to you.

After putting up with all the drama, dealing with all the tension, it's your time to release aggression.

But, just one problem. It's not a little problem; it's a HUGE problem. It's just that—well—it isn't becoming the punishing force you intended in the heat of passion when the urge was rising.

Now, there she is laying there—submissive to you—expecting you to make her lose control.

You try to talk to yourself, in your head. You're like, "Man; I got this. C'mon... pull it together... remember when it did work and how she loved it."

But, just one problem. Today isn't your day.

You scan your memory bank for some excuse to lay on her, in the place of the solid pipe that didn't get served, to console her, to pretend that she'll just remember that one time, the heated time when she couldn't stop obsessing about your c*ck.

You want to keep her there! In that space where she is under your spell. You know if you can, she's not looking elsewhere.

But, something went wrong.

Women don't work that way. They are moment-to-moment creatures. If you don't lay the "D" on her the way she likes it, she's going to think something's wrong.

Most likely, she'll obsess about how she's not pretty enough. Or, young enough. Or, good enough anymore.

Think real hard, this turns into her stirring up resentments and jealousies that you don't need in your life.

My God man! You've got to pull it together, you aren't that old, yet. Most likely, you realize your testosterone might be a bit lower, but, you haven't got a clue HOW it happened—so you wonder?

Perhaps there is something medically wrong with you? That thought has crossed your mind a dozen times, but it's embarrassing.

So now what?

Get a prescription of the "blue pill" or some other dangerous drug?

I mean, it could be worth it to save your relationship... but, at what expense?

Then, there's the rub, explaining to her that the "window of opportunity" is approaching a peak and it's time to use the artificially propped up manhood like a wig.

Underneath, you fear the stigma of "aging" and how it affects her perception of you. It's true, in fact.

The reptilian brain of the human organism is hard-wired to "reproduce and survive." It's the only DRIVING FORCE behind the "deep-seated" unconscious mind that drives her engine.

You know it, she knows it, and to admit you need "assistance" is a defeat that acknowledges "the man who once was is now a shadow of himself..."It's not the reality you wanted to face. We all age and our testosterone and drive fall off, and yet—some men seem to GO STRONG and SERVICE their partners every day, sometimes many times!

Women talk.

So, the last thing you want is for her to share a wine-story with a friend who does nothing but brags about how her MAN can't keep his erection down around her.

The pleasure she experiences by listening to that story should be the GLORY of YOUR NAME flying around the table!!!

So, let me tell you WHY you're here and who I am... so you know WHY you should listen to me.

First of all, I'm not your doctor. I'm not here to play "internet" doctor either. I gave up on Western medicine a long time ago... back in 2012.

You see, I went in for a routine doctor visit due to a headache I'd had for several days.

Some young hotshot doctor used my body as a testing ground for a chemical concoction that almost left me paralyzed.

For months, I went into somatization episodes and had to revisit the emergency room, over two dozen times.

My last straw with doctors and their "zero liability waivers" you sign, giving them the right to use ANY DRUG they want to, regardless of the damage, ... this was the last straw for me.

I became the damaged party who couldn't have a voice.

My name is Matthew David Hurtado. I'm the CEO of Complete Ascentials and Alpha Upgrade—a new company, designed to support MEN (and women, too).

Men like you and I, who know what the dangers of "modern medicine" can be... and we desire to find NATURAL SOLUTIONS that work.

I'll tell you more...about me, later.

Right now, this is about MANLINESS in the bedroom and HOW TO HAVE A POWERFUL STAFF.

I'm not afraid to call it what it is... this is what a woman wants. She wants you to "BEAT IT UP!" in the bedroom.

Not make excuses. Your mate needs it for her emotional state of satisfaction, so she can be the one who whispers in their ear, drinking wine and getting loose, telling THEM how you are so turned on by her that you lose control—leaving her on the bed legs shaking when you've finished.

She wants to loosely slip out of her mouth, "He gets me off several times and the sheets need to be cleaned"... it's some gold-standard thing where she is slightly 3-degrees above her friends when she can tell this story.

Her friends get to stew in their stale relationships and wonder...

Who is this MAN who she got hooked, and they become curious... You sense it when they come around.

In the back of their minds, they are fantasizing about your c*ck, betraying their friendship. They can't help it. It's human nature to be deceitful in a relationship.

You've been alive long enough to recognize this by now. You're either the ALPHA and she knows it, and fights to keep the other sexual-predators (her friends) away from you... or, the OTHER MAN gets the crown of glory.

He gets the stories told about him. He gets the fantasies about HIM channel-surfed in the neighborhood.

All the women have this SECRET "imaginary life" they live... in their minds. It's time to PENETRATE this realm of imagination once and for all!

I can say these things to you, *man to man*, because I've experienced it all take place. I've been there. On BOTH sides of the "stories" going around the table at ladies night...

My journey into TANTRA allowed me to discover some crazy "DARK HORSE" stuff... this stuff, I am going to reveal to you.

You see, you and I are going to get acquainted with each other in a few moments.

I'm going to ask you to visit **http://www.BeatItUpSolution.com**

The three ingredients I'm going to tell you about can PUT YOUR STAFF IN "MOSES" POSITION... commanding the RED SEA to part, or at least something will be apart more often.

My journey into self-healing exposed me to over 10,000 hours of natural health research. Not to mention, millions-in-sales with products... that kick ass.

I'm going to tell you about BEAT IT UP!

It's a 3-compound blend of Butea Superba, Bacopa, and Tongkat Ali.

This MALE ENHANCEMENT BLEND is the PERFECT COMBINATION of proven ingredients. The ingredients are backed with ample scientific studies to answer the question you've been asking, *"Is there something natural that works?"*

The proof is in the bedroom. That's why I back up the formula with a 100% no questions asked guarantee. For 30 full days.

I want you to say, "Matthew knows his shit man." when she says to you "*you're are a frickin*' ANIMAL!"

Look, if you want the BEAT IT UP! product, visit the website at http://www.BeatItUpSolution.com.

I'll tell you all about the ingredients and how to use this formula to assist you in having the best sex, ever!

On the next page, you'll get 3 Keys to Maximize Performance in The Bedroom.

Right now, I'm going to GIVE YOU CUTTING-EDGE INFORMATION that can help you get ROCK-SOLID results.

You're going to get 3 KEYS to MAXIMIZING PERFORMANCE IN THE BEDROOM, plus a few bonus tips.

3 "SECRET" Keys, explained...

These are the three secrets that you can use in the bedroom. I've discovered these through trial and error and much study. Each one has been applied with extraordinary results achieved.

Since I have done these, and it's my life's work and passion... I'm ready to share.

I love fitness and wellness. You know becoming fitter and becoming more healthy at the cellular level will make you more powerful and more potent in the bedroom. I call these "SECRET" keys because they don't directly pertain to sexual performance.

You get the rewards, catch my drift?

Believe it or not, there's a vital mind-body component that ties into it as well. A "psyche thing," if you will.

Now, we're going to get to the three keys, immediately, and this is going to be a short overview. Just learn and consider using whatever feels right in your situation.

SECRET KEY #1: this is something you can do at home. It's something that you can do without buying anything or investing in anything, but it's going to take a little bit of willpower and discipline on your end.

It's called intermittent fasting.

Intermittent fasting is one of the things that allowed me to transform my life and get the lean, chiseled look. Not to mention, listen to what many experts agree can also happen, if you're willing to sacrifice some "eating" for more male potency...

Dr. Axe on YouTube talked about how intermittent fasting can raise your testosterone substantially. If this doesn't perk your ears, I'm afraid this book is not for you. If so, check out how it's done as we go forward.

Now, MORE TESTOSTERONE was something that I wanted because I was turning the decade around to age 40.

I realized that my workouts were getting a little bit more challenging and I had a huge goal in mind. I was training for the SEALfit Kokoro Warrior Camp. And I knew that I was going to have to workout two to three times a day. So, the more testosterone, the better. Let's explain intermittent fasting.

Here's how it works: In a nutshell, when you look at your day, you have 24 hours available to you. Out of these 24 hours, usually, you're working for 8, or maybe more.

You have time "off work" or more awake time, typically leaving you with sleep time. For most people, it's around 6 – 10 hours of sleep. So, for most people, 16 hours of the 24 hour period they are AWAKE—investing in consuming nutrients, calories, food, junk, etc.

In other words, they FEED for 16 hours and FAST through the night, while they sleep.

Now, with intermittent fasting, instead of having just an 8-hour window where you are not consuming any food while sleeping, you're going to reverse this and FAST for the 16-hour portion of the day.

You're going to put all of your daily caloric intake into an 8-hour window. You eat, then stop eating. 2/3 of the day (16 hours), you are FASTING.

So, I started doing this and eating from 3 p.m. till 11 p.m. I didn't focus on trying to cut calories back. But what I did was, I focused on getting all of my protein requirements in and essential fatty acids.

These were the things that were most important to boosting my testosterone, in my opinion.

Combining intermittent fasting with the next secret, really turned things right side UP, in a hurry...

When you see the next secret I'm going to share with you; it may contradict everything your doctor has told you. Be warned. I'd advise you to explore the work of other doctors if this is the case.

One of the magic foods that I put into my intermittent fasting eating schedule helped me out tremendously in the area of sexual performance. And muscle building, too.

Here it is...

SECRET KEY #2: Dr. Joel Wallach, one of the greatest minds in natural medicine, talked about eating whole eggs every single day. He mentioned that ALL steroid hormones in the body are made up of cholesterol.

So, all of the doctors out there that are labeling cholesterol as a bad thing and using all of these cholesterol-lowering drugs.

In Dr. Wallach's opinion, these are doing a great disservice to male and female patients.

My experience has been profound using "BEAT IT UP!" and staying on a monthly regimen of "PROSTATE RESET."

You can get your FIRST BOTTLE FREE if you want to try PROSTATE RESET, today – just visit http://www.PROSTATERESET.com

I eat six to ten whole eggs every single day and try not to overcook them. So, in essence, this means "soft-boiled," or lightly cooked with the yolk still soft.

So, each day I eat on average six hard-boiled eggs. I put a little bit of Himalayan pink salt on them. Also, I consume enough essential fatty acids.

One of the things you want to do is to make sure that your omega 3:6:9 ratios are corrected. This ratio plays a huge role in the inflammation process and can affect hormonal balance.

Most people in the United States have a 1:17 ratio of omega 3 to omega 6 and 9.

And the ideal ratio is 1:1. In short, we lack sufficient OMEGA 3s to counterbalance the high amounts of 6:9 we consume.

So, with most of the meats that we consume and most of the foods in the Standard American Diet (S.A.D.), things get heavy on the omega 6 and 9.

But, the omega 3s are the most critical component to balance...

The way that I do this is to minimize the amount of processed meat and dairy that I consume on a regular basis.

The reason why is because these are loaded with Xenoestrogens that can cause weight gain and especially if they are also fast food meals, there's SOY in there—awful stuff, and I'll tell you why.

AVOID FAST FOOD AS MUCH AS POSSIBLE (due the processed oils and soy).

What I do is, I take an ample supply of omega-3 fatty acids from a high-quality source. I get them through my company, Complete Ascentials.

So, for the first two weeks, I recommend taking 15 grams every single day to get your levels back up to the optimal standard.

Then, space these out with your meals throughout the day... try to get at least 5 grams per day, total. I'll show you a trick to do this on a budget.

I use 2 – 3 soft gels from our Complete Ascentials (choose whatever high-quality brand you prefer) line, every morning. Then, throughout the day, I use "sprinkled flax seeds" on my meals.

This method is very cost-effective. You have to have a balance. Flax seeds can promote estrogen dominance if you consume vast amounts.

Grinding flax seeds in a coffee grinder... you can carry them and sprinkle a bit on every meal that you have throughout the day. They are high in omega 3 fatty acids.

This way you're always balancing your omega 3:6:9 ratios. Very important! I can't stress it enough...

Lastly, key number three is about avoiding the things that are catastrophic to male potency and sex appeal (not to mention, health).

SECRET KEY #3: Avoid commercially processed soy. I know the media tells you that soy is healthy and that it is beneficial for you, but this is B.S. in my opinion.

If you want to be LEAN and CHISELED, understand the dangers of commercially processed soy!

Consuming soy milk and getting packaged foods with soy in them; protein powders with soy isolate; and soy sauce, etc. These things are likely to cause cellular damage and most likely make you fat and out of shape.

Worst of all, it could nose-dive your testosterone levels. You won't *beat it up*, then. I've been there.

Look at it this way: the reason why commercial farmers use soy for livestock is to fatten up the animal as quickly as possible. So, is that what you want to be? Do you want to be fattened as quick as possible?

And have your hormone levels thrown off and your testosterone levels and estrogen levels way out of whack. Of course not.

Another thing to avoid is high fructose corn syrup (HFC). In a book called Body Rx, by Dr. Scott Connelly, he mentions how high fructose corn syrup (which is found in mostly condiments like ketchup, barbecue sauces, salad dressings, bread, boxed foods) alters the metabolic pathways in your body.

HFC makes your body want to store the calories as fat!

IS THIS A FAT-LOSS SECRET THAT PUT KEVIN TRUDEAU IN JAIL, BECAUSE HE CALLED IT A "CURE?":

Now, a little-known secret that I'm going to tell you about is the use of H.C.G or Human Chorionic Gonadotropin.

If you are in a situation where you have more than 20 pounds to lose, and you need to get yourself in your best shape ever, I recommend RESEARCHING the use of injectable H.C.G.

Disclaimer: no, I didn't say it was a cure or that results are guaranteed. Some people experience ZERO fat-loss.

Now, H.C.G is something that has been around for over 60 years. I got H.C.G injections as I began doing intermittent fasting.

My calories remained quite "high" for the typical H.C.G. diet. I won't diet to 500 calories per day.

No way.

Kevin Trudeau got put in jail for 10 years. He wrote a book called, "*The Weight Loss Cure They Don't Want You To Know About.*"

For me, H.C.G. was a miracle. Always consult with YOUR DOCTOR first. I get my legal H.C.G. here: http://www.HCGSupplier.com (Real H.C.G. Injections).

My doctor prescribed me a round of H.C.G., so I never advocate getting it outside of the legal channels, you won't know what you're getting and it could be "fake."

I focused on keeping my calories moderate, below baseline, around the 2000 calorie a day mark.

My goal was focusing on getting my muscular development optimized by doing weight training and some high-intensity short cardio workouts.

Stubborn body fat that was hanging on year-after-year "melted away" and I dropped three inches off my pants in a few months.

So, today I can take off my shirt, and I have a six-pack, and I can even see the veins coming up from my groin area through my stomach.

You know those muscles that women find super sexy in the groin area? Those are shredded now.

Women (and men) love a sexy, tight and firm stomach. It symbolizes "health" to their reptilian brain.

When you optimize your sex life, and you get your stomach shrunk down and focus on getting yourself healthy, you're going to have so much more enjoyment in your life.

I'm not a doctor, and you should always check in with your doctor to make sure that it is advisable for you to consider doing H.C.G.

These strategies are militant and powerful; these strategies transformed my body fast.

Here's a final tip about coming off H.C.G.

If you return to eating in your old ways (assuming you modified your diet while on H.C.G.) and gain back more than 2 pounds, here's the idea to help "reset" and drop those pounds again—which many people have tried successfully:

Fast for one day. Then, the following day at dinner time, have a four-ounce piece of steak and one apple.

Then fast through the night again.

Check the scale. See if the weight came off!

I only recommend researching H.C.G. if you are about 20 lbs. overweight or more. It's a drastic method, but I experienced no side-effects.

So, with that said, those are the 3 SECRET KEYS to Maximizing Performance in The Bedroom!

Now, notice how it had nothing to do with anything related to the bedroom. Instead, it had everything to do with ***getting off the excess weight, getting yourself lean, getting your hormones optimized and most importantly, to feel confident***.

Getting yourself to feel good about yourself is CRITICAL, because as I said—the psyche is so essential.

When you feel confident, and your hormones are "on point," and your testosterone is optimized... Life is delicious!

Especially in the bedroom.

Bonus Tip - Increase Blood-Flow

Now, another little-known secret that I'll leave you with is to IMPROVE YOUR CIRCULATION and VASCULAR SYSTEM.

Here's a super idea: I recommend you increase your intake of polyphenols. Polyphenols are things like grape seed extract, green tea, white tea, and others. Research them online.

You want to INCREASE POLYPHENOLS and DECREASE LECTINS.

SUPER TIP: you can add in two supplements called, L-ARGININE, and CITRULLINE malate.

A protocol for MALE ERECTIONS I picked up online (very useful information suggested Take 3000 milligrams, which is equal to 3 grams, of L-ARGININE a day).

I recommend getting it in a powder form just mixing it with water. Add in 1,000 milligrams (1 gram) of CITRULLINE malate powder. You can use both in capsules or powders.

It's not going to taste that great, I'll warn you. You can buy capsules if it's easier to consume.

L-ARGININE and CITRULLINE malate can increase your nitrous oxide (and blood flow). For most people, this helps get more blood into the penis (and other areas, too).

It's a great combination for developing bigger "pumps"—know what I mean?

You can aim at cleaning up a lot of the mess if you've done damage to the arteries, etc. Just INCREASE your intake of polyphenols and DECREASE your consumption of lectins.

Doing exercise will probably help, too—if you find yourself mostly sedentary.

CONCLUSION: Your electrical current can be enhanced by maintaining a healthy, lean and muscular body. You can influence your SEXUAL ENERGY and ALCHEMIZE this energy into creating all sorts of new experiences.

The ONLY creative energy in the universe is SEXUAL ENERGY, or what I call "electricity-squared!"

In the next chapter, let's explore the FOUNDATION of your "electrical energy body" and discuss ***Minerals, The Currency of Life!***

CHAPTER 11.

Monatomia - ORMUS, Minerals, and Super-Currency

Your spirit and body work together; you can't improve one without affecting the other, and vice-versa. It goes both ways. The "physical-you" won't work if the spirit is "sick." You're a spiritual being, having a 3D experience of reality.

For example, did you know that the spiritual cause of allergies is a broken heart? Dr. Henry Wright of *Be In Health Ministries* figured this out[3].

Dr. Wright is a medically trained physician, and he's also a minister, and he's brilliant. He took on the case of a woman who was allergic to nearly everything. It was at the point where she had to live in a sterile environment in a bubble.

---

[3] http://www.beinhealth.com/

When he was on the plane going to see her, he was praying and opened his Bible. He saw scripture that led him to the answer. When he got to her, he asked her, "Who didn't love you who was supposed to?" She broke down crying. She cried and cried, and they worked together spiritually, and she was healed. She got set straight in her heart and the body aligned with wellbeing.

I have this mantra that I used when I was young, and I think it might be helpful here:

"I am healthy, wealthy, happy, wise, rich, and totally free for now until eternity."

I love that! It rings, it rhymes, it's positive, and it's true. These days, I'd REVERSE SPEECH my affirmations, but back then it was catchy to rhyme my affirmations.

I want to talk to you about the connection between health and wealth. If you're going to get *life by the tail*, the first thing you have to do is **escape mind control**. I know that sounds a little crazy and woo-woo, but hear me out.

Let me tell you a little story. When I was recovering from Lyme disease, and I was carrying around a lot of extra weight, my body didn't move very fluidly.

The irony is, Lyme disease made me skinny to the tune of 158 pounds and also fat to nearly 220 pounds. My studies of German New Medicine revealed insights into why this happened. For the scope of this book, let's just say it all pertains to WHICH CONFLICTS are most active at the time.

As you know, Lyme disease is a death sentence for most people's psyche because once you believe that you have this awful disease and you're never going to get over it, it creates a perpetuating adrenaline cycle. It's called an ***existence*** conflict in German New Medicine.

Mainstream media can keep you living in fear; our datasphere bombards us with mind control "cages" that keep the masses influenced and controlled. The word "**govern-ment**" means "**control-mind.**"

Everything is out in the open, so there aren't any startling secrets that you can't see for yourself once you're awake.

Back to our idea of an **existence conflict**, which can be triggered by a constant lack of money, diagnoses, the threat of violence or persecution, etc. Our kidneys can be affected by an existence conflict, according to German New Medicine.

Look at the word: kid-neys, or KID-NEEDS.

#SeeReality #OpenYourEyes

Now you have constant torment as your companion which will suppress your immune system quite substantially. This emotional upset can create all sorts of additional conflicts in your psyche.

Regarding German New Medicine:

Dr. Ryke Hamer, a German Physician, spent his life and career studying the connection between psyche and disease. He said, "Through the millennia, humanity has more or less consciously known that all diseases ultimately have a psychic origin and it became a 'scientific' asset firmly anchored in the inheritance of universal knowledge; only modern medicine has turned our animated beings into a bag full of chemical formulas."[4]

I don't know about you, but I feel like I am more than a bag full of chemical formulas.

Let me make a disclaimer right here: I'm not a physician. I'm not a doctor, and I'm not giving you medical advice. I'm giving you my opinions which base themselves on research and personal experience, and I can't legally say that they will cure, treat, or diagnose any disease. My views are my perceptions, and while I might hold them very firmly, they are for entertainment purposes.

I can only tell you what happened to me and what I've seen with my own eyes.

I think that most of the medical community practices are what I call "Rockefeller Medicine." Think of this—what does the word "medicine" even sound like to you? Medici. And who or what were the Medici's?

The Medici family was an Italian banking and political dynasty in the late 1300s and early 1400s. They controlled the money at the time. Just like the Rockefellers and their ilk controlled the "LEGAL" CURRENCY in America at the turn of the century. [p.13] My opinion is that they are more concerned with your money than your health. Sickness is profitable whereas a cure is the end of money spent to treat the condition.

---

[4] http://www.newmedicine.ca/german-new-medicine.php

Most people can't believe any of these ideas, dismissing them as "conspiracy theory"—it's a shame that most people cling to ignorance. It is negligent to inject poison into innocent children without reading the insert and discussing potential dangers vs. benefits (if any) of vaccinations.

#VaxxedMovie #ForcedVaccination

How did we get so *dumbed-down* where we stopped questioning the intentions of our self-appointed decision makers?

According to the vast work done by Kenneth Cousens; six corporations run the entire world educational system, the medical system, and the media.

These six corporations trace back to a few families who have kept it all for centuries.

#Medici

Their goal is to maintain their power, not educate, cure, or inform you. Again, you may or may not appreciate the "conspiracy theory" here... remember, these are my OPINIONS based on research I've done.

The reason I share this with you is that I have skepticism towards "experts" in the mainstream. An expert these days is someone with a shiny-degree who propagates the collective narrative.

So when you look at all these *so-called* experts, and you read all of their scientific journals and papers, does it ever cross your mind how come they never manage to solve the problems they are trying to get more funding to research?

How come there is no cure for cancer (according to them) in the mainstream medical system?

Let me ask it another way, if Raymond Francis—who is an M.I.T. trained biochemist who wrote the book, *Never Fear Cancer Again*—says we DO know what causes cancer and how it can be reversed, who do we listen to anyway?

All it takes is one weaponized-media attack of someone influential, and the character assassination destroys them -- unless there's no one to attack, like Bitcoin. It has survived over a dozen alleged "deaths" touted by the mainstream media.

My point is this: if you don't think you are mind controlled, influenced to believe in a certain way, then how is your fellow man paying half his wages in taxes? Dave Champion, who wrote the book *Income Tax - Shattering The Myths*, claims that most tax attorneys don't even know the law.

Dave has studied the tax code for over two decades. While I'm not an advocate for picking a fight with Goliath (IRS)—hoping your slingshot works that day—is it possible that most people are so credulous they can be "experts" and not have a clue what's going on?

How come the "educated" M.D.s say that nothing can undo diabetes; just give people insulin, forever, while other health researchers like Dr. Joel Wallach and Raymond Francis allege otherwise?

Who is the expert? Where did we get our programming to believe our culture code, according to Clotaire Rapaille: *doctor = hero*. If the hero tells you to vaccinate your child dozens of times, **most people will comply** without questioning any of the potential dangers or side-effects. #WAKEUP

We get our programming from television, movies, schooling, and most importantly; our desire to be accepted and fit into our cult-ure (GUILT programming) sidelines our reasoning with cognitive dissonance instead of critical thinking.

We can no longer think for ourselves because of our pressure to "fit in" and the possibility that non-compliance would cause us violence, threats of violence, persecution, or even death.

Remember, even a loss of a job or income can register as a perceived "death" to the reptilian brain—the part of us that always wins in the decision making process. The reptilian brain only cares about survival and reproduction.

Well, I don't believe any of the so-called talking heads who subscribe to defeatism, and that has always been my position. I don't listen to them or consider their use of "mustard gas" (chemo) as a treatment for cancer makes any logical sense.

Remember what Dave Champion said, how a legal professional in the business of helping you with taxes may not even know the tax law? Would it surprise you that a "health" professional may not know anything about health, nutrition, or any of the studies done about reversing **cellular malfunction**—the *disease* process?

Again, in my opinion, the institutions who fund and conduct "certain" studies may have a vested interest in keeping you from escaping their profit-machine. If you get *well*, then you can no longer be their guinea pig running on their little wheel or be the milk cow for the medical mafia.

So let me tell you the good stuff, the stuff they are not telling you when you get your medical checkup.

We refer back to our friend Dr. Joel Wallach, Dr. Fred Bell, Raymond Francis, and other brave souls who have challenged conventional "thinking"—which is a misnomer.

Dr. Wallach, one of the most brilliant minds in natural healing[5], calls minerals "the currency of life."

Remember in Chapter 7 how we examined the laws of electricity and series vs. parallel circuits? Again, we choose our framework of mind—or **it** programs us—and all POWER flows into that BEING CHOICE.

Where do you think we get this power? We derive this power from electrical current. Minerals are conductors for the current in our bodies. Without adequate mineral stores in our body, our power diminishes, and we can suffer biological "malfunctioning" in our cells.

Here's what I know about minerals. Minerals are mostly depleted from the soil today. It's been that way for over two decades now.

You need to have 90 essential nutrients in your body at all times. If you don't have at least the minimum requirement of minerals, your body organism, and your body mind can't function properly.

---

[5] http://youngofficial.com/dr-wallach/

Consciousness is a direct result of our capacity to conduct CURRENT into our hologram, metaphysically speaking.

Another expert who speaks the same truth is the late Dr. Fred Bell, Ph.D. His work clued me in that minerals (and enzymes) were the foundational piece of health. If you didn't have these bases covered, vitamins wouldn't absorb properly, and cells wouldn't function properly. Consequently, hormones would also become impaired, and HORMONES contain CONSCIOUSNESS.

It's vital understanding, and like most things, that's where the power is, accessible openly—in plain sight, where we will never see the truth.

If you want your body to act as a receiver for the CURRENT, you need to manifest (electricity-squared) your desired outcome; you need "the currency of life."

Without these minerals, your lamp will grow dim.

I repeat: your body conducts electricity. Minerals are essential for this to happen correctly. *Nuff'* said.

I looked at Dr. Wallach's work, and then I studied Ken Rohla's work about fulvic acid. Combining these studies with Raymond Francis' work and Dr. Fred Bell's, I discovered the common denominators I was searching for, to obtain my complete recovery.

Going beyond recovery, the ability to train like a pro athlete today is a gift from God. I'm here to tell you: before my body began getting the required minerals (in the proper form), my recovery was stagnant, and my lamp was undoubtedly dim.

You require vitamins and enzymes, and there are other nutritional requirements as well. But, guess what? Without the minerals—everything else is like having a sports car without the oil in the engine. You may have 12-cylinders under the hood, and it won't matter one bit when the engine seizes and locks-up, would it?

My company—Complete Ascentials—uses fulvic acid in our minerals. It was a breakthrough! Fulvic acid aids in the body's absorption and use of minerals.

I discovered how fulvic acid and volcanic ash could be spun inside a vortex using a blender with magnets. This next piece is where I pick up our conversation about monatomic gold I alluded to earlier when I said there was a better way to get monatomic minerals. I call these "Monatomia."

WATCH HOW YOU CAN DO THIS AT HOME, WITH A BLENDER AND MAGNETS : http://www.Monatomia.com

In this way, I could create ORMEs[6]. By using fulvic acid and ionic minerals. I do this because I want to supercharge my nodes (meridian system acupuncture points: Chakras are collective hubs of nodes). I want my CURRENCY to generate a POWERFUL magnetic field and ATTRACT what I desire.

[6] ORMEs are Orbitally Rearranged Monatomic Elements.

I recognize Western medicine would think this idea is "humbug" — and, I'm not trying to convince you otherwise.

My discovery rests on a personal application in my life circumstances. Ken Rohla's work allowed me to see this "missing piece" to what I extrapolated in the work of the other health pioneers mentioned, earlier.

My question that led to the breakthrough I was looking for was this:

"How do I get monatomic ORMEs into my body without the ridiculous ascension challenges that traditional monatomic gold brought into my experience?"

Beginning with the foundational base—using Complete Ascentials ionic, angstrom minerals and combining fulvic acid, made the process work in a way that delighted me.

Look, I understand you may be thinking, "Oh this is a clever pitchman here... he is selling me now."

You're right, I am. If you're not getting your minerals in your foods, where are you getting them?

Just like if you had a car and you took it into the shop because it kept flashing a red indicator light, and someone said, "Your oil is leaking. Replace it. We'll give you a new oil pan; it's broken."

It's your choice if you want to keep driving the vehicle in the condition it's in, or just fix it now. At the same time, you don't have to buy from my company. There are many reputable suppliers in the world. Naturally, I am biased.

This process is how I got the body that I have now. Before I began with minerals, my body never had any stamina or ability to overcome the complex challenges I faced. Taking supplements wasn't very useful, the damage done by Lyme disease was devastating.

Overcoming the "series/serious/SIRIUS" thought that kept me ensnared in a prison of the five senses, wasn't possible. Hence, the reason I use the saying, "my lamp was dim." My CURRENT was weak; the POWER SUPPLY was low.

Your mind ties directly into your body. I've simplified something you will read about in a moment that I heard from Clif High on YouTube. Here's my short explanation: "Willpower only lasts as long as the body does."

To entrain yourself to REMAIN out of the old BEING CHOICE that kept you stuck in undesirable circumstances, you must use willpower. *Willpower that is not tempered with wisdom is madness, whereas willpower with wisdom is freedom.*

If your body is starving for nutrition because you're not getting adequate minerals to absorb your nutrients, **hormones** will suffer compromise. You may find yourself "CRIBBING" (munching all the time, possibly gaining weight). It is possible to be STARVING and OVERFED.

A sick person is the easiest person to control via fear and mind-programming. Especially someone whose lamp is dim.

Once the body goes, so does the willpower. ***Tired eyes never see a bright future.***

#OurCurrentStateOfAffairs

My health transformation wasn't about competing in a fitness competition. I wanted to be free from disease and be in a body that can **move through life with unstoppable energy**!

Again, nowadays, I put on a 20-pound weight vest and run five miles. A lot of it is sprinting. I go uphill and downhill. Sometimes I need to stop and catch my breath; I'm *hasty*.

After this cardio training, I do another full-on, intense weight-room workout—almost every day.

Practically every day, I do two challenging workouts. I'm 41 years old now, as I write this. Take a look at these pictures: which person looks healthier and happier?

In the picture on the left, I was 30 years old. I could barely walk around the block. I would go into what they call "somatization[7] episodes."

My body would shake, and I would become terrified. I lost control of my body. *Damn right* I was scared! Everything would hurt. After attempting to do a workout, I'd have to call an ambulance and go to the E.R.

I tried to push through the pain and go do what I love — to **move my body and express physical freedom**—only to find out that my body was so depleted, and back then I didn't know it was a "deficiency" issue.

A lot of people with diseases like Lyme disease understand what I went through. Unfortunately, it hurts very badly and is scary. While (ACT) may have addressed the "bugs" to help me overcome Lyme disease, there was a reason my body wasn't RESPONDING to my attempts to build power, speed, stamina, and be *mighty* in my spirit, too!

I learned self-coaching tools to eliminate fatigue and exhaustion, and yet—my muscles would cramp and weaken far too soon. It's all about RECOVERY, and if you're deficient, hormones and vital processes in the cells won't work correctly.

You may be sick right now like I was at one time in my life. You feel like you are going to die. Quite honestly, it's probably not good for you to be weakened and push as I did. I'm just unreasonable about quitting.

---

[7] Somatization is the physical expression of mental phenomena. See http://www.merckmanuals.com/professional/psychiatric-disorders/somatic-symptom-and-related-disorders/overview-of-somatization

I'm not sure what caused the somatization or other issues I faced, maybe the Lyme pathogens were obstructing the nutrient uptake, and there was an imbalance of unhealthy bacteria in my system?

All I can tell you is this—my body began to STRENGTHEN the minute I started using angstrom[8] sized ionic minerals and combining them with fulvic acid.

Why did I choose to use the "smallest" particles for taking in my minerals?

Angstrom-sized particles are small enough where they absorb without having to pass through the digestive system. If you ask most natural health practitioners, they would likely tell you most people have impaired digestion. Common digestive issues may be because of disease or poor eating habits or the over-use of antibiotics.

Your body's electrical system needs minerals for your cells to communicate with each other.

#Think

Clif High also talks about the importance of minerals in one of his YouTube interviews. He mentioned in a broadcast something along the lines of...*whoever controls the food supply on the planet can also control the minds on the planet.*

---

[8] An angstrom is a unit of length. It is 1/100,000,000 of a centimeter. It is used to measure inter- and intra-atomic distances and wavelengths.

Clif said something about the CIA and an idea along these lines: **"Willpower lasts as long as the calories in your body and the sleep in your system."** As in, they can break anyone by just waiting out the body's ability to supply itself with energy.

I surmise that the big companies know that if they control the food supplies, they can control "disease" (profits).

My question is: is there a valid reason minerals used to inhabit in our food supply, but they aren't anymore?

Our agricultural practices over the past century have deprived the soil of these minerals. We stopped growing our food. We stopped using wood ash from cooking stoves to supplement the earth.

Fast-forward a few decades, today we have a lot of diseases. Metabolic syndrome, for example, and the recent surge in diabetes. Our standard of health is why Raymond Francis likely called his company, Beyond Health.

This next paragraph ought to open your eyes:

"Americans are eating plenty of calories, but they're starving to death for nutrients. This is causing an unprecedented epidemic of chronic disease where more than 3 out of every 4 Americans have a diagnosable chronic disease, including children. More and more children are on prescription drugs, and children as young as six are getting strokes. Government surveys have found that most people are deficient in at least several essential nutrients. If you are chronically deficient in even one, you will get sick. That is a guarantee. If that weren't bad enough, much of the food we eat is loaded with toxins. So

right there you've got the two causes of disease—nutrient deficiency and toxicity." - Raymond Francis

It's hard to get academic doctors to understand. It took years to get academic doctors to understand even the simple nutritional fact that scurvy could be resolved with the vitamins in citrus fruits.

The big problem here is: since virtually nobody recognizes this tragedy we call our "food supply," they go to the doctor when they eventually notice signs of deficiency and toxicity. All too often, the person ends ups with a drug—like an opioid. A drug is another toxin that all too often causes further depletion of nutrients, more deficiencies.

#WTF

Are we clueless? Are evil agendas behind all of this? I can't answer these questions for you. The world you live in is a direct result of two things:

Your consciousness.

Your energy.

Let's address each point, briefly.

First of all, here's how the quantum structure of the universe works. It begins with GOD-CONSCIOUSNESS that permeates all of existence. All religions tell us this foundational truth. We can call this POWER "God-consciousness, life force, chi, prana, *The Force*" or whatever you prefer to call it. It is creative power, and it is "electrical" in nature.

This POWER flows from the galactic (*Rishi* self) in towards the crystalline structure you call the "physical body."

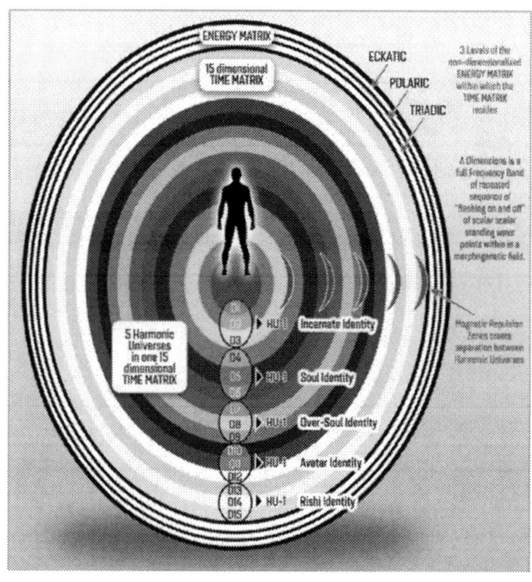

As God-consciousness flows into your BEING CHOICE—*who you are choosing to show up as in your You-Niverse*—it comes in the form of scalar wave energy.

Your "physical body" has a meridian system (used in acupuncture; **nodes**) and Chakra system (hubs of nodes) filled with SUPER-CONDUCTOR minerals—*ORMEs*. Your body collects these deposits of minerals, and they act as AN INTERFACE for the FLOW OF POWER to express itself in your DNA.

Your DNA is like antennas that RECEIVE this GOD-CONSCIOUSNESS and PROJECT out your hologram or external reality. If you FEED YOUR BODY these SUPER-CONDUCTOR minerals, you can increase POWER (prana; chi; life-force; God-consciousness) flowing in—called "Ascension."

If your body is VOID OF the minerals it requires, your *lamp becomes dim*. Your FREQUENCY weakens. You become *less* potent and more susceptible to false-reality matrix "programming," unconsciously re-acting.

We could say, "you have a lower consciousness" to someone in this condition.

Bear in mind, once you RAISE YOUR POWER by giving your body more ORMEs, your THOUGHT-FIELD is amplified. You must be more discerning. Unconscious negativity you have not "cleared" can ABRUPTLY confront you. You cannot ascend without clearing, or learning life lessons you incarnated to grow beyond.

Remember how I warned against using monatomic gold (in most forms, especially "white powder") because Ascension can cause CHAOS in your vibrational field?

The solution is to manufacture your ORMUS from minerals, volcanic rock powders (for growing vegetables you can consume), and fulvic acid, spun in a vortex-field (blender).

A process I've dubbed, *MONATOMIA* is what I've been doing for a couple years now. It's safe, as it requires only water, minerals, and fulvic acid. Again, a demonstration is here: http://www.Monatomia.com

Now, let's talk about energy. Your LIFE consists of energy. Your body is supposed to have vibrant LIFE-FORCE, by FUELING it with proper nutrients.

Your body requires these essentials, in this order: **enzymes, minerals, vitamins, essential fatty acids, proteins.** If you are getting all these needs met, assuming you are not overly-toxic and diseased; your body will give you ENERGY.

I've addressed all these issues and compiled a compendium of knowledge you can get at the links below.

If you want to explore my WELLNESS research, along with my healing journey, from being bedridden with Lyme disease to working out like a pro athlete—over 10,000 hours of research, distilled down to the BEST IDEAS I've discovered is yours, FREE to obtain immediately.

My WELLNESS blog site - FREE Membership, plus: ***The Ultimate Blueprint for Perfect Health!*** http://www.CompleteAscentials.com

My company website for **Complete Ascentials products**:

http://www.CompleteAscentials.com

CHAPTER 12.

You, A Crypto-Currency Millionaire?

In observation of the ongoing bankruptcy of THE UNITED STATES OF AMERICA, INC. (chapter 11), I decided to write about the potential antidote—individual sovereignty over his or her currency.

Here's something I read at www.AnnaVonReitz.com:

THE UNITED STATES OF AMERICA, INC. is now in Chapter 11 bankruptcy. It is owned and operated by the newly revamped FEDERAL RESERVE—another international banking cartel operating under the law of the United Nations City State. Its franchises are named like this: OHIO, NEVADA, FLORIDA...

It's an interesting read, regardless of whether you believe what Anna is saying, or not. If what she points out is correct, your FREEDOM is in serious question, in the "land of the free."

I'm not going to debate this argument as it's not my expertise. However, being AWAKE and AWARE means that I see a pattern that repeats throughout history; great empires fall under the weight of tyranny, the kind of "lawlessness" we've seen escalate in the past several decades.

My concern has to do with the future of my children. I believe we are on the precipice of massive change—heading towards totalitarian control over humanity, or a long-awaited LIBERTY.

After all, it's our last chance at freedom.

#SadButTrue #FascismIsHere #TotalitarianismNext

2008, as I mentioned earlier, was the year that many Americans got bent over (without any vaseline) as the economy screwed them, while banks got bailed out by their friends in the "public servant" profession—with your consent, of course.

"All that is required for evil to triumph is for good men to do nothing." –Edmund Burke

It's okay. I am taking complete responsibility (within myself) for the markets crashing and "clearing" on it, now. So don't think that I'm pointing the finger at you or anyone else.

I'm going to assume some of your loved ones weren't too happy if they lost their home, job, or life savings.

I lost it all that year. Including my health.

I bankrupted right along with the market crash, so my excuse was that I was surfing the collective wave. However, while the world mourned and people lost everything (including me), the following five-year stretch was filled with millions of dollars flowing into my online ventures.

We don't have to surf the collective wave if we choose to exit the dream of learned powerlessness. We VOTE with our CURRENCY and where we INVEST it, matters a great deal.

Bitcoin emerged following the 2008 collapse, which alludes to the idea it could be a "*Problem-Reaction-Solution*" scenario designed to bring in a cashless society.

If you haven't heard, Bitcoin is the world's first decentralized digital currency. The key word: decentralize. It's the opposite of centralization.

Centralization is like playing Monopoly with your friends and the "banker"—well, let's just say he gets to do whatever the heck he wants. In fact, he's arrogant enough to say out loud, "*I care not who makes the rules, so long as I control the money!*"

Centralization is when we put our trust in institutions, governments, and people. How's that worked out so far? It is a scam.

"Absolute power corrupts absolutely," as they say. Remember the sub-prime home loans pre-2008?

In 2006, my wife and I were able to get a mortgage on a home with practically ZERO money down and no proof of savings. All my wealthy friends at the time were mortgage brokers; anyone with a pulse and a stack of leads could close a six-figure income. It was easy to sell mortgages when all the potential clients were approved, regardless of financial stability or proof of income.

Then, ***crash***... the 2008 market bust left money-grabbers (banking cartels) getting their payday, while everyone I knew lost their asses.

If you haven't figured out that all **market manipulation** is planned and executed to **steal the wealth of "everyday people**," you probably have all your money in an IRA, 401K, and the stock market. If you still trust putting all your money in the bank, just try something "honest" and see how "dishonest" you're made to feel: go and ask to withdraw all your savings (if it's over $10k).

Banks rarely keep any substantial cash on hand, and they will potentially report you for a "financial crime" if you try and take out YOUR money. You are guilty, remember? The whole con-game is to make you feel guilty while *they* commit the crimes.

As long as centralization is something allowed, believing in the "good faith" of some government or Federal Reserve—we're screwed. It is alleged that *the Cabal* (unelected *powers that be*) control 173 of the world's most powerful banking institutions.

The Cabal refers to a clique of global-scale plutocratic manipulators who control governments and economies to siphon off the wealth and enslave the entire planet into their stranglehold. While, *them worshipping Satan* is one thing, and *being above the law* is another thing; do you think "they" care whether you get ahead—or lose everything for their gain?

How do you think they do it? **By controlling the money via centralization**. Centralization exists because of this: a collective belief in government, institutions, and people whereby we TRUST someone else to manage our affairs.

An entire book could be written on this subject matter, but I'm interested in explaining the opposite of centralization: belief in "data" as it pertains to **decentralized**, sovereign currencies.

Regarding playing games to understand reality...

Interestingly enough, I had a mentor once who told me a secret about choosing a business partner. She said, "How someone plays a game, is how they will do business."

She encouraged me to play Monopoly with any potential future business partners. She said, "How they do anything is how they do everything!"

Look, all banks themselves aren't bad. Rivers have banks. Following suit with how you BIRTHED into a DOC's hands and your CURRENT is your CASH-FLOW, having a BANK isn't such a bad thing.

It becomes a bad thing when ZERO accountability and all the "*rules*" that apply to people (who must use the BANK), are BANKING their "trust" on the security of their money—and the rules **don't apply** to the banker.

In other words, we need transparency and decentralization, or things are going to get worse—far worse.

Decentralization would REMOVE the corrupt bankers from this entire scenario by obsoleting him. Without their ability to operate unscrupulously, they wouldn't be able to ROB the public with made up bullshit (paper derivatives and other instruments backed by nothing).

It's all done with fancy words like, "quantitative-easing" and "fractional-reserve-banking."

My mentor always says, "When you are confused, there is a deceiver in your midst." Do you feel slightly confused when economists talk about money and how they're always working to solve problems?

These economists are so full of ***chutzpah***, dolling out Keynesian ideologies all day; leading to the destruction of every fiat currency due to hyperinflation.

Here's what is needed to make right the wrongs we have endured in this "rigged" system we're forced to operate in:

The TRANSPARENCY of TRANSACTIONS across a distributed ledger. It would force a **public servant** to remain—*honest*. And, it would force a bank to have assets to cover its loans.

If I were a betting man, my bet wouldn't be on anything positive happening for quite some time regarding politics. Parasites usurp a living off the backs of honest people because we still trust in "people" and governments to take care of us.

And, although I'm a fan of cryptocurrencies, the battle for FREEDOM is going to be an arduous one. #CLEARING

Central banks aren't going to go away with their tail between their legs. If your strategy is to buy Bitcoin and ride it to $1,000,000.00 per Bitcoin—I hope that this happens to you.

Before we talk about my opinion on cryptocurrency and its future, let's explore what it is and why it offers new hope.

So, what is currency and why should you care about CRYPTOCURRENCY?

The currency has evolved over the centuries. Merriam-Webster defines currency as "something that is in circulation as a medium of exchange."

In other words, currency is just something that we use to buy things or exchange one thing for another. Currency does not necessarily in and of itself have any worth.

Over the centuries we've gone from coins, shekels, slaves, paper cash, legal tender, and eventually credit cards. The one thing that these things had in common was centralized control—usually the king or the government.

A central agency—either a banking institution or the government—would decide what the currency was going to be and then manage it accordingly.

Cryptocurrency is the next step in the evolution of currency. The only difference between, say, a ten dollar bill, and ten dollars' worth of cryptocurrency, is that a ten dollar bill is controlled by the U.S. Federal Reserve, and the **cryptocurrency is a product of the free market.**

At least, it was *initially* intended to be this way.

Why is a ten dollar bill worth ten dollars? Because the government says it is. And why will ten dollars buy us ten dollars' worth of goods and services?

We've all agreed that taking that ten dollar bill is a fair exchange for what we are buying.

Cryptocurrency is no different, except without government intervention. So far, that's the case.

The free market determines what the worth of the cryptocurrency is and what it can be exchanged for.

This market is in its beginning, and now may be the time to get in—if you're into *high risk, high reward.*

I'll be upfront; *these are the two fastest ways to become a millionaire in cryptocurrency: start with nothing, or start as a billionaire.*

With HUGE volatility spikes that would make you more at ease on a roller coaster, you could create massive wealth or lose a fortune, overnight. I've seen both sides of the "coin" in this space.

If you're hoping for the "inside expert" to give you the ultimate crypto pick, and that's why you're reading this, it will be a letdown. I've paid thousands-of-dollars to get the best picks from top traders, only to find *they* don't even have a clue.

Overall, the market has been great for long-term holders, but things are changing now. I'll tell you more about this later on.

So, *please* NEVER assume that I'm giving you financial or investment advice. If you can't afford to lose it, crypto is not the place to store it.

The reason I'm writing this is not to give you the "coin" that beats them all, or my top 10 picks. Instead, I'm going to address the VIBRATIONAL ALIGNMENT I've discovered WORKS for most people, who have done well.

I'm talking about the METAPHYSICS of "diving into a turbulent sea of red, or green," that may change its flow in a New York minute.

It's important to realize how early you are if you love the idea of cryptocurrency, whether it's for SOVEREIGNTY or for making money by investing in this new space.

Remember back when the internet was first launched? There was this tremendous growth potential. You had all these millionaires that minted overnight. There were a lot of legitimate opportunities, and there were also a lot of scams.

You had this big tech bubble. A lot of these companies came and went. They're gone today. But a lot of them stuck around and are hugely profitable—think Amazon, Google, eBay, etc.

The ones that stuck around are the big behemoth companies that we spend our time and energy focused on studying. We know that they dominate the world. If you invested early in these companies, you'd have done well for yourself.

The currency revolution and the innovation connected with it is the next phase in that domination.

My thought is, if you're not getting up to speed with cryptocurrency, you're missing out on a huge opportunity. At least begin to learn about it, if nothing else.

#DistributedLedger #Blockchain #Cryptocurrency #Hashgraph

Here's where we are in the midst of this evolution of currency, happening right before our eyes. Throughout history, there have always been three cycles in every boom phase.

Cycle One: This is when the early adopters get in. They're savvy, and they're going to take it over. At this point, it is usually an easy entry.

Cycle Two: This is when the smart money starts to move in. The people who have the power and the influence to bring the masses onboard begin to get involved.

Cycle Three: This is when something is well known and established, and the masses get involved.

Between cycles two and three is where all of the real wealth suddenly appears. Cycle one is too risky. Cycle two is where it proves itself. But by the time you've got to cycle three, it's too late.

We're just shy of Cycle Two, in my opinion. We've seen colossal BULL markets and MASSIVE corrections—but, it's still early. The overall cryptocurrency market is tiny compared to its potential. I'm talking 100X or more potential for growth.

This rapid growth is what happened with the internet. The internet was first getting popularized in the mid-1990s. By 1998, people were talking about it on television and the news, etc. It wasn't that huge until the early 2000s.

That's when the third phase kicked in, and it started to take off like crazy. A lot of people made a lot of money and a lot of people also lost a lot of money.

At the time of this writing, 46% of all ICOs (Initial Coin Offerings) in the cryptocurrency space have failed, or are about to collapse. There have been numerous schemes, frauds, and it's to be expected in a "wild west" environment that had very little regulation.

The big reason so many people are getting ripped off, in my opinion, is because GREED works both ways: "*There's a sucker born every minute and someone willing to exploit this fact.*"

It is this INTERPLAY—the vibrational current of the volatile ocean of "crypto-space"—where I'm doing my teaching. I'm qualified because of my experience in KILLING IT in the cryptocurrency arena, and also going against my better judgment and LOSING A BOATLOAD, fast.

So, if you're early enough to appreciate what I'm about to tell you—this message is for you. You see, once I corrected my ATTITUDE towards crypto, it rewarded me in a way that was always there to enjoy. When I got carried away (GREED), the losses started to pile up.

I'll explain as we proceed further down the path of market phases and cryptocurrency "timing."

In these early stages, as with every boom industry, there will always be legitimate opportunities, and there will also be scams. Cryptocurrency is chalked-rich with scams.

You have to KNOW SUPPLY AND DEMAND: there are VERY FEW qualified "blockchain" developers. Perhaps a few hundred. There are THOUSANDS of projects. Do the math. How will a working product be developed and deployed amongst all these ventures when there's so few who are qualified for the job?

I'll leave you with that sobering insight, while we keep heading to real-time and get my point across.

Regarding cycles: the same thing happened with the housing bubble. All bubbles have these three phases or cycles, as I talked about above.

There are legitimate opportunities, and there are scams – and the trick is being able to tell which is which. Which, you probably won't in the cryptocurrency space if you watch YouTube personalities shill their favorite coins.

Finding a reliable project that will last as a good investment is easier said than done in the cryptocurrency space. Bitcoin could go to $100.00 as quickly as it could go to $100,000.

How, you might ask? Innovation. The tech could be obsolete and government intervention in new ways, making the use of Bitcoin as currency—illegal.

People who profess that it could never happen are not using their history to remind them of how powerful governments genuinely are. What if, say, the IRS can not get more than .04% of Bitcoin users to pay their taxes, willingly? Don't you suppose the government would be a bit upset and take dramatic measures to change this by "outlawing" Bitcoin as a currency?

I'm just saying, it's possible.

Now, on the positive side of things, let's hope for the SOVEREIGN FREEDOM that may, one day, emerge from the technology itself.

Especially now, if you can get in at the right time and in the right place, you can make an absolute fortune.

We are in that sweet spot right now with cryptocurrency. We are in the second phase, about to go into the third phase, probably within the next two or three years.

All sorts of hedge fund managers and people that control trillions of dollars have taken a keen look at Bitcoin and other cryptocurrencies. At the time of this writing, PayPal has filed a patent for an expedited cryptocurrency transaction system. You can opt to use Bitcoin and other cryptocurrencies to buy virtually anything you can think of already—we're still very early.

And, this is where things may be a bit rocky. I'm just going to say what's on my mind:

It is my opinion that "big money" players are already manipulating the cryptocurrency markets by artificially pumping them (creating a bubble inside the market to attract new money)—then dumping them.

Most people buy at the wrong time, getting in when the mainstream media is telling them how fast the price is soaring. By this time, the experienced "whales" are looking to sell the "news." The savvy investors buy low and sell high, every time.

It should be common sense, but it's not emotionally easy to do. When a stock or crypto tanks in the red-sea of a "correction," most people try and get out while they still can!

The smart money then rebuys at the new bottom, repeating the cycle over and over—siphoning new investor money into their pockets.

So, if that's the case, what's the appeal?

Like Bill Gates said, "Cryptocurrency is not going away. It is the future." Cryptocurrency will control the economy.

The currency market is a $150 trillion market.

That's $150,000,000,000,000.00. It has to be filled by technology, and in a way that corresponds with the times that we are living in today.

We are in the digital, technological age. Cryptocurrency is the future. Right now there are fortunes to be made—and lost.

By having the right education, you can start to see exactly where you can fit into this innovative stage and plant your flag—if you like *high risk.* Not everyone does. Now may or may not be the time for you to get a piece of the action.

You'll require a healthy degree of emotional intelligence and investment savvy, just be warned. Your investment could double or triple in a week—or less. It could also do the opposite.

What is a sound cryptocurrency? What does a person look for in a solid "coin" or "token?"

There are only two legitimate purposes for cryptocurrency, and it's essential that you learn what they are:

A CURRENCY OR A UTILITY

CURRENCY: If you are looking at a currency (coin), I'd ask the hard question: what makes it better than Bitcoin? If you can't come up with a solid answer, it's probably a con-job coin that will go to zero value in a year or less.

There are issues with Bitcoin which leave room for improvement: the main problem is "privacy" at this point. With Lightning Network allowing the *scaling debate* and *high transaction fees* to be put to rest, there are not many other flaws in Bitcoin's present use as both a store-of-value (Gold 2.0) and as a currency.

UTILITY: There are many projects where you can use the tokens inside their platform. Another utility is that specific projects can be used to build on top of—like Ethereum and EOS. These tokens offer value because they help build the infrastructure of other projects.

My personal opinion is as follows:

***Utility tokens** are more valuable to me in considering"potential big winners" because of their PURPOSE and the PROBLEM THEY ARE SOLVING. As I said a few moments ago, unless we're getting complete privacy—like ZCash, ZenCash, and Monero—what possible advantage would the project offer that Bitcoin can't accommodate?*

I am a fan of one particular company, called Stellar Lumens. At the time of this writing, it is $.30 per token, and it checks out on many areas of due-diligence I've done (for opportunity to make gains).

I'm not recommending that you go out and buy into this project, or any other I've listed. It would be foolish for you to dive into something without doing your research.

If you can understand WHAT PROBLEM a token or coin solves, you'll be able to weed out probably about 90% of the currencies that are showing up on the ICO[9] lists, as they happen today.

I mean, for Christ's sake, why do we need a coin for dentists? It seems about as far-fetched as creating one for my son's basketball team. And, this can be accomplished in about an hour.

---

[9] Initial Coin Offering

Yes, I could build on Ethereum and create the next shill coin to hype in the market for my son's basketball team. The good news is; it would fail miserably. "Those days" are soon to be forgotten with new SEC regulations and investors becoming far more discerning. Smart money will LEAVE the useless projects and move into only the real players that solve legitimate problems.

WHAT ABOUT THE "GET RICH QUICK" ICO LAUNCHES?

Most of the ICO's fail to sustain their presence and evaporate their value towards zero, quick. It's frightening to the speculator who gambles in this space.

You're thinking, "Matthew, so far you've told me that I'm probably going to lose my butt in this deal, so where is the actual appeal!?"

You already know, the opportunity is just as exciting as the fear over the potential of losing money. And, it is this very dynamic—VIBRATIONALLY SPEAKING—where I'm going to interject my observations and experiences, from being involved in cryptocurrency investing.

If you can get into the right place at the right time with accurate information, it is common sense that you have a vast potential of opportunity to *make an absolute killing.*

What you have to capture that's different than most other markets, is that a month in "crypto space" can be the equivalent of a year or several years in the old economy.

Things can move so fast that it is imperative that you get either or both of these two things: helpful advice from someone who has been successful in the space for at least a year or longer and spends time learning. You have to learn how to protect your cryptocurrency and keep it safe.

I'd also recommend exploring your exit-strategy in advance. By not taking "profits off the top" at the height of a BULL MARKET, you might kick yourself. Things could go south fast, and massive gains can be wiped out in days or hours sometimes. Are you going to hold long-term? Or dollar-cost-average your way into positions on the way down and take profits off the top on the way up?

Have a plan and stick to it. That's emotional intelligence. Your strategy is more important than anything else.

You can join my Facebook group if you'd like to get my latest insights into this space, or share your own!

Join my private Facebook Group **A.U. Crypto** at:
http://www.AUCryptoGroup.com

Can you use the law of attraction to be a Cryptocurrency Millionaire?

Now that you know the basics about cryptocurrencies and the law of attraction, how can you combine the two to become a cryptocurrency millionaire?

As I mentioned earlier in the book, my friend Joel is a cryptocurrency millionaire. He has had some of the biggest names in social media—people who run multimillion-dollar enterprises—consult with him about investing in "crypto."

Joel immerses himself in the world of cryptocurrency and gets out there to meet people in the space. Others, like Teeka Tiwari and James Altucher—who offer memberships to access their knowledge—can be helpful.

You're probably busy, so leveraging other people to do the digging can save time and money, too. Remember, many people who've never made a dime in their lives can easily give out crypto investment advice. They'll tell you "this is not investment advice," and the next minute; they shill out the new coin they bought telling you to buy it, too.

While it seems harmless, you have to remember the FACT that whatever kept them broke in the past, will probably be the reason they unconsciously chose a project that goes south in the future—or, something will happen to keep their "status quo" in their financial affairs.

How can I say something like this? Look, it's simple. There is no magic bullet—not even cryptocurrency—that will make your "average Joe" suddenly become a wealthy and flourishing individual. Unless, of course, he also changes his BEING CHOICE and allows a new identity to emerge. Yes, I've seen it happen. It's not too commonplace.

I prefer to find advisors in the space who have been very comfortable with millions of dollars in their reality, or at the least—several hundred thousand. If they have a PROVEN track record of being right, not based on "lottery luck," but reliable intel they receive, my ears are usually listening.

Many of these investors have private groups you can join or gain access. Just be careful of "pump and dump" schemes. Some groups exist to merely recommend a ***shitcoin*** and get everyone to pump it, while the gambler inside of their prospect's mind goes "all in" only to realize he's late to the party.

These days, I don't touch ICOs. At one time, not too long ago, you could invest in just about any ICO project and have a chance to get at least 2x as soon as the coin hit the exchanges.

Here's an example: I got excited about a project called Electroneum, back in October of 2017. Electroneum is a British-based cryptocurrency.

I predicted it would be a 10x play—imagine earning ten times your initial investment! Guess what, when it hit the exchanges and officially launched, it soon reached a pinnacle point of 20x (to the date of this writing).

I sold my position in Electroneum at 10x as it was cooling off, knowing that this was my strategy all along. The value of each ETN (Electroneum) is around $.06 at the time of this writing, down from an all-time high of $.20.

Unfortunately, I do not hold a strong opinion of the long-term potential for this project. That's not important. The 10x multiplier is what mattered. In other words, having a plan to pull out profits when a coin is "breaking out" may be worth considering.

It looks like this: example, "xyz fake coin" (made up).

Current price on CoinMarketCap.com: $1.00.

I'm expecting it to break out after a recent dip (market correction) where I feel it is now undervalued. As the price was dropping below my "buy in" price ($1.20), I picked up positions at $1.20, $1.07, $1.00.

The all-time high for (xyz fake coin) was $1.55.

I'm expecting the value to go up over the next few months, based on advancements in the project. I'm hoping they'll be announcing big news about strategic partners any time now—so this "fire sale" is a good buy, in my opinion.

My strategy is as follows:

Exit point #1: $1.30 (25%)

Exit point #2: $1.40 (25%)

Exit point #3: $1.50 (25%)

Exit point #4: $1.60 (25%)

If the price drops below $.85, I pull out of this project and cut my losses.

Of course, the numbers I used are entirely make-believe. But, the overall strategy of HAVING A PLAN and STICKING TO IT helps me avoid getting swayed with "FUD" (fear, uncertainty, doubt) and "FOMO" (fear of missing out).

Every time I've lost money in cryptocurrency, or made tactical mistakes that could have been avoided—here's what I did wrong:

Invested more than I could afford to lose. This gamble is by far, the worst thing anyone can do. Greed has taken the reigns and disaster is likely. *When they say "size matters,"—think position size if you're going be in bed with a cryptocurrency.*

Bought into FUD or FOMO. Scanning YouTube or having someone tell me about an ICO or coin that's going to go parabolic (*to the moon*, as they say), without any foundational reasoning for the project to even exist; remember the only valid purpose of a cryptocurrency is either as a **utility** or **currency**. The other way I lost was buying into fear; panic selling is what it's called. This inevitable "FUD" is why you have to stick to your plan!

One of the people I look up to for financial advice is Doug Casey. He described cryptocurrencies as "trading sardines"—you don't eat these sardines, you trade them.

I grabbed this next paragraph from Doug's website:

It's like that old joke about sardines. You've got eating sardines and trading sardines. Commodity currencies are eating sardines. Fiat currencies are trading sardines. Of course, there's no guarantee that Bitcoin is going to be accepted a year or two from now. It's a high tech innovation, and maybe a Version 2.0 will collapse the value of the current version. So in a few years, we may find that Bitcoin fails the store of value test. But it's accepted at the moment.

MOST PEOPLE WANT TO "HODL" THEIR BITCOIN

Most people want to hold their cryptocurrency, what they call "HODLing." I don't particularly feel safe doing this.

It defeats the purpose that underlies a SOVEREIGN CURRENCY. Look, by "not" spending and using it—declaring it mainly as a store of value—you remove the potential of DISPLACING THE MODEL (centralized banking) that eliminates your sovereignty.

If you participate in cryptocurrency, spending is the only way to build the use of a currency. **If it doesn't circulate, it stagnates.**

#Think #CurrentStagnation

I'm not into HODLing for the long-term. I'm also not into ICOs anymore. The SEC classifies cryptocurrencies as "securities"—making ICOs mostly out of reach for the average U.S. citizen to participate in, post-2018.

If that wasn't bad enough, the IRS decided to pour salt on the wound of the bleeding hearts (over ICOs) by imposing a tax on trading or exchange of the cryptocurrencies. All I can say is, "*Are we ever going to find a way to exit the over-reach and outright **fleecing** of the public in the USSA?*"

We are sitting at the Monopoly table I described at the beginning of this chapter. It's nearly impossible to be 100% compliant if you are a cryptocurrency trader—so where's the silver lining in all this? We'll get to that shortly, be patient.

A myriad of forces are at work AGAINST cryptocurrencies, and they're also just cumbersome as heck. It's a pain in the butt to store cryptocurrencies and *safeguard* your seed words. Yes, it's complicated.

HERE'S THE SILVER LINING YOU WANT TO HEAR

There will be more fortunes made in cryptocurrencies.

The party is not over. Round two of the BULL MARKET is likely just around the corner. At the time of this writing, the entire market cap is below $400 billion. We were up over 100% back in early December of 2017.

Warning: the game has likely changed since 2018.

The most effective strategy before 2018—*for the average person*—would have been to hold the top cryptocurrencies, like Bitcoin, Ethereum, Litecoin, and a handful of other prominent cryptocurrencies.

Again, if crypto (currency) is not a currency, rather speculation only, and THOUSANDS of them flood the market—where is the actual value? What are you HODLing?

Today, there are THOUSANDS of cryptocurrencies and new ones that make Bitcoin's speed and efficiency look like a typewriter in an Apple computer store.

This competition doesn't mean Bitcoin isn't going to win the race, some of the best developers in the world are committed to Bitcoin's long-term potential.

Here's my observation: I like to tell people—**scared money never made money**. There are a lot of people out there that are so afraid. They should not invest, in my opinion. Stuffing their dollars under the mattress is "safer" for them.

Scared money not only doesn't make money, but it also creates the environment for *market manipulators* to eat someone else's lunch.

This manipulation began **profoundly** impacting the cryptocurrency markets in late 2017. My objective is to fit my message into the gap of "what to do about all this manipulation?" After all, the CORE of it FEEDS off *greed,* and it's subsidiary impulses—"FUD" and "FOMO."

More than half of all Americans have less than $1,000.00 in a savings or investment account[10].

If you're down to your last few dollars, this is NOT the time to aim for the fence. Instead, *take a position size that allows you to FEEL safe, and opportunistic.* This "less resistance" is the VIBRATIONAL SPACE you need within yourself to ATTRACT MORE prosperity. You MUST feel rich to manifest riches.

Speaking of "scared money don't make money," I know a man who has a health condition who tried socking everything he owned—almost $1M—into a cryptocurrency that he believed would give him "F YOU" money, in no time.

[10] https://www.cnbc.com/2017/09/13/how-much-americans-at-have-in-their-savings-accounts.html

He was sick of sitting at our metaphorical Monopoly table with the bullies rubbing his face in the dirt. So he risked it all at the peak of the last bull market. #Greed #Fomo

He lost it all. Every penny. As the crypto he got involved in was dropping to zero, he frantically ("scared money" style) sunk it into another project that took every dime. #Fud

He could have approached his strategy level-headed. Perhaps by having a stop-loss (where he moved back into fiat), that would have prevented him from losing it all?

There are many others just like him who allowed GREED to drive them into unreasonable *re*actions, trying to navigate EMOTIONALLY TURBULENT waves—without a life preserver.

#Gamblers #TheyPlayToLOSE #Unconsciously

In my early days of coaching, I had a gentleman come to me and ask for help. He couldn't afford to hire me and my time is valuable. Due to his recent divorce and the fact he was living virtually homeless (because of a gambling addiction), I offered three hours of my time to assist this man.

It was a grave mistake on my part. Since this man wasn't paying for the advice, he didn't <u>own</u> the advice. When he asked me, "Why am I addicted to gambling?"

I told him, "You are playing to lose. In your case, to lose it all." I felt his energy; I'm clairsentient—his life story emerged in my "knowing"—so, I asked him to tell me what his dad had in common with him.

He was startled, "How did you know that my dad was a gambler and he brought hardship on our family?"

I told him, "you didn't come into this world to take his karma, but you are trying to resolve it for him."

He hung up on me. We never got our three sessions in that I offered him. The truth wasn't what he wanted to hear.

Several months later, he called me and invited me into a business opportunity with him. He found a new way to gamble. Instead of acting the role of coach, I told him to let me think it over. A couple of weeks later, I signed up underneath him in a Network Marketing venture to help him out.

He called me to thank me for enrolling, and he was on an optimistic high, having experienced some success with a few people getting involved. Deep down, I wish he would have been OPEN TO RECEIVE mentoring. He was still gambling, and the only reason most people **bet** "high risk" for is to lose.

About a month later, I get a call, and it's law enforcement. They were calling all the recent numbers this man dialed in the past several weeks. He was missing. His ex-wife had not seen him for quite some time. She was worried. His phone remained, and no further trace of him led to any clues.

Nobody ever called me to tell me what happened. I felt a nudge inside to look up his name about two weeks after I got that call. He was found dead. This man committed suicide, or so it appeared.

While I don't know the story of what happened, I felt what was inside of him. During that first brief call, before he hung up on me, I could see what he was doing. He wanted to make others suffer for what he felt his entire life; he took his father's karma (in the womb).

When I saw the news online and read about what happened to him, I cried. His pain was very unconscious. He wouldn't allow me to help him, and I wasn't familiar with the "clearing" power of Ho'oponono. The reason I'm telling you this story is because UNCONSCIOUS SABOTAGE caused him to approach every opportunity TO LOSE. He was addicted to gambling.

Many so-called "investors" in cryptocurrency are gamblers who haven't explored what they're doing.

While they may not take their lives in such a dramatic way as the man I told you about, they could easily be seduced by the allure of "get rich quick" profits with a "scared money" mentality. Money is scared to be around them.

Why? It's energy. We are our MONEY. It's our CURRENT that we have CHOSEN to represent itself as OUR SELF WORTH, based on our BEING CHOICE.

If I could have helped this man for the 3 hours I offered, we would have focused 100% of our time NOT involving external opportunities—instead, choosing to BE SOMEONE who magnetizes wealth because money can't stay away.

CRYPTO: THE GREATEST WEALTH TRANSFER?

It doesn't matter if you are involved in THE GREATEST WEALTH TRANSFER IN ALL OF HISTORY if you're the one who is transferring your wealth to market manipulators, does it?

SCARED MONEY TYPE 1: This type of *scared money* is where money is scared to be around you, and it flees as soon as you let it out of your reach. "FUD" and "FOMO drives this impulse."

SCARED MONEY TYPE 2: Hucksters use the saying "scared money never made money," to convince others to hand over the loot. This impulse is pure GREED (where the victim meets the victimizer unite) and "FOMO" takes over logic and reasoning.

SCARED MONEY NEVER MADE MONEY

It means this: **if you are afraid you're going to lose, you will. Somehow it will happen.** You create it to occur in the vibrational field you are in—<u>your state of being</u> is in "failure" mode.

The best experts I pay attention to in finance, like Teeka Tiwari, James Altucher, Jeff Berwick, Doug Casey, and others who invest in cryptocurrency—use RATIONAL POSITION SIZES.

Remember how I said that "**if you make it okay to fail, you also make it okay to succeed?"**

Do you remember that little saying from earlier?

Now, tie it in with this age-old investment advice:

TO BUILD WEALTH, NARROW DOWN.

TO PRESERVE WEALTH, DIVERSIFY.

If you desire wealth building, here's what has worked for me in the cryptocurrency space: narrowing down to the "best picks" and holding rational position sizes to BUILD WEALTH.

Having a strategy is critical. Like I wrote earlier, what is your exit strategy or stop loss? To PRESERVE WEALTH, you may need to consider Doug Casey's analogy of "trading sardines"—you don't eat them, you trade them.

This idea is demonstrated where I showed you an example of "xyz fake coin" and the strategy used to "pull profits out" and park them elsewhere. Where is elsewhere, you ask? You answer the question: where are your eating sardines?

Do you feel safe having dollars in the bank? Gold? Silver? Investing in Pot Stocks? What's your plan to DIVERSIFY to PRESERVE once you've built the wealth?

If you captured what I shared with you, you gain the advantage of my "first year in cryptocurrency" and the experiences I've had. The most important thing you'll gain is by learning from my mistakes.

You see, I've made a lot of money in cryptocurrency—in spite of the fall off that occurred in late December of 2017. You'll gain nothing from those experiences, other than the fact that I got involved in SOLID PROBLEM-SOLVING COINS/TOKENS that grew over the course of 2017.

You can gain more from my mistakes, again they all occurred when something emotional inside of me took over: GREED and FEAR, straying me away from a "rational" strategy.

It can happen to anyone if you fail to stick to your plan.

#EmotionalIntelligence #FinancialIQ

Now, let's gaze into a crystal ball before we leave this chapter and explore what the future could be...

You are again at the Monopoly table, as you have no other choice but to play. This time, things are a bit different. There are several bankers at the table—each one of them validating the other's transactions. The arrogant bully who yelled out loud, "I care not who makes the rules, as long as I control the money!" He's gone. People got sick of him and decided to innovate the game to include many "sets of eyes" to spread control over the money far and wide.

You notice another change that occurred; the "rule maker" is also gone. He has been replaced by a distributed-ledger-like series of "rule makers" who keep everyone accountable to the same rules. As strange as it seems, the game looks fair—you can play and win.

As everyone takes their turn and rolls the dice, a perfect accountability system makes the game fun and enjoyable. The mischievous "banker" who stole everyone's wealth (working in cahoots with his "rule maker" friend), are long gone and yet, never forgotten.

Looking back, all the players at the table reflect on how they lost every time in the past: they gave away their power to centralized authority-figures who didn't play the same rules. By incorporating a decentralized model of "banking" and "rule-making" accountability, the bullying stopped. People weren't afraid to prosper and play the game anymore.

You smile and think that your decision to OPT-IN to the idea that "the game could change" by removing centralized control over the MONEY SUPPLY—it worked!

You feel a sense of gratitude that your kids and future generations may learn from the mistakes your great-grandparents made, back when they agreed to "bullying." They didn't have a choice.

Today, the technology to obsolete that reality is right here, and you've got first-mover's advantage. It's not just about making a short-term profit. It's about SUPPORTING an EVOLUTION of CURRENCY. It's about moving you back into the SOVEREIGN and out of the false-reality matrix.

In a FREE MARKET, you can rise to MILLIONAIRE STATUS on the virtue of the VALUE YOU PRODUCE. If you allow this freedom to erode by remaining a "victim" to a bully "banking system"—totalitarianism will capture the hour.

CHAPTER 13.

The Ultimate Daily "Cleanse" to End Self-Sabotage - For Good

I received a revelation that came to me a couple of weeks ago. It completed itself on February 22nd, and I wanted to put it out today.

As I write this chapter, a signed copy of *AT ZERO* just showed up in my mailbox. Synchronicity? You bet. After all, this chapter is about Ho'oponopono — many thanks to *Dr. Joe Vitale* for making it "famous" and spreading it for us to discover.

Hint: you can use this method to "cleanse" anything in your world, including the things we covered in the last chapter.

And this is going to be transformational if you just pay attention and just check within yourself. Look through the history of your life and see if it lines up.

See if there's wisdom that brings you to a place of remembering and knowing that what I say is true.

If not then you know maybe this isn't for you. But I'm pretty confident if you line up thought and circumstance in your life, you'll discover that what I'm saying is spot-on...

Okay, it all begins with the Bible in Romans 8:28. What that says in the King James Version is:

"And we know that all things work for good to them that love God; to them who are called according to his purpose."

I'm gonna dissect this and show you how it translates into real life application as well as you putting to use in your life.

Dr. Ihaleakala Hew Len (Dr. Len) and Dr. Joe Vitale talked Ho'oponopono in the book *Zero Limits*. The book is all about Ho'oponopono.

In short, H'oponopono is a tradition where you are doing healing on everything that comes up in your life, and you're healing yourself only.

In essence, you're taking complete responsibility that everything that shows up in your world is an out-picturing of your consciousness.

Now that's quantum physics 101. So that's not even "old-timey" Bible type talk. But I'm going to show you how old-time Bible talk has been saying the same thing.

Here's what Dr. Len said is the magic; how he healed patients without ever seeing them. He took on the task of treating some of the toughest cases—people that were in a criminally insane ward who are some of the worst criminals out there. Many of them were considered "throw away cases."

How did he do it, you ask?

Dr. Len would look at their files, and he would recognize that everything that showed up in his world—including them and their problems—was really inside of himself.

He didn't treat anybody else other than himself, nor did he have an opinion about who, what, where, when, why, or how... In other words, Dr. Len didn't put a judgment out into the universe; that's important to understand.

He looked within himself, thinking about that person or that situation, and said "I love you." Repeatedly.

Fascinating, isn't it?

Saying "I love you" is the short version. Or, "Thank you." The complete Ho'oponopono is "I love you, I'm sorry, please forgive me, thank you."

Before I tell you another compelling story about Ho'oponopono, here's a link to Dr. Vitale's short article about Dr. Len and his miraculous work: http://bit.ly/2FItTPX

Another miraculous story about Ho'oponopono is about a woman who began studying law of attraction. She followed her excitement through to a few various teachers.

A message about getting very specific about what she wanted came to her loud and clear; she wanted $40 million (or something better).

The other thing she realized: she needed to get "clear." The one thing she wanted to convey was that she went to bed saying the following four statements ever night: "I'm sorry, I love you, please forgive me, thank you." Just not in that order. Here's a link to the video: http://bit.ly/2owTYdp

It's all about getting clear.

Let's go back to Romans 8:28 where it says, "And we know that all things work together for good to them that love God."

It doesn't say "we think we know," and it doesn't say "we have a theory." It says, "WE KNOW." In other words, this is how it works.

It says all things work together for good to them that love God. Now that's precisely what Dr. Len is doing. He's looking to the God within himself and loving God.

Can you see it? Are you registering the eternal truth that has been written thousands of years ago? That's how you solve the unsolvable problems in your life.

I'll show you where they're coming, and how to shift into parallel universe's... but, CLEARING is the "missing link" to it all.

You don't look at the problem situation with problem consciousness and solve it with that same mindset. Einstein said, "You can't solve the problem with the same level of consciousness that's creating it."

So this is deep, but here's how you get out of the conundrum: you turn to the God within, recognizing that every situation, person, problem, perceived challenge or anything that's bothering you is your response-ability.

What you want to dissolve is coming from within you. It's being projected into your hologram, by what I call "The Memory Stick."

These are the karmic memories you've been storing in your DNA. All the "junk" in life is merely our interpretation of phenomena that our consciousness is bringing forth to heal.

We must begin our manifesting process from the following understanding:

You are the deity. God is expressing itself as you. You're the puppet and the puppeteer at the same time. So turn within to God. Here is what the scripture says, "All things will work together for good to them that love God."

So, if you love God, turn within and keep saying, "I love you" in regards to anything that shows up in your You-niverse that requires cleaning up.

Whatever is happening in your life is neither good or bad until you make a judgment. These judgments are the karmic debts we are paying in the first place!

So, put them to rest and let the "dead bury the dead."

Whatever situation arises, think about it then turn within to say "I love you, I'm sorry, please forgive me, thank you."

Let me tell you how this worked out in my life...

The first time I had to work through a lot of these issues was as a teenager. I had a problem with depression, and I was angry all the time.

To make a long story short; it was when I started thinking about God (talking to God) within my mind saying, "God's gotta be the solution here because I've heard about God... and this has got to be my answer."

When I reached a place of love, as in feeling "clear" and back in harmony within myself... even though I thought God was still outside of me, the challenge resolved itself.

My healing came moment-by-moment as the universe laid out the blessings for me to receive. It will always do this when you get clear!

Fast-forward to my late teens. I developed what "they" called eating disorders. Over five years I suffered from bulimia and anorexia hanging over me, like a guilt-complex from hell.

It seems that I forgot my earlier miracle. Instead, my focus was on using the mind. I read over 700 self-help books, yet nothing was getting me out of that sickness.

Things got worse with every new rule and opinion some new author gave me, deepening my (misunderstanding) of what was going on inside of myself.

Look, I'm going to be blunt. Most self-help thought leaders are trying to tell you something. In other words, one person would say that the cause of my eating disorders was a food intolerance, and the next author would say it was because of trauma.

Before I knew it, my mind was so full of crap that I had over 1,000 wrong answers that led me to give up and surrender ultimately. As my willpower gave out, it just so happened I rediscovered this same "clearing" ability to release the eating disorders—just like the depression.

We all intuitively know how to release these things. The problem is; the world is so full of B.S., and we hand over our power to so-called "authorities" who try the impossible: to live our life for us, by the rules they set up.

We all do it.

We discover something that works, and then, we share it with someone else. It's just a matter of time before someone says, "it did nothing for me."

Or worse, "it gave me a bad reaction." I've discovered the golden rule (if we're going to make rules) is NEVER to advise unless someone asks. Otherwise, we're imposing, and it usually ends up in tears.

You are the cause and solution to whatever challenges you are facing!

You see, you can't use your mind to solve a problem that the ego is creating. Further reinforcing the problem with "other minds" that conjure up books of information on the subject, leads us to one fact alone: the path to the result is never the same for two people.

The only caveat is; we can ALLOW someone's opinions to become "permission slips" for us to use. If we do, we can experience our version of their rules in our (belief) experience. What we believe is what we see.

I give a warning about this because it works both ways. We can listen to a doctor tell us a condition is permanent or fatal just as quickly as we can look to someone to tell us it is nothing at all to be concerned over.

A perfect example is the work of Surprise Sithole, a pastor who has raised over a dozen people from the dead.

No, I'm not making this up. Even better than this, this man has trained others how to do the same with proof-positive results.

I'm talking about people being dead for days or weeks... who were raised from their dead, cold (so-called physical appearance) and resurrected!

After hearing about Surprise a few years ago, I reached out to him through his ministry. At the time, I had been ill for several weeks—going on three months—with mononucleosis. My kids had it, too.

I asked Surprise to pray for us. He obliged, joyfully. Within a few days, after he prayed, we were all well again.

The day after he prayed, I began having hot flashes and feeling changes happening in my body. I could sense my ALLOWANCE of his faith in

Jesus (to heal), was something I accepted. In other words, I received his belief, and the miracle ensued.

Just how powerful are you, you might wonder?

Let me share another story as I segue into this for a moment. I want you to grasp the sense of WHO you are.

When the pinnacle of Lyme disease had me bedridden in 2009, I began doing the ABC Break Process that's described in my book *ALLOW - Mastering The Law of Least Effort to Receive Your Desires!*

One day, someone turned me onto the work of the late Phineas Parkhurst Quimby. A nineteenth-century clockmaker by trade turned "master healer" out of necessity. To make a long story short, he was healed of a fatal condition called consumption.

Quimby's body was weakened and frail, and according to the belief of the day, he would have drowned in his fluids with this disease. It was a terrifying experience for Quimby.

The miracle came while he was sitting on top of a hill. He heard of someone curing the same disease by riding horseback.

Quimby knew of another man who experienced healing this way. In essence, what I'm saying is this: it was a permission slip, offering Quimby a shift in consciousness.

While on the hill, something startled Quimby's horse. He recognized that he wouldn't be able to get back down the hill by his strength alone —if the horse left without him.

As the horse demonstrated its intent to run off, potentially leaving Quimby up on the hill (to die), he grabbed ahold and hung on for dear life.

When Quimby reached the bottom of the hill, a miracle happened. He recognized his strength had returned, and he was suddenly in a body that seemed well again.

This experience was a breakthrough that inspired him to discover mesmerism and the truth about man, which he described as being under the influence of beliefs, or better said;

"Human misery universally arises from some error that man admits as true. We confound our fears with the idea feared, and place the evil in the thing seen or believed. Here is a great error, for we never see what we are afraid of."

—Phineas Parkhurst Quimby

Since P.P. Quimby was born on February 16, and my birthday is February 17, the "woo woo" side of the Aquarius in me became fascinated by his work. I studied his work for years.

On that note, let me share one last idea and story with you. This information all pertains to how "The Memory Stick" is the cause of all the problems (perceived) we experience. It's our job to clear and rewrite the software that engineers our reality.

Remember, it's a hologram illusion built on opinions (lies), and when we distill it down to a few truths—like God being you; all power within you—we take our power back.

Here's another example that indirectly ties into Quimby's work. A woman with a lifelong history of illness came to him. She wanted to heal from a severe injury, or so she thought. In three days, she recovered after having a conversation with Quimby.

That's how he did it; Quimby healed through a conversation on two levels of being. He spoke to the (mortal illusion) of the physical man, correcting the mind of the lies. Quimby believed any idea that didn't bring about happiness and peace of mind was an opinion, or lie.

In parallel, Quimby visited the place (a trauma where he alleged the person remained "bound" in consciousness) and brought the person to NOW-TIME and out of their fear, which the woman he healed in the above example called: the fountain of all disease.

"Fear is the fountain of disease." –Mary Baker Eddy

Mary Baker Eddy's formula was simple: destroy the lie causing the false appearance of disease and remove the fear associated.

When something was stuck, there was often a MORALITY issue involved. In other words, if we choose to break our own rules (doing something we believe is not good for us or others), we suffer. I'll lay out a perfect process for dealing with guilt at the end of this book.

Back to Mary and her work:

Mary Baker Eddy was the woman who Quimby healed, who became the protege and torch-bearer for his methods. She was the founder of

Christian Science. Not to be confused with Scientology or some other similar name.

Mrs. Eddy was able to perform the same conversational miracles as her mentor, Phineas Parkhurst Quimby—both of them alleging they rediscovered Christ's healing technique.

Remember, Jesus taught his disciples to heal and expected them to also raise people from the dead. We still have people on this Earth today who possess this knowledge and can apply it, effectively.

It is this discovery that gave me my life back, repeatedly when I was stricken down with incurable illness several times in my life. I don't call it Christian Science or subscribe to a religion to honor God—if I did call it something, it's closest to Ho'oponopono.

This scripture has been my life's journey, given to me in a prophetic dream. A Bible opened up to Romans 8:10 and I heard God speak to me, telling me this was my path. It led me to Surprise, Quimby, Eddy, and several others to reinforce the wisdom of the scripture:

Romans 8:10

"But if Christ is in you, then even though your body is subject to death because of sin, the Spirit gives life because of righteousness."

So, how powerful is this discovery? Let me remind you of what I'm talking about, in case you think I'm referring to religion or something. I'm not. I'm talking about YOU discovering the GOD WITHIN.

Just like Quimby who heard about horseback riding curing an acquaintance of a fatal disease, only to have his own experience derive from that "permission slip" into a new revelation.

Quimby also discovered healing from the same formula, but subjectively very differently than his colleague's; he understood why it worked and how to replicate it, repeatedly. It had nothing to do with the horse.

His colleague obtained a miracle, and Quimby ascertained the mechanics of the same wonder, beneath the surface appearance.

I'm talking about leading you to the source of your sorcery so that you can be impervious to the sting of venomous scorpions, just like this woman: http://bit.ly/2HYd0kT

Now that I've laid some groundwork for how LITTLE the so-called educated ones on this planet know about reality, and perpetuate B.S. to enslave their colleagues in the same cult-ure of ignorance, let's carry onward to a solution.

The reason why (the mind is creating our perceived problems) is because of our record of judgments in "The Memory Stick."

Like Quimby says, "minds mingle." We can pick up opinions stored in our Memory Stick that we have no clue as to how they got there. Our job is to clear them, all the time.

It's like the bank where you keep your judgments and judgments are held there until they are cleared. That's what we have to remove, and this is how you remove them—through non-judgment, or *surrender.*

Let's finish my story about the overnight healing of a five-year bout with eating disorders:

At last, the eating disorders left in the twinkling of an eye!

So how I resolved it was to begin shifting my focus away from studying all kinds of nonsense. Like Quimby discovered, it was all lies and opinions.

I didn't need to entertain my mind further to do what it does best—beat me up with negativity.

I could write an entire book about why the mind does this... the short answer is this: our language is corrupt from the beginning. Since our language is corrupt, we derived one-thousand-and-one industries to live off the corruption.

Corruption is status quo. Just look at the work of :David-Wynn: Miller on YouTube. (No, the full colons are not typos).

Let's get back to the scope of this subject matter...

My miracle came to me by being with God and loving God within. The first domino to fall was the decision I made to STOP JUDGING MYSELF for BEHAVIOR that was just that; it was behavior that was neither good or bad.

Domino one fell. I released the idea, or opinion that my behavior was indicative of a disorder. It meant nothing. It was just a phenomenon. (Remember what Mrs. Eddy's formula was—first, remove the lie).

Once I removed the judgment, my attitude softened towards myself enough to begin the SELF-LOVE required to orchestrate an overnight miracle. (Mrs. Eddy's second part of the equation—remove fear).

The fear of the illness disappeared almost instantly when I disassociated with having a condition. My attitude was gentle and loving toward myself, and I acted as PURE AWARENESS, the same way Ho'oponopono does.

The next morning, the so-called eating disorder was gone from The Memory Stick. A few weeks later, I realized it had been not only hours, or days, but weeks—without a binge and purge. I knew my healing was complete.

It took five years to struggle. It took less than an hour to release it all. For good.

Here's a reminder of the truth to capture:

Our reality is nothing more than our ATTITUDE towards life reflecting itself back to us.

It was receiving this miracle when I started to realize that God was within. Before being set free from the eating disorder program in The Memory Stick, I began learning from Deepak Chopra and Wayne Dyer's work.

Consequently, not everyone who tries to "tell us something" is full of garbage. Spiritual teachers are all around us if we're ready.

A real spiritual teacher leads you to yourself. How do you know you're ready? You seek and begin picking up the bread-crumbs.

Remember: life is a projection that you are experiencing, based on your ATTITUDE towards life, or yourself. You're ready when you surrender.

True surrender means you are in control. In other words, just keep doing Ho'oponopono on everything, and it will lead you into real ALLOWING, being at the level of "zero."

You have the advantage of using this technique. Before it was available, I had to take an alternate route to the same outcome.

A few months before my instant healing, my consciousness shifted by meditating on ancient wisdom.

I found a program by Deepak Chopra called *Everyday Immortality*. I listened to it about a hundred times, every night. I would drive and dedicate this time to the God within.

I started to hear some of these esoteric truths about God being inside of me and about the world being inside of me. What broke the camel's back (the ignorance causing my dis-ease) was meditating on the sutras in Everyday Immortality, which caused a shift in consciousness.

Again, there is more than one path to the desired result. Today, I revisit these sutras from time to time... in addition to using Ho'oponopono. Both methods address the inner-world at the level of cause.

As I would drive and dedicate each night to my spiritual growth, using ancient Vedic wisdom (the sutras in Everyday Immortality), every piece of the puzzle that was supposed to happen came into my life.

I loved God, within me… adhering to Romans 8:28.

"And we know that all things work together for good to them that love God."

God will handle the details. You are here to enjoy the experience!

The sequence of events played out automatically. I met someone who loved me, brought me to the family's home (to live in her basement), and her mom loved me, too; I had so much love. They were an Italian family who loved to cook.

At first, this presented a challenge with my resistance towards eating (I had too many food rules from all the nonsense in the bodybuilding community about calories and food).

However, as the dedicated time to growing my consciousness took hold, and MY ATTITUDE shifted toward LOVING MYSELF, I performed the same miracle that Dr. Len did with Ho'oponopono.

The beauty of Ho'oponopono is the efficiency and speed at which it performs miracles, by shifting your consciousness. It clears "The Memory Stick." Back then, I didn't know about this method.

My instinctual ability to do Ho'oponopono (saying "I love you" to myself the last time I binged and purged, removing my judgment and simply repeating "I love you" to myself, to the God within), made the miracle happen. Overnight. One last binge, and purge and it faded away—for good.

Now again, it's saying "I love you" as you turn to the divine, turning within instead of trying to solve a spiritual problem with an *earthly* solution.

You turn within to the divine. Whatever this problem is, the solution is "I love you. I'm sorry, please forgive me, thank you."

You're repenting, first of all. Next, you're asking for forgiveness. Finally, you're removing the judgments out of "The Memory Stick."

If you look at the work of the early classic, *As a Man Thinketh*, you can see that it says, "man is belief expressed." It all stems back to Quimby's discovery and the beliefs shared by Jesus.

Quantum physics says that 99.99997% (approximate number) of what we call "matter" is *empty* space. So what you see with your lying eyes is an illusion.

If you actually look at the physical matter that's in the Earth (taking out the non-physical *empty* space), this planet would be the size of a softball.

Here's another fun observation your lying eyes can't see...

You can fit three human beings on the head of a pin (again, removing the empty space and leaving only the matter). So how can you tell me what you see with your lying eyes is true?

It's not. It's a hologram, a projection that is coming from within you.

You never hear what the universe is saying if you are always re-acting through judgment, which means: re-presenting data in a way that distorts your vision. Your world is inside of you. Let that sink in.

So how do you change the distortion? How do you see what's missing?

Repent, ask for forgiveness, remove judgments all in one fell swoop!

The most important one is Romans 8:28, "And we know that all things work together for good to them that love God, to them who are called according to his purpose."

Again, what does that mean?

You are the deity, and the purpose in life is to love more; the expansion of your life is to LOVE more. It will make you happier, it'll make you healthier, and it'll make you wealthy.

BONUS AUDIO & TEACHING - Instant Karma Clearing.

In this bonus material, I wish to offer you a final breakthrough. An instant karma clearing process that will keep you PROGRESSING forward.

Your journey into the unknown is where you meet you, and only you. With this said, THE MOTIVE IS THE MEANS IS THE END means:

How you go into anything determines how you will end up experiencing the outcome.

I'm going to provide you with a fascinating string of ideas, to consider. Instead of telling you what to do, my motive is to cause your mind to EASE OFF the gas, so you can live—free at last.

In her book, *The Easiest Way to Live*, Mabel Katz describes a lesson she received from her mentor—Dr. Ihaleakala.

We have all heard the story about the Garden of Eden and eating the "forbidden fruit." However, the interpretation offered in this context is something I appreciated.

It goes like this: God created the Earth where he put Adam and Eve. He told them it was paradise, and they didn't have to worry about ANYTHING.

God gave them free will and also told them he would provide EVERYTHING. In other words, it's an all-inclusive V.I.P. paradise—compliments of the Creator of all of existence.

In addition to offering paradise, God created the apple tree. He told Adam and Eve that the tree was called "thinking." God said, "you don't need it."

In essence, God was saying to them, "You can live your life care-freely and remain in paradise, or choose to live carefully and think."

Am I saying that thinking is wrong? In the way most people use the mind, it is detrimental. Look at the word: detri-mental. Detri means "wearing away," and mental means, "mind."

Just reminisce about what you learned about series or SIRIUS thinking in chapter 7. Here's what all too often happens when we engage the mind:

Since the mind is reactive, we trigger unconsciously by the "*Luciferian program matrix*" in FEAR. As you'll hear in the audio I'll be sharing shortly; the controllers keep you triggered emotionally —targeting the Amygdala.

The Amygdala is the instinctive part of your brain that, when triggered often enough (danger), can set itself like a thermostat to perpetuate an anxiety disorder.

This Amygdala discovery was something I learned in Charles Lindon's anxiety course—when he reverse-engineers the process of developing an anxiety disorder.

Interestingly enough, you'll hear about how this Amygdala triggering keeps people controllable. An audio link will be provided, below.

I cannot reveal the name of the man who shared this information with me; you'll have to remember: this is all for entertainment purposes only (disclaimer). *We are going to take cover in public incredulity to protect our message.*

Now, here's what happens inside of you when you RE-ACT in a thinking process after you've triggered (psychologically) via the Amygdala's "danger" signaling:

First, your ATTENTION goes into the thought impression. An example is when someone experiences a loss of a job.

Immediately, the person engages their mind—putting attention on the "what if" thoughts. The mind is predominantly negative, by its nature.

Next, ATTENTION also means A-TENSION. We suppress and collect these traumas (Amygdala danger-threat signals) in our body-mind.

We develop a tension. If you look at the word emotion, you see E-MOTION. Electrical motion. We are electrical beings of light.

So, what do we do with this A-TENSION we store in our bodies? My analysis suggests that we STORE CELLULAR MEMORY inside ourselves; this is the "programming" that turns ON and turns OFF different STATES-OF-BEING.

#QuimbyDiscovery #ParallelUniverse #Cells

Funny how we understand how electricity LIGHTS a building and flows as a current, yet we fail to see the obvious: the universe is a hologram. *Every part of the "whole" must be present in every other facet of our projection.*

You are part of existence, so you are ALSO being LIT UP with electricity—the same force animates you.

ENTER: Dr. Bjorn Nordenstrom, MD

TOPIC: ELECTRIC MAN

SOURCE: Discover Magazine, 1986

Dr. Bjorn Nordenstrom discovered the following outcomes when treating late-stage cancer patients (for experimental purposes):

As soon as he put a positive charge on the needle in a tumor (he could put the ground anywhere on a person's body)_the swelling (tumor means: swelling) always dissipated.

Dr. Nordenstrom was reversing terminal cancer over and over again. He found a previously "unknown" electrical universe in the human body. His work got him in hot water, and his peers ostracized him. Nothing gets attacked faster than the truth.

ENTER: Dr. C. Samuel West, DN, ND

TOPIC: Applied Lymphology

SOURCE: My Experience in Self-Healing

Mr. West is the father of Applied Lymphology and discoverer of the Sodium-Potassium Pump. (The "Electric Generator" provides the "POWER" for cells to function and makes life possible).

When the medical community almost took my life with an experimental cocktail of six drugs—injected into my arm—I had to find a miracle to heal myself.

The story begins with my mistake of entering a "hospital" (which my mentor at the time called: a military testing facility). I had a migraine that persisted for several days, so I went in to get examined and find answers.

#BigMistake #Drugs #SideEffectsARETheEffects

After the young, arrogant medical "student" decided to TEST an experimental combination of drugs on me, I lost the use of my legs.

I remember sitting on the table and losing consciousness. As I became conscious again, I tried standing up to use the restroom. My legs gave out and wouldn't function.

The doctors who came to check on me became angered and told me that it was all in my head.

I went into shock almost three to four times each week after this poisoning at the medical facility. Thanks to many healers who worked on me, and the discovery I'm about to show you—I survived and fully recovered.

However, the six-month battle to use my legs and become NORMAL again was the most intensely terrifying experience of my life; far worse than Lyme disease.

I looked up the drugs they gave me online (six drugs, including Phenergan, Toradol, Benadryl, and three more) and discovered that people had lost their lives undergoing the same "testing" they did on me. Death by "medical error" is more common than most people expect.

I knew that my life was barely hanging on by a string when I left the hospital that day. The hell that followed was beyond anything I'd known, previously.

My miracle finally came in two discoveries. The first one saved my life. I found Dr. Ezra West's (Dr. EZ) teachings about the lymphatic system.

There were examples of people who overcame similar experiences I had encountered. I worked on my rebounder and "Lymphasized" daily—only able to do between 15 seconds and 1-minute, max.

I was at death's door. My body was weak.

During this time, I required the help of a full-time caregiver. Fortunately, my income could support this, and I give credit to God for taking care of me—through my tithe covenant.

Each day, I would activate the POWER PLANTS in my body to turn on the ELECTRICAL PUMPS.

This self-healing was done by using a mini-trampoline (to bounce) and using Dr. West's method. It kept me alive and steadily improving.

It wasn't an overnight fix, but I'm confident I would have died without using it. This discovery came at the perfect time.

The final piece that helped me overcome the poisoning and recover was the use of brown-seaweed extract. We use this extract in our Complete Ascentials MAGIC FORMULA as a detox kit.

I was informed about brown-seaweed extract (the same species used in the Chernobyl radiation cleanup), by a woman who claims she cured her multiple sclerosis.

This woman told me she was wheelchair-bound before using brown seaweed extract. Within two years, she was walking again and experiencing health.

As fabulous as this may sound to you, I'm not making any medical claims that brown seaweed extract (or MAGIC FORMULA) will cure you of any disease.

Instead, MAGIC FORMULA is designed to support the body with nutrients and assist the body to detoxify.

I obtained some brown seaweed extract and began using it, in conjunction with my daily Lymphasizing. Within a few weeks, I was in the gym again, doing squats.

I'm not kidding.

And, while I'm not suggesting that these results are typical or to be expected, this was true for me in my circumstances.

A healer I had known for several years told me that the poison lodged itself in my spine. He told me to find a way to detox this out of my system. I tried using several things until discovering brown seaweed extract.

I believe it was the combination of DAILY LYMPHASIZING and finding a method to assist my body (providing critical minerals and detox support) that unlocked my healing.

Today, when PAIN occurs in my body (by lifting heavy weights or injuries, etc.) I can usually rid myself of it in minutes or seconds, sometimes. I use the techniques I discovered in Dr. West's Applied Lymphology course.

Keep in mind; I'm not paid to promote Dr. West's work. I'm telling you because THE MOTIVE IS THE MEANS IS THE END.

My motive is to **GIVE YOU POWER** or <u>UNLOCK</u> the POWER you already have—inside. My teaching wouldn't be complete without telling you about this discovery.

YOU DO have "ELECTRICAL PUMPS" in your body, as discovered by the late Dr. C. Samuel West.

Remember when I told you about how minerals are the currency of life?

It just so happens that the brown seaweed extract provides an excellent source of minerals; previously undiscovered in my healing regimen.

Once I began SUPPLYING MY BODY with MISSING MINERALS and then ACTIVATING THE ELECTRICAL PUMPS to cleanse itself, things shifted rapidly.

Let's explore something else that I learned during my tenure with a few very advanced souls: **you access parallel universes through the cell.**

Look, at face value, I'm guessing you are skeptical. By now, you're probably a bit more open-minded. You likely have a ways to go before you "believe" this could be possible, or accurate.

Experience will be your friend, as you apply some of the things I'm sharing. You'll have a new experience. Then, you KNOW. When you KNOW, you don't require "thinking." At least, not nearly as often.

If you're going to RAISE YOUR FREQUENCY using monatomic ORMUS, as described earlier in this book—you might want to know how to ERADICATE NEGATIVITY INSTANTLY from your field, right?

As I recommend you consider a lifestyle of Ho'oponopono to remove judgments, I also recommend Lymphasizing to GET YOUR CELLS INTO THE DRY STATE, as Dr. West describes in his work, Applied Lymphology.

If you're going to ACTIVATE PARALLEL UNIVERSES consciously, choosing the vibration you sustain, consider "the cells" as being critical to this process.

In essence, you must make sure your cells are "happy and healthy." As Raymond Francis, author of *Never Be Sick Again*, discovered: there is **only one disease, a malfunctioning cell.**

KEY INSIGHT: If I were to tell you that Quimby would describe a disease as a STATE-OF-BEING, this means that THE CELL is where the "wormhole" or "portal" to a parallel you-niverse opens.

Remember, it's all a WHOLEogram. Your cells are YOU. I believe that PROGRAMMING INTENT while Lymphasizing ACTIVATES POWER—*especially if you're using monatomic ORMUS!*

GET INSTANT CLEARING - ON THE SPOT?

Now, I invite you to listen to the recording found at **http://www.KarmErase.com**.

As the future unfolds, you're sure to discover that humans already do time-travel. What you see in movies is usually already REAL technology, just kept away from the general public.

When I began my journey, each layer of understanding primed me to shift my awareness.

These days, I can easily *surrender my will* to hear God's instruction or "channel" what my higher self is saying.

With less thinking, ACTIVATED BY AN ATTITUDE OF NON-JUDGMENT, you reclaim this ability.

Like Dr. Ihaleakala's story at the beginning of this chapter, you SURRENDER to a greater INNER-STANDING.

It comes from within you. You are the deity.

Soon, you will think less and KNOW more.

Thank you for reading this book.

I S.A.L.U.T.E. you!

Conclusion

There's a lot of information to be found in this book. A lot of these ideas are completely contrary to what your parents and teachers may have told you.

Your mind will resist acceptance of what I've told you. It will tell you that what I'm saying doesn't make sense and that it won't work because it doesn't follow the rules of logic.

Logic is not what achieves success. Vision does. Seeing yourself where you want to be and tuning your vibrations in to that goal.

There is harmony in the universe, and no amount of hard work will get you to harmony with your goals unless you tap into the vibrations of your best excitement.

Remember these takeaways from this book, and use them as mantras if you need to:

Only the good is true.

You are the source of your own sourcery.

You are a manifestation of the God-force within you.

Go and be successful. You already are, because you already see yourself that way. That's all it takes.

If you'd like to FEEL the vibrational STATE-OF-BEING I was in while LIVING THIS BOOK, a collection of songs I wrote (performed by two amazing artists) is at the link below:

http://www.LOVEISMYLEGACY.com.

ASK UNTIL IT IS GIVEN!
Reader Reviews:

"By the first paragraph, I was already hooked, pausing for reflection and making personal discoveries. You're topics lead me down the google search rabbit hole more than once. I devoured this book and can't recommend it highly enough."

- Amanda Hannon

⋆ ⋆ ⋆

"The book is amazing the two chapters that stand out for me are where you mention the SALUTE method and also The Safe Touch Method. The information is unlike anything I've read anywhere else. Not only is it insightful but very tactical as well."

- Gilberto Rosas

⋆ ⋆ ⋆

ASK UNTIL IT IS GIVEN!

"Matthew David Hurtado's second offering Ask until it is GIVEN! is truly paradigm shifting. In essence, it is the blueprint to developing openness within a restrictive being. A well- streamlined approach to cultivating wholeness and ascending like a boss. #Transformation."

- *Endalk Hailu*

⁂

"On March 4, 2018, I had an 'inner prompting' to do a Google search for any information regarding the relationship of 'Anger and Poverty.' One of the items of information I received from that Search was your YouTube video on the topic of Anger as the cause of Poverty. I have been spending a few hours a day 'with' you ever since then. Currently, I am on my second reading of your book, 'Allow.' Is it a coincidence that the title of the first chapter in your newest book, 'Ask Until It is Given' is about Anger being the Cause of Poverty? I don't think so. I was 'divinely' guided to this information and to you. Both of your books are a Confirmation for me that I have been and am on the 'Right Path.' From the Sri Yantra on the cover of 'Ask Until It is Given,' to the information about Reverse Speech, to the ancient wisdom of the practice of Ho'oponopono, etc. the Message 'between the lines' for me and everyone else is, *what God/the Universe/Source Energy has done for you is also being done for me*...and MORE. All that is required is that I Believe...Allow...and Receive!"

- *David von Braun*

⁂

"Matthew David Hurtado's 'Ask Until It Is Given,' is a must reading for those who are open to and seek an alternative view of reality that will surprisingly bring a wealth of benefits. It will offend sensibilities, as I am offended on a few occasion being a Catholic faithful, but that is no reason to seek understanding of the deep truths he unravels. His work is a blend of eastern philosophical, spiritual and esoteric thoughts and leading-edge scientific research and insights that will stretch your mind. But the core is who you come to understand, believe and accept as your true identity determines the kind of life and the world you experience. What makes his work worth the effort of understanding is that he has demonstrated in his life amazing results. For the courageous hearts, I say go and read 'Ask Until It is Given' and be pleasantly surprised even if you may be offended."

- Norbert Isles

* * *

"I read Matthew's Book, 'Ask Until It Is Given' in 3 days! The information contained in the book was so eye-opening that I could not stop reading. I have read many, many Law of Attraction and Personal Development books. While most books contained useful information and made me very excited after reading it, the progress in my life was happening very slowly. This is likely because I did not practice changing the core emotions that are needed to experience a change in my reality more quickly. I often heard others talk about how they had changed their beliefs and experienced their desires and wondered why it was not happening as quickly for me. With Ask Until It Is Given, the information contained gives you the core principles and methods that will allow you to experience a shift within days. It also breaks down the meaning behind them. I was able to feel better immediately by practicing the Safe Touch Method and letting go of guilt and shame that had plagued me most of my life. I began experiencing synchronicities and opportunities on the first day. I have also made some changes in my food choices for better health and more energy with the information that Matthew teaches. This book has given me the wisdom and methods to begin experiencing my desired life. Thank you, Matthew!"

- Romica Prasad

⁂

"This amazing book feels like a divine download of the most effective soul cleansing and healing tools delivered in such a clear-minded and brilliantly comprehensive language by D.M. Hurtado! I have read quite a lot of spiritual books, but the way he efficiently condensed all the diverse existing methods plus his own developed techniques into this book, blew me away. My favorite aspect of the book are all these inspiring cleansing rituals. Thank you, Matthew David Hurtado!"

- Karima Djabelkhir

⁂

"I'm going to keep this brief because I know its supposed to be a book review (at least I'm going to try!). First of all, I want to say that I've been following you for a while and aspire to be where you are. You live life on your own terms and most importantly have FREEDOM, and that is exactly where I desire to be. You are one of the only people that I've found that actually gives practical, how-to information along with your messages. And that is probably why I read and watch just about everything you put out there. I read your previous book 'Allow' and absolutely loved it. But 'Ask Until it is Given' just blows all of that information out of the water... and not in a negative way, just kind of like the WOW-factor is huge! The book is 330 pages jam-packed full of inspiration/information. I mean it really blew me away! Here are some of my favorite parts of the book:

—I always knew there were hidden meanings in logos but never knew the extent to which symbols affected our psyche. This is something I'm going to delve into more so I can empower myself by wearing symbols that reflect the core of who/what I want to be. This is exciting information!

—I really loved the S.A.L.U.T.E. information. That is something that I'm going to start implementing right away, and I can see how that would almost cause an immediate shift. And what a novel way to practice by using index cards! So simple yet can make such a profound change.

-- I also loved the information on Self-Entrainment. The thought of putting yourself in a parallel reality where you are being and doing exactly what you want to do. I've always been interested in this type of thing and you can bet I'm going to be doing this exercise daily!

-- And last but not least Ho'Oponopono! I have been practicing this lately and love the information and your suggestions on use. For me, I feel most of my blocks and challenges stem from some kind of unforgiveness on my part (mostly for myself). I've already felt a shift just by doing it a few weeks. I think in time I will see more changes happening.

And honestly, there are so many good nuggets of information in this book that I could just go on and on. But the above is what stood out FOR ME.

Now that I'm finished with the book, I'm going to go back and read it again and this time VERY slowly. Also, I can't wait until all of your videos are finished and included in the material! I want to do and try everything!

And Matthew, you can use as much or as little as you want from what I've said. Or rearrange it in a way that will fit the format you are wanting to use.

I will keep you apprised of the miracles happening in my life. I can literally feel shifts are coming. I have the feeling of anticipation and like something huge is about to happen.

Thank you for being in service all the time. You are the definitely the definition of S.A.L.U.T.E.!!"

- Jo Karol Dean

* * *

"What you hold in your hand's is a manifesto of epic proportions. A masterpiece in the true sense of the word. I have spent the last eight years reading countless books, listening to countless podcasts, watching countless videos and diving head first into countless rabbit holes regarding all things self-help, relationship, spiritual, esoteric, history and health. This is truly the end all be all. Matthew has not only dropped the mic, he has taken said mic and smashed it into a million pieces."

-Craig Scott

* * *

"I think this is a very interesting book. Subjects that I have been studying for years, come together in this book. We are all connected at an energetic level. It is not me and you, it is US! As a result, what you do to someone else is what you do to yourself. In this book, handles are provided to become the best version of yourself. The best version in health, mind-set, mood and in actions. The better you feel, the friendlier and more helpful you are. You start to spread more loving divine energy and, therefore more energy comes your way. Energy in all kinds of forms: happiness, wealth, abundance. What you sow, you will reap. This book is a must for anyone who wants to know the real law of attraction."

- Fiona Onos

* * *

"It is time to be sovereign again...we have the capacity to be Gods again... All my life I was looking for the solutions to my problems in my head... but it is the other way round. All you have to do is to forget what your mind is offering and ...relax. You have to give Universe\The Source\ The God the time to offer the best possible solution for you and for you only. You have to jump and let go and it will come. Matthew gives you different ways (S.A.L.U.T.E) how to achieve everything you desire in the best possible way. Not only that. When you read this book you receive a view on current ongoings that rule the current world. A "must -have" knowledge, especially for American brothers and sisters.. and those who are already 'awake'... Many thanks, Matthew."

- Marzena.B.Nowak

* * *

"What an amazing book. If you are looking for success and extraordinary wealth, then this is the book to have. It's not like any other book with the same old stuff, it goes DEEP into the HOW, and yet in a very simple way. You will learn the habit of Honor and S.A.L U.T.E .the true and Magic way to receive Abundance and achieve your Destiny. This book will show you how to use symbols, and how to harness your sexual energy, and use it in all areas of your life. Its so amazing, and there is so much knowledge in this book that it will empower you in many ways. It's a must read, I highly recommend it."

- Joshua Flores

* * *

"I am sorry I was not able to finish your book, only halfway, the reason being is most self-help books I usually read the whole book in one sitting and most of them were really good, but once I put the book down I did nothing with the information, your book is different for the first time I feel compelled to slow down really let the information sink in, do the exercises, and put in practice what I have read before moving on to the next chapter, this is such an amazing thing for for me and I feel myself already changing for the better. The information in the book puts together all I have learned on my own journey of healing and self-discovery in an easy to read format that anyone who reads will get benefit from. So if you will allow me to once I finish I will leave a more detailed review on Amazon, with the hopes that many people read and buy this book, I S.A.L.U.T.E you Matthew and thank you for sharing your amazing healing journey with all of us."

- Jonathan Paulat

* * *

"Just finished reading ask until its given I think it picked up where allow left off I did all the exercises in the book allow and it was life changing and look forward to doing the exercises in asked until it's giving thank you, Matthew, for this easy to understand gem."

- Elvis Raposo

* * *

"I really enjoyed your readings, I learned about my God-like Power and being in control."

- Booker Anderson

* * *

"Hey, just finished reading your book and I want to let you know it is phenomenal! I mean it..."

- Malik Saidawi

* * *

"This book not only brought out my pen and notebook but it gave me the courage and knowledge needed to finally decide to change every aspect of who I AM!"

- Nigel Adrian

About The Author

MATTHEW DAVID HURTADO is the #1 Amazon best-selling author of *ALLOW*. He is the Minister of ALLOWING.

Learn more about Matthew at: http://www.matthewdavidhurtado.com

Connect with me on Facebook:
https://www.facebook.com/matthew.hurtado

Complete Ascentials: http://www.completeascentials.com

Alpha Upgrade: http://www.alphaupgrade.com

Love is My Legacy: http://www.loveismylegacy.com

ALLOW - Mastering The Law of Least Effort to Receive Your Desires!

http://www.allow.ws

Made in the USA
San Bernardino, CA
21 July 2018